SOCIO-ECONOMIC PROFILE OF RURAL INDIA

Volume One
SOUTH INDIA

Socio-Economic Profile of Rural India

Vol. I : SOUTH INDIA
Andhra Pradesh, Karnataka, Kerala, Tamil Nadu

Vol. II : NORTH-EAST INDIA
Assam, Manipur, Tripura, Nagaland

Vol. III : WESTERN INDIA
Gujarat, Maharashtra, Rajasthan

Vol. IV : NORTH AND CENTRAL INDIA
Punjab, Haryana, Himachal Pradesh, Madhya Pradesh

Vol. V : EASTERN INDIA
Bihar, West Bengal, Orissa, Uttar Pradesh

About the Editor

V.K. Agnihotri, an IAS officer of 1968 batch, belongs to the Andhra Pradesh Cadre of the Service. Born on 25 August 1945, he obtained his Masters degrees in English Literature and Political Science from the University of Allahabad, Allahabad. He obtained his Ph.D. in Public Policy Analysis and Design from the Indian Institute of Technology, Delhi. Before joining the IAS, he was on the Faculty of English Studies at University of Allahabad. He was recipient of several awards and honours during his distinguished academic career, and has been a Visiting Fellow at the Queen Elizabeth House, University of Oxford, in 1991-92.

Among several responsible positions with the State and Central Governments, Dr. Agnihotri has held posts of Collector of Visakhapatnam District, Director of Handlooms and Textiles, Government of Andhra Pradesh and Development Commissioner for Handlooms (Ministry of Textiles), Government of India.He was with the Lal Bahadur Shastri National Academy of Administration, Mussoorie from 1992 to 1998, initially as the Joint Director, and later as Professor of Public Administration.

Currently, he is Additional Secretary in the Department of Administrative Reforms and Public Grievances (Ministry of Personnel, Public Grievances and Pensions), Government of India. His areas of specialisation are public service quality, public policy, administrative reforms, e-governance, rural and cottage industries, panchayati raj and primary education. He has several publications to his credit, including books entitled **Environment and Development**, **Skills for Effective Administrators, Public Policy Analysis and Design** and **Dimensions of the New Economic Policy.**

SOCIO-ECONOMIC PROFILE OF RURAL INDIA

VOLUME ONE

SOUTH INDIA

Edited by

Dr. V.K. AGNIHOTRI

Published for

Centre for Rural Studies

L.B.S. National Academy of Administration, Mussoorie

by

CONCEPT PUBLISHING COMPANY, NEW DELHI - 110 059

ISBN 81-7022-743-7 (Vol. I)
ISBN 81-7022-742-9 (Series)

First Published 2002

Published and Printed by
Ashok Kumar Mittal
Concept Publishing Company
A/15-16, Commercial Block, Mohan Garden
New Delhi-110059 (India)

Phones: 5351460, 53541794
Fax: 091–(11)–5357103
E-mail: publishing@conceptpub.com

CONTENTS

FOREWORD

At the time of India's independence, the then Prime Minister, Shri Jawaharlal Nehru, in his famous 'tryst with destiny' speech had declared that one of the foremost aims of independent India was "*the ending of poverty and ignorance and disease and inequality of opportunities*". In the initial two decades after independence, it was believed that growth of the economy would reduce poverty through a trickle down effect. However, the trickle down effect was negligible, overwhelmed by the prevalence of a host of socio-economic obstacles such as low literacy rate, lack of awareness, low quality or inadequate health facilities, lack of modernisation in the agriculture sector, inequality of income, social tensions, etc.

Thereafter, there was a paradigm shift in the strategy of rural development and poverty alleviation and it was decided to target directly the persons below the poverty line through a series of schemes. Over the years, these schemes have changed in nomenclature and to some extent in substance too. Broadly these schemes aim at:

(a) providing employment to the rural labour force, especially during the lean agricultural season;
(b) targeting small and marginal farmers providing for subsidy for irrigation facilities etc.;
(c) generating income through provision of assets to the poor at subsidised prices through credit linkage;
(d) providing food security through a public distribution scheme
(e) providing targeted care including nutrition to pregnant mothers and children till the pre-school age;
(f) providing basic necessities like housing, drinking water, etc.,

(g) schemes targeted towards the vulnerable sections of society especially the old and the disabled.

It should therefore be evident that while some of the schemes aim at providing a security net for the poor, the other schemes aim at bringing about development of the poor.

Poverty, in its most rudimentary form, can be defined in terms of food availability. In India, even after fifty years of Independence, we are not able to provide food security to all. There are still reports of starvation deaths occurring in few parts of the country. The starvation deaths in Kashipur block of Rayagada District of the state of Orissa in the month of September 2001 have forced the government, policy makers and policy implementing agencies to think again about the definition of food security. The most paradoxical feature of food security in India is that, while on one hand the FCI godowns are facing the problem of storage of food grains, on the other hand starvation deaths are occurring in certain parts of the country. It can be inferred that the shortage of food grains is not a problem, the real problem area lies elsewhere. This phenomenon throws up the immediate need for rethinking our strategy towards rural development and security nets for the poor. Studies have shown that casual labourers engaged in agriculture were found to be the poorest. Poverty is also higher among SCs and STs when compared to the general category. People are poor because of want of entitlements, physical and/or human, lack of access to agricultural land, paucity of work on land and non-availability of education, lack of capital and of effective security nets.

Even after three decades of implementation of these schemes, the latest NSS data (1999-2000) shows that nearly 26% of Indians, numbering 260 million fall below the poverty line. No doubt, there has been some progress in reducing poverty; however, there is an urgent need for accelerating the process of poverty reduction. The overall progress made at the national level also masks substantial differences at the state level. There are wide variations in poverty ratios between different states. Varying from 6.16% in Punjab to

47.15% in Orissa. It is also apparent that poverty is becoming more and more concentrated in certain areas, which can be termed as backward. These regions which fall prominently in the BIMARU States are characterised by a predominantly subsistence agricultural economy, lack of physical and social infrastructure, illiteracy, high incidence of diseases, weak institutions, poor governance and low people's capacity for organisation and action. Such areas would need focused and concerted action to break out of the vicious circle of poverty.

Historically, social factors have been affecting economic factors in determining the standard of living of different sections of people in the society. The caste-class relationship has maintained its hegemony since long. Despite interventions at different levels, social factors have dominated and affected the rural development strategy and efforts adversely. As a result, development programmes have bred corruption and mismanagement. A new class of middlemen has been amongst the major beneficiaries of the schemes. It is a well-known fact that the benefits of economic growth have reaped by sections of the society, who are neither in need nor eligible to benefit from such programmes. Thus, money meant for the poor gets subverted on the way. In fact, an ex-Prime Minister was candid enough to say that hardly 15 paise out of every one rupee spent by the Government for poor people reached to the real beneficiaries.

The performance of poverty alleviation programmes (PAPs) has been mixed. The PAPs have undergone changes over the years. But more and more it seems like old wine in new bottle. Targeting and identification of the poor are the two main issues, which have attracted the attention of the critics of poverty alleviation programmes. It has been realised that the localised identification of poor families are the best from the point view of targeting, implementing PAPs and adopting suitable policy measures. The involvement of local people in the process of identification of poor families through participatory methods inculcates diversified views and these diversified views also provide vital inputs for strengthening policies. It is expected that after the 73rd Amendment, Panchayati Raj Institutions will play major roles in this context. However, socio-political factors at local level may contribute to the violation of the principles of democracy at the grassroot level. A committed and impartial social concern by bureaucracy and other functionaries of the government are vital for ensuring democracy at the grassroot level.

In the near future, "markets" will have a greater role to play in the economy. Economic liberalisation too presumes a field where "markets" can function in an effective manner to maximise the welfare of the society. However, it is a well known fact the people who are better endowed in terms of physical and human entitlements are placed in a far better position to take advantage of the opportunities thrown open by liberalisation and markets. It is these social and economic "asymmetries" which will need to be addressed by the Governments. More and more emphasis will have to be paid on education and health and for sometime till inequalities reduce, strong effective security nets have to be provided by the Government to ensure that vulnerable sections of society are not adversely affected.

One of the major objectives of Lal Bahadur Shastri National Academy of Administration, Mussoorie, India, which imparts training to IAS (Indian Administration Services) officers at various levels, is not only to sensitize the IAS officers towards the plight of rural people, but also to equip them with an in-depth understanding of rural issues. The IAS officer trainees are required to prepare a village study report as a part of their district assignments after conducting extensive questionnaire based house-hold survey. The South-India volume of socio-economic publications contains papers of the states Andhra Pradesh, Karnataka, Kerala and Tamil Nadu prepared by eminent senior bureaucrats and academicians. The basic ingredients of the state papers are borrowed from the village study reports of the IAS officer trainees. The effort of the Centre for Rural Studies (CRS) to publish such kind of book is really commendable, because the valuable firsthand information and findings of IAS officer trainees would have been confined only to the four walls of the Academy if this kind of books are not published. I hope and trust that this book will be widely read and well received by academicians, policy makers, administrators and all other concerned.

The book is the first volume of the series of publications Socio-Economic Profile of Rural India. The authors of different state papers of this volume are senior bureaucrats and Academicians. Many of the authors are directly involved in policy formulation at different levels of Government of India. Undoubtedly, the state papers prepared by them are of high quality because the state papers are enriched by inputs from their long experiences in the field of rural development. It may not be possible to thank them individually. The only thing I am mentioning here is that I am short of good phrases, to express my gratefulness to them, one and all.

The task of publishing the volumes of Socio-Economic series was initiated by the Village Study Unit (VSU), which was later merged with Land Reforms Unit to form Centre for Rural Studies (CRS). I must congratulate Shri Amarjeet Sinha, IAS, who was the Co-ordinator of VSU, when the task of publishing Socio-Economic series was initiated. The efforts of Manoj Ahuja, IAS, the present Co-ordinator of Centre for Rural Studies and Shri Subhransu Tripathy, Assistant Professor, Centre for Rural Studies to bring out this book are praiseworthy and I am looking forward to the publication of the remaining volumes in this series.

Wajahat Habibullah
Director
Lal Bahadur Shastri National Academy
of Administration,
Mussoorie – 248179,
(INDIA)

13th December 2001

1

ANDHRA PRADESH

V.K. Agnihotri and S.V. Subramanian

1. INTRODUCTION

Regional Classification

The State of Andhra Pradesh was constituted on November 1, 1956, comprising parts of the then Madras Presidency and the erstwhile princely state of Hyderabad. The Madras state had 11 Telugu-speaking districts, namely, Srikakulam, Visakhapatnam, East Godavari, West Godavari, Krishna, Guntur, Kurnool, Anantapur, Cuddapah, Nellore and Chittoor. Another nine Telugu speaking districts formed part of the Hyderabad state. In accordance with the recommendations of the States Reorganisation Commission, the nine Telugu speaking districts of former state of Hyderabad were merged with the 11 districts of Andhra state, to create the new state of Andhra Pradesh. At present the state has 23 districts, the three newly created districts being: Prakasam, Vizianagaram and Rangareddy.

Conventionally the state comprises three distinct regions, namely, coastal Andhra, Rayalaseema and Telengana, with a total area of 2,75,000 sq. km. This regional classification is largely based on natural and geographical features as well as socio-cultural aspects. The coastal Andhra region consists of nine districts with a total area of about 93,000 sq. km. The districts falling in this region are: Srikakulam, Vizianagaram, Visakhapatnam, East Godavari, West Godavari, Krishna, Guntur, Prakasam and Nellore. The largest district in this region is Prakasam, while the smallest is Srikakulam. Rayalaseema region with a total area of 67,000 sq. km., has four districts. The largest one is Anantapur with an area of 19,000 sq. km. (it is the largest district in the state as well), followed by Kurnool, Cuddapah and lastly Chittoor. The Telengana region is the largest region in Andhra Pradesh with an area of 1,15,000 sq. kms. spread over 10 districts, namely, Rangareddy, Hyderabad, Nizamabad, Medak, Mahabubnagar, Nalgonda, Warangal, Khammam, Karimnagar and Adilabad.

The coastal Andhra region is the most prosperous and is also rich in terms of its natural bounty. This region, which has fertile lands, is often described as the "granary of the state". Large perennial rivers like the Godavari and the Krishna pass through the region and form rich deltas. As a corollary Visakhapatnam, Guntur and Vijayawada have emerged as major urban complexes. The east coast is a polarised region. It comprises of, at one end, the port of Visakhapatnam thriving on heavy and power intensive industrial base and on the other the deltaic area is dominated by agricultural activities.

The Rayalaseema region, the stalking ground of famines, is a sparsely populated and economically vulnerable part of the state. The region is drought-prone and is characterised by dry tracts, rocky soils and scanty rains. It is observed that during 1900 to 1960, some part or the other of this region was a victim of famine with an average frequency of once in five years. Dry land farming and proper utilisation of mineral resource base are the only viable solutions to hasten the process of socio-economic development of this region.

The Telengana region has a princely heritage having been ruled by Nizams for centuries. This region is relatively well-developed industrially as compared to the other two regions. This development could largely be attributed to the presence of the capital and metropolis of Hyderabad. However, a feature typical of urban-based development in third world countries can be noted wherein the polarised Hyderabad exists with no positive relationship to its rural hinterland.

Physical Resource Base

On account of its geographical situation, Andhra Pradesh occupies a place of significance among the states of India since it is centrally located and serves as a link between the southern, eastern and northern parts of the country. The two major rivers of the state are Godavari and Krishna. The river Godavari, 1,450 kms. long, is the longest and broadest river in south India, and Krishna, with a length of about 1,300 kms. is the second longest. Both these rivers flow eastwards through the eastern ghats to the Bay of Bengal. They are fed by the two monsoons (south-west and north-east) and are perennial. The other rivers of lesser importance are Penner, Vamsadhara, and Nagavali. The Godavari and Krishna traversing through almost the entire breadth of the state provide irrigation to large tracts of land and are important sources for generation of hydro-electric power in the state. These two rivers alone have a hydel potential of 2,500 to 3,000 MW at 60 per cent load factor. There are 55 irrigation projects, of which seven are major projects like Nagarjunsagar, Sriramsagar, Thungabhadra etc.

Andhra Pradesh receives an average rainfall of about 90 cms. during the months June to September and most of it is through the south-west monsoon. The maximum annual rainfall of 110.17 cms. was recorded at the Kakinada meteorological station in the coastal Andhra region, while the minimum of 55.79 cms. was reported from the Anantapur station in the Rayalaseema region – a dry and arid zone. The maximum rainfall region lies in the north-eastern part of the state along the forest belt covering Telengana and coastal Andhra and the rainfall decreases as we move from the north-east to south-west. Most of the areas of Telengana and coastal Andhra regions receive fairly good rains, while the Rayalaseema region receives less rainfall.

The soil surveys of the state indicate the presence of 11 distinct types of soils. Red sandy soil occurs most extensively. It is mainly found in the regions encompassing Rayalaseema and Telengana and the two districts of coastal Andhra, namely, Prakasam and Nellore. Among the other major soils of the state are deep black soils and mixed red and black soils. The coastal Andhra region has the most fertile soil, namely, the deltaic alluvium and coastal alluvium soils. The other soils occurring in small patches are medium black soils, red loamy soils, laterite soils, coastal sandy soils and saline soils.

An area of 6.5 million hectares, which accounts for about one-fourth of the total geographical area of the state, is covered by forests. The state ranks fourth among the states of India as far as the extent of forest area is concerned; the other three with higher rankings being Madhya Pradesh, Orissa and Maharashtra. Most of the forests lie in the Telengana region which accounts for 45 per cent of the total area under forests in the state. The coastal Andhra region constitutes 30 per cent, while Rayalaseema region has the remaining 25 per cent of the forest area in the state. The forests can be classified into four distinct categories - tropical littoral and dry evergreen forests, tropical moist deciduous, tropical dry deciduous, and tropical dry thorn forests. Bulk of the forests (45 per cent) belong to the category of tropical dry deciduous and are mostly found in the districts of Telengana. Teak and sal are the important species of this type of forest. Tropical moist deciduous (25 per cent) and tropical dry thorn forests (25 per cent) are the next important types of forests. The former mainly occur in the eastern ghats region where the annual rainfall exceeds 125 cms. The major species of this type are mango, *jamun*, *konda, tangedu, yerakarra* etc. The tropical dry thorn forests are characterised by dwarf and medium-sized trees of thorny growth like acacias, zizyphus, cassias, albizzias, randia etc. They occur mainly in the districts of Guntur, Nalgonda and Anantapur. Only 5 per cent of the forests in Andhra Pradesh fall in the category of tropical littoral and dry evergreen forests and are mainly found at the mouths of the rivers, Godavari and Krishna, and on the eastern sea coast, mainly in Nellore district.

Although forests constitute around 23 per cent of the total area of the state, it is still way behind the national target of 33 per cent. According to more strict and scientific estimates, forests cover only 18 per cent of the area, while more than 40 per cent of the total area is covered by scrub land. Bamboo and *tendu* leaf (used for making *beedis*) contribute more than 80 per cent of the total forest produce

Coal, manganese, bauxite, iron ore, mica, barytes, asbestos

and a variety of silica products and clay are the major mineral resources of the state, which is the second richest in this respect in India. These resources have a high potential for industrial development. The state has large reserves of bauxite and mica and enjoys a virtual monopoly in chrysotile asbestos. It is the only southern state with coal reserves of the type ideally suited for thermal projects, railways, cement plants etc. Manganese, mica and potassium are mainly exported. The mineral industrial base of the state is weak, partly because most of the minerals are of low grade. In the last three Five-Year Plans, the state has laid emphasis on tapping minerals to accelerate the rate of industrial development which, when compared to the neighbouring states of Maharashtra, Tamil Nadu and Karnataka, is quite low.

2. DEMOGRAPHIC AND SOCIAL STRUCTURE

Demographic Characteristics

In 1991 Andhra Pradesh was the fifth largest state in the country with a population of 665 lakhs. The rural population of the state was 486 lakhs and the urban population was 178 lakhs. The growth rate of the population increased marginally in the decade 1981-91 (23.91 per cent) as compared to the preceding decade 1971-81 (23.1 per cent). This led to an increase in the density of population from 195 persons per sq. km. in 1981 to 241 persons per sq. km. in 1991. The rate of growth of population among the three regions of the state was varied. The districts of coastal Andhra experienced the highest growth rate followed by Telengana and Rayalaseema.

Table 1.1 : Density of Population

Regional	Persons per sq. km.	
	1981	1991
Coastal Andhra	256	312
Rayalaseema	174	174
Telengana	176	226
Andhra Pradesh	195	241

Source : Census of India, 1981, 1991.

The distribution of population in terms of their gender reveals no significant change from 1981 to 1991. In 1991, the sex ratio expressed in terms of females per thousand males stood at 977 as compared to the 1981 figure of 975. While Rayalaseema had the lowest sex ratio (959), in coastal Andhra it was the highest (987).

Rural Andhra Pradesh has a birth rate of 25.9 per thousand population, death rate of 10 per thousand population and infant mortality rate of 76 per thousand live births. On an all-India basis the infant mortality rate, which was 92 per 1,000 live births in 1957, decreased to 71 in 1992. The life expectancy for the state as a whole is 60 years.

Considering the close correlation of urbanisation with development in general, it would be worthwhile to assess the changes in the level of urbanisation, defined as the proportion of urban population to the total population. In 1981, the state's urbanisation level was 23.46 per cent which increased to 26.89 per cent in 1991. It may be noted that the level of urbanisation in Andhra Pradesh is in close conformity with the all-India average, 25.4 per cent, though marginally higher. Rayalaseema as per the 1981 as well as 1991 census, was the least urbanised region of Andhra Pradesh, with 20.34 and 23.16 per cent of its population in urban areas, respectively. Telengana continues to be the most urbanised region of the state with about 30 per cent of its population living in urban areas. The presence of the metropolis of Hyderabad is no doubt a major factor in the high level of urbanisation of Telengana region.

An analysis of rural settlements in Andhra Pradesh reveals that 32.35 per cent of the villages are in the population range of less than 500, 19.1 per cent are in the range 500-999 and 44 per cent are in the range 1,000-4,999. Only 4 per cent of the villages have a population of more than 5,000. While such a distribution pattern holds somewhat true for the regions of Rayalaseema and Telengana, in coastal Andhra the rural landscape is dominated by small villages, i.e. villages with a population of less than 500. It is interesting to note that almost 63 per cent of the small villages and a majority (58 per cent) of all the large villages in Andhra Pradesh are in coastal Andhra (Table 1.2).

Table 1.2 : Percentage Distribution of Villages by Size of Population, 1981

Regions	Small (less than 500)	Small Medium (500-599)	Large Medium (1000-4999)	Large (5000+)
Coastal Andhra	43.5	15.3	35.5	5.7
Rayalaseema	17.5	19.1	58.2	5.2
Telengana	24.0	23.8	49.2	3.0
Andhra Pradesh	32.35	19.1	44.2	4.4

Source: Census of India, Andhra Pradesh, 1981.

About 70 per cent of the surveyed villages belong to the large-medium (1,000-4,999) category, followed by large (5,000+) which accounts for 17 per cent. A perusal of the socio-economic surveys further reveals an average size of 5 persons per household across all the three regions of Andhra Pradesh. No significant change is noticeable between 1983 and 1993.

Social Structure

Any analysis of the structure of society in the Indian context cannot be devoid of the caste factor, although parameters like literacy, mortality, availability of social infrastructure etc. perhaps are more important. According to the 1991 census, 15.9 per cent of the population in Andhra Pradesh was classified as Scheduled Castes while 6.3 per cent was Scheduled Tribes. While the proportion of the Scheduled Castes to the total population does not vary significantly across the three regions, the Scheduled Tribe proportion does indicate a variation. Telengana has the highest proportion of its population (8.5 per cent) as Scheduled Tribes and Rayalaseema has the lowest (2.7 per cent).

The socio-economic surveys indicate that the majority of the villages in all the three regions are dominated by Backward Castes (different from Scheduled Castes and Tribes). On an average about 70 to 80 per cent of the villages had a Backward Caste population exceeding 50 per cent, prominent among these being Polavaram, Pachipenta, Vemulapudi, Patur, Kothur, Routhulapadi, Rellivalasa (all coastal Andhra), Palampalli, G. Singavaram, Korrapadu, Guttur (all Rayalaseema), Mandalapally and Venkatapuram (both Telengana).

Although there are signs of the old hierarchical and rigid caste system paving way for a more liberal structure, nevertheless the correlation between caste, class and power exists (for example, in Nandivelagu and Patur of coastal Andhra among surveyed villages). Brahmins, despite their ritual superiority, are not the dominant caste in most of the villages surveyed. In fact a ritually lower or intermediate caste, more specifically the *Reddis*, are the dominant caste in rural Andhra Pradesh. They are found to be the strongest in the Rayalaseema region, but are equally strong in the Telengana and the coastal Andhra regions as well. Such dominance essentially rests on two factors, i.e. land and numerical strength. These two factors have helped this caste to acquire both economic and political power. Another caste of considerable politico-economic significance is that of the *Kammas*.

Of late the state has seen a resurgence of Backward Castes demanding concessions of various sorts, a trend being witnessed in India at large. Backward Castes like *Kapus* (called the *Balijas* in the Rayalaseema region), who have also gained considerable economic clout, are now demanding a greater share in the polity. The caste polarisations are now getting strengthened at the village level, with different caste groups becoming more conscious of their identities.

The practice of untouchability was not found to exist in either a physical or institutional form in most of the villages surveyed, but the same cannot be said of the mental disposition. Even now the concept of untouchability very much exists in the mental psyche of the upper castes (as specifically reported in the surveyed villages of Moram, Palluru, Chinna Tumbalam, Kanuparthi, Palampalli and Bychegiri, all belonging to Rayalaseema region, and Polavaram of coastal Andhra). The upper castes are still conscious of their superiority and separation. In other words, there is hardly any social mixing in the true sense. The upper castes have a feeling that they are being given a raw deal *vis-à-vis* the Backward

Castes. This, in general, might lead to heightening of social tensions in the villages.

Evidence of bonded labour and other similar forms of exploitation has been reported mostly in Telengana region (e.g. Mandalapally, Venkateswarlabavi) and that too even as late as in 1993 (Kothapalli). Child labour has been found in all the three regions, viz., coastal Andhra (Nandivelagu and Rangapuram), Rayalaseema (Bychegiri) and Telengana (Yashwantapur and Irukulla).

The literacy rates in the surveyed villages ranged between 15 per cent to 32 per cent, a figure much below the state average, especially for the female population. According to the 1991 census, in the state as a whole, 46.8 per cent of the male population and 27.9 per cent of the female population was literate. A perusal of the surveys indicates that the variations in rural literacy can be explained by the proportion of Scheduled Caste and Scheduled Tribe population to the total population and the proportion of agricultural labourers to the total workers. The higher these proportions the lower is the literacy rate, for these are the sections most deprived of the benefits of education. The surveys also point to the wastage in educational expenditure that occurs primarily due to socio-economic background and institutional factors.

Social Infrastructure and Institutional Support

The institutional factors essentially relate to the provision of education, health, housing and other social infrastructural facilities. From a review of the surveys it is clear that almost all the villages have a primary school. However in certain cases, the condition of these schools is unsatisfactory, with no proper provision of accommodation, teaching equipment, drinking water and toilets. Lack of good teachers is common. The presence of high-school facilities was noted in less than 5 per cent of the villages. The attendance of children in schools has been a major area of concern. Here, the mid-day meal scheme is noted as providing a major impetus in increasing children's attendance in schools (Ammapalem, Irukulla, Gudem and Ponnalur).

Socio-economic factors contribute to a very high drop-out rate. The findings of the surveys indicate that the drop-out rate increases as one goes to higher standards especially after the fifth standard. Further, it is clear that the drop-outs are specific to certain groups of people. The drop-out rates are found to be highest among the Scheduled Castes and Tribes, agricultural labourers and women, in general. However, in certain surveys a large number of people expressed a sincere desire to continue studies if facilities were made available.

The surveys confirm the state figure of a high rate of participation of women in rural areas. Majority of these women not only work in the fields, but are also involved in household chores, child rearing, fetching water, fuelwood etc. An obvious indicator of the status of women is the low literacy rate amongst them. It is observed that social and infrastructural barriers contribute to lower enrolment and a high drop-out rate for girls. Surveys also indicate a positive correlation between low female literacy and high population growth rate. This in a way indicates the failure of family welfare programmes in making a significant impact on improving the status of women. On the adult education front, less than 10 per cent of the villages had some form of adult education facilities.

The delivery of health care facilities to the population at large is again far from adequate. In the coastal Andhra region, the villagers have to travel an average of 12 kms. to avail the services of a primary health centre. The average distance travelled in the Telengana and Rayalaseema regions is 10 kms. and 11 kms., respectively. It is clear from the surveys that the health care services provided in the rural areas are inadequate as well as inaccessible. Further, with the average age of marriage for females being 17 years, it is imperative to have adequate maternity services.

Absence of protected drinking water supply has been specifically highlighted in several surveys, particularly those of Kothur, Pedur, Pachipenta, Routhulapadi, Seethanapalli, Rellivalasa, Mamidipalli, Koppolu, (all in coastal Andhra region), Venkateswarlabavi and Venkatapuram (of Telengana region). It would appear that on account of greater development, the expectations of the people of coastal Andhra region are higher and absence of protected drinking water supply is perceived as a problem, whereas in the less developed regions of Telengana and particularly Rayalaseema they are still coping with the scarcity and non-availability of drinking water.

Rural Governance

The rural local bodies, particularly the gram panchayats, do not appear to be serving their basic objective of empowering and organising the poor, though as we scan the findings of the surveys, there seems to be greater involvement of the underprivileged sections of society. Nevertheless most of the local bodies are still heavily biased in favour of the influential sections, dominant factions, large farmers or the upper castes, as the case may be. Therefore, in practice, irrespective of the composition of the panchayats, the largest land-owning classes, who are also socially and economically dominant, control all decision making between them. If there exists a division among the dominant groups, a phenomenon characteristic of almost all the villages surveyed, then the weaker among them take sides and the power of each faction determines the nature of public investments in the villages. Financial constraint remains one of the weaknesses of gram panchayats, although one major reason for this problem could be the malfunctioning of the politico-administrative systems operating at the grassroot level.

Cultural Life

Regarding cultural aspects, the findings of the surveys reflect a lack of participation of the villagers in recreational activities. On one hand this could be attributed to poverty, and on the other hand to the lack of recreational facilities. Cinema continues to be the mainstay of their recreational activities. Idol worship of screen personalities is common, a phenomenon true of south Indian states in general, with the exception of Kerala.

Marriages and festivals are occasions of great revelry. Expenditure on marriages is often quite enormous, and, by any standards, not commensurate with the economic status of the families concerned. Dowry is still rampant (Kanuparthi). Some of the major festivals celebrated in the villages of rural Andhra Pradesh are *Ugadi, Makarsankranti, Dussehra* and *Deepawali.* In addition, *jatras* honouring local deities are celebrated with great fanfare.

One of the undesirable features of the cultural landscape of rural Andhra Pradesh is the consumption of liquor. This, which perhaps is true for most of the Indian poor whether they live in urban or rural areas, is perceived as a means of relieving their tensions. In this regard it may not be right to simply blame the villagers. Instead, a positive intervention through proper education and mobilisation of the people, coupled with prohibition, could yield better results.

3. AGRARIAN RELATIONS

An Overview

After the end of the colonial rule, the *ryotwari* system of land tenure had predominated in the Andhra area (part of former Madras Presidency), with pockets of semi-feudal land tenures. In the Telengana region, feudal and semi-feudal form of land tenure, with medieval forms of exploitation of the working peasantry prevailed.

In the Andhra area, about 39 per cent of the agricultural land was under different forms of landlordism such as *zamindari, mahalwari, inamdari, mokhansadari*, and *muttadari* systems, while the remaining was under *ryotwari* land tenure. With absentee landlordism rampant, the peasantry of the Andhra area was heavily burdened with land revenue and other taxes. In the Telengana region, 40 per cent of agricultural land was under the *jagirdari* system, and another 10 per cent of the land belonged to the Nizam's own estate *sarf-e-khas*; the remaining 50 per cent land was under government land revenue system.

In Indian agrarian society, and Andhra Pradesh is no exception, land ownership and caste status are decisive elements for any structural analysis. Going through the surveys one can identify some elements, common across all regions, which shape agrarian relations. They are: (a) size of land holding; (b) extent of tenancy/share cropping; (c) degree of exploitation through high rent; (d) role of usurious money-lending; and (e) pattern of utilisation of surplus.

Land Reforms

After independence, the Estates Abolition Act, 1948, of the Government of Madras abolished all the *zamindari*, *mokhansadari* and *inam* estates in Andhra area over a period of 15 years. In

Telengana, after the police action in 1948, all *jagirs* were abolished, and the Nizam's *sarf-e-khas* lands were taken over by the state.

In 1950, the Hyderabad Tenancy and Agricultural Lands Act was passed with the objective of protecting the interests of the tenants. As a consequence, a class of protected tenants was created among whom only a small number were able to acquire ownership rights on the tenanted lands. However, it is quite clear from a review of such legislations, that unenthusiastic implementation of land reforms by officials, on the one hand, and the resort to *benami* methods by landlords, on the other, have defeated the very spirit of land reform legislation. Such a viewpoint, although a truism, is substantiated by the fact that only 7.29 lakh acres in the state were declared surplus by the land tribunals (as on January 1, 1992) which, even going by liberal standards, according to some, was only half of the expected surplus. Out of the declared 7.29 lakh acres of surplus land, 5.49 lakh acres were taken into possession and only 4.63 lakh acres of land was actually distributed to about 3.96 lakh beneficiaries. Andhra Pradesh was one of the states to launch a special drive to distribute ceiling surplus land during the period October 1991 to February 1992. During this period 30,905 acres of land was distributed to the landless (Land Reforms Unit, 1995).

Land Holdings

An inverse relationship is obtained while analysing the ownership pattern and the extent of average holding in different size-classes

Table 1.3 : Percentage Distribution of Farmers Holding Land and Average Holding

Class	Size	Farmers (%)		Extent of land (%)	
		1983	1991	1983	1991
Small	Less than one acre	41.00	24.60	7.20	6.80
Small Medium	1-5 acres	39.00	38.66	25.50	36.60
Large Medium	5-10 acres	10.00	28.65	17.10	34.00
Large	More than 10 acres	10.00	8.09	40.20	22.60

of holding. In the case of land ownership pattern, the distribution is highly skewed, wherein a large number of farmers own small land holdings and *vice versa*. A significant increase is also noted in the extent of land holding in the 5-10 acre category. Simultaneously a significant decrease is also noted in the extent of land owned by large farmers.

From a perusal of the survey data it is found that, by and large, across the three regions, 54 to 80 per cent of the farmers belonging to the small and marginal category (i.e. owning upto 5 acres of land) own between 21 to 34 per cent of the land in the villages, as shown in Table 1.4 below.

Table 1.4 : Per cent Distribution of Numbers and Holdings of Small and Marginal Farmers

Village	Year	% of Holders	
		Small Farmers	Marginal Farmers
	Coastal Andhra		
G. Mamidada	1983	87	72
Ponnalur	1984	65	27
Gandipalem	1985	90	70
Vemulapudi	1985	58	21
Koppolu	1986	68	26
Iruvada	1991	58	24
	Rayalaseema		
Kalagatur	1992	78	39
Chinna Tumbalam	1993	65	22
	Telengana		
Dharmapuri	1983	80	32
Ammapalem	1984	67	34
S. Itikyal	1984	70	32
Mandalapally	1986	40	7
Venkateswarlabavi	1986	43	16
Mustibanda	1988	58	24
Repakagommu	1991	54	6
Venkatapuram	1991	63	43
Kothapalli	1993	77	32
Kothur	1993	73	62

However, no trend in terms of increase or decrease in the numbers or share of land held by this category of farmers is discernible from Table 1.4. In any case the surveys pertain to different villages. There are no doubt a few oddities like Mamidada, Gandipalem (coastal Andhra), on the one hand, and Mandalapally, Venkateswarlabavi and Repakagommu (Telengana) on the other.

Common Lands

As common land is distinguished by common use, information and data on landuse categories is useful in understanding its occurrence. In the context of Andhra Pradesh, out of the nine-fold standard landuse classification, the following may be designated as common lands: (i) all forest lands, except those under regeneration, new plantation or sanctuaries; (ii) culturable waste; (iii) permanent pasture and grazing land (SPWD, 1990).

The surveys indicate that people depend heavily on commons for grazing, standing cattle and firewood collection. There are of course other functions like burial, cremation, playgrounds, farms etc. In most of the villages, there has been a constant decline of common land, either through encroachment and/or assignment.

State ownership of common resources is predominant through its forests, revenue and irrigation departments. The Department of Forests enjoys absolute control over forests, while granting certain privileges and concessions to the village population. Wasteland is under the purview of the Revenue Department. The structure of tanks and the water-spread area are administered by the Public Works Department and Irrigation Department, depending on the size. These departments are also responsible for repair and maintenance of water sources. In some cases responsibility for water distribution, repair and maintenance of small tanks has been vested in gram panchayats.

The only remaining common land which is wholly vested in panchayats are *porambokes*, which include grazing land, tank foreshore, beds of ruined tanks, threshing floors, burial and cremation ground, cattle stands etc. There is, however, a provision in the

Andhra Pradesh Gram Panchayat Act, 1964, that such *porambokes* may be resumed by the government by an executive notification in the Andhra Pradesh Gazette.

According to landuse statistics (1986-87) the total common land in the state was 75,81,458 hectares. Following a similar general pattern in all three regions, forests are the largest type of common land. Coastal Andhra has the lowest percentage of its area as common land (25 per cent) with a range of 15 per cent (Srikakulam) to 43 per cent (Visakhapatnam). Rayalaseema averages 28 per cent with district figures ranging from 16 per cent (Anantapur) to 38 per cent (Cuddapah). Telengana leads with an aggregate of 31 per cent which varies from 15 per cent (Medak, Nalgonda) to 53 per cent (Khammam).

It is quite evident that there has been a steady decline in the area under commons for reasons which include diversion of land for agriculture, industrial, or institutional purposes. From the available literature it is clear that agriculture and forest projects are the major beneficiaries. Regularisation of encroachments, once popular, has declined in the past few years. Between the period 1970-71 to 1986-87, the estimated loss of common land was of the order of 85 per cent. This decline is in turn explained by an increase in the area put to farming, housing, building, industries, roads etc. (SPWD, 1990).

The future diversion of forest land will be slow and cumbersome in view of the legal restrictions. Thus armed with legal protection and in several areas traditional commitments to judicious use, forests should retain their status as common land. Hence, land under culturable waste is usually targeted for distribution to the landless. This is a reflection on the government land distribution policy and is further entrenched in the philosophy and activities of NGOs in Andhra Pradesh. In addition, the *porambokes* too can be used for the purpose of welfare of the resident village communities, such as for distribution of house sites.

Animal Husbandry

The relative importance of different types of livestock to the people in a specific region is influenced by the prevailing culture, agro-climatic conditions, farming system and support structures. According to the livestock census (1987), the largest category is of bovines (64 per cent), followed by sheep (21 per cent) and goats (15 per cent). Comparison of livestock per 100 households across regions shows that Telengana leads in bovine population, Rayalaseema in sheep and goat, while coastal Andhra trails in all the three. This reflects in certain ways the order of priority accorded to livestock across the three regions.

Table 1.5 : Distribution of Livestock per 100 Households Across Regions, 1987

Region	Total	Adult Male	Adult Female	Young Stock	Sheep	Goat
Coastal Andhra	195	48	83	64	48	38
Rayalaseema	254	78	103	73	133	91
Telengana	325	111	104	110	101	69
Andhra Pradesh	251	75	94	82	82	58

Source : SPWD, 1990.

Sheep and goat, constituting one-third of the total livestock population, are important in several districts, particularly in Rayalaseema. Of the adult bovine population, 56 per cent are female and 44 per cent are male. There has been an 8 per cent decline of females between the period 1983 and 1987, while the male population has remained steady (SPWD, 1990). Although animal power for agriculture may be diminishing in importance because of increasing mechanisation, nevertheless, for small and marginal farmers, dependence on animal power continues. The population of female cattle and buffalo is larger than that of the males in 12 out of 22 districts, notably so in the delta region of coastal Andhra, Rayalaseema (excluding Kurnool) and Khammam in Telengana, which points to the likelihood of dairying. In other words, ownership of female buffalo is another indicator of the extent of dairying. Cross-breeding is also associated with dairying, but crossbred females are only 3.9 per cent and 3.5 per cent of the female cattle and buffalo, respectively. It should, however, also be pointed out that the simple fact of abundance of female bovine population does not automatically imply the propensity for dairying, as they may have been kept for dung or breeding purposes. Similarly the extent of availability of a market network and nature of pricing are also factors which would impede or promote dairying in a particular region or a village. In summary, the nature of animal husbandry in the state presents a picture of strong regional variations.

Closely related to animal husbandry is the issue of availability of fodder. Competition between the large and the small livestock is restricted to grazing. Smaller livestock, such as goat and sheep, are exclusively dependent on grazing, though the former are often fed leaf fodder. For cattle and buffalo the principal sources of feed are crop residues, cultivated fodder, green grass and, to a lesser extent, tree lopping.

The pattern of feeding shows a seasonal variation. During the monsoons grazing and grass collection are at a high, while as the climate turns drier grazing provides less and poor quality forage. Correspondingly it may be deduced that the nutritional status of livestock is best during the monsoons and dips sharply by the end of summer.

In 1986-87, 1.57 lakh hectares were under fodder crops, which constituted a mere 2 per cent of the net sown area of the state. Of the 1.57 lakh hectares 90 per cent was in coastal Andhra, 8 per cent in Telengana and 2 per cent in Rayalaseema. It is also clear from the available literature and the socio-economic surveys, that fodder cultivation is restricted to those having large holdings. Given the skewed distribution of land holding, it would then be restricted to a few large farms. It is, therefore, here that preservation and augmentation of community grazing land becomes imperative to enhance fodder availability to meet the requirements.

The institutional support services for animal husbandry activities also need to be assessed. Some of the major parameters would include: provision of veterinary services, breeding centres, artificial insemination etc. Based on the information available in the surveys, it is seen that in almost 80 per cent of the villages there is no veterinary dispensary. In the villages of coastal Andhra and Telengana region the average distance of a veterinary dispensary from the village is about 5 kms., while in Rayalaseema it is about 8 kms.

From Table 1.6 below it is clear that there is not much variation across the regions. For every 1,000 livestock, on an average only 1 veterinary dispensary is available. Also from the surveys it is clear that the status of support services for animal husbandry is quite inadequate in Andhra Pradesh. In the surveyed villages, a distinct regional pattern is discernible. In the coastal Andhra region, there is mention of shortage of fodder and lack of grazing facilities time and again (G. Mamidada, Pedur, Madepalli and Kumardevam). Telengana and Rayalaseema village surveys stress the animal husbandry potential of the region but bemoan lack of adequate veterinary facilities (Bhagepally, Konapur, S. Itikyal and Korrapadu).

Table 1.6 : Availability of Veterinary Services, 1987

Region	Number of veterinary dispensaries	Number of Livestock	Services per 1000 livestock
Coastal Andhra	1574	1,23,59,508	1.27
Rayalaseema	820	78,47,757	1.04
Telengana	1713	1,55,29,067	1.10
Total	4107	3,57,36,332	1.14

Source : SPWD, 1990.

Agricultural Practices

Andhra Pradesh continues to be a predominantly agricultural state. Seventy per cent of its population is dependent on agriculture and 40 per cent of the net domestic product of the state is generated from this sector. Over 70 per cent of the gross cropped area is used for the production of food grains, followed by oilseeds, which account for 16 per cent of the area. Rice is the most important food crop, while oilseeds, sugarcane, chilli, tobacco and cotton, are important commercial crops.

Food grain production in Andhra Pradesh increased from 6.35 million tonnes to 9.32 million tonnes during 1956-1981. While this is an impressive absolute increase, the share of Andhra Pradesh in all-India food production declined from 8.6 per cent to 7.7 per cent during the same period. If we compare the share of food grain production in Andhra Pradesh to total output for the country, *vis-à-vis* its share in population to total population, we find that the former is lower than the latter.

The abolition of various intermediaries was followed by an expansion of the agro-technical base in rural areas. Large investments were made in major, medium and minor irrigation projects. As a result of such massive investment the state's irrigation facilities, both government and private, have increased greatly. The net irrigated area increased from 23.43 lakh hectares or 24 per cent of the net sown area in 1950-51 to 35.22 lakh hectares in 1984-85 or 33 per cent of the net sown area. The total irrigated area in the state in 1984-85 works out to 44.69 lakh hectares which is 34 per cent of the total cropped area (Reddy, 1991).

Although the increase in the total irrigated area in the state, both gross and net, has been impressive during the last 30 years, there are large regional variations as is evident from Table 1.7.

Table 1.7: Percentage of Net Irrigated Area to Net Sown Area

Region	1955-56	1984-85
Coastal Andhra	47.0	53.6
Rayalaseema	12.0	18.5
Telengana	15.0	21.7
Andhra Pradesh	24.3	33.0

Source: Bureau of Economics and Statistics, AP (1984-85).

Rayalaseema region suffers not only from inadequate irrigation facilities but also from scanty rainfall, when compared to coastal Andhra and Telengana. As a matter of fact, 56 per cent of the area in Rayalaseema is drought prone, while in Telengana and coastal Andhra it is 13 per cent and 3.5 per cent respectively. In Andhra Pradesh, as a whole, 16.5 per cent of the total area is prone to drought and 16.1 per cent of the population of the state is affected by such drought conditions. The population affected by drought in Rayalaseema is almost 60 per cent; while the comparative figures for Telengana and coastal Andhra are 11.9 and 2.4 per cent, respectively.

However, taking the state as a whole the extension of irrigation facilities has been impressive. Vast areas of the state which were previously rainfed, particularly districts like Nalgonda, Karimnagar, Warangal and Khammam in Telengana region, and parts of Prakasam district and the uplands of Krishna district in Andhra region, have been provided canal irrigation from Nagarjunsagar and Sriramsagar projects. Over the last two decades nearly 5 lakh wells were energised and another 2 lakh were fitted with diesel engines. Incidentally, Andhra Pradesh occupies first place in energisation of wells.

Analysing the information on the sources of irrigation it is noted that in the villages of Andhra Pradesh as a whole, 50 per cent of the net irrigated area is through canal irrigation, followed by tanks (22 per cent), wells other than tube wells (19 per cent) and tube wells (5 per cent). A regional analysis, however, reveals a pattern somewhat different from the state pattern. In the coastal Andhra region almost two-third of the net irrigated area is irrigated by canals, followed by tank irrigation. In Telengana, both canal and tank irrigation are major sources of irrigation, while in Rayalaseema, wells (other than tube wells) are the chief source of irrigation.

A perusal of 71 survey reports, for which the data could be tabulated, reveals that while 18 out of 35 villages of coastal Andhra region have reported wet land in different proportions, the figure for Rayalaseema is interestingly 8 out of 14, and for Telengana, expectedly, it is 4 out of 22.

To sum up, it can be said that on the whole at least two-thirds of the sown area is completely dependent on the vagaries of weather. Even in the case of irrigated lands only 50 per cent of the cultivated area has assured irrigation. The balance of the irrigated area is covered by tanks and wells, which depend on rains for replenishment. This is further corroborated by the fact that although the state has one of the highest percentage of irrigated area, it also has large areas which are drought prone. In this context it becomes imperative to develop ground water sources and to promote dry farming in the state.

Cropping Pattern

Approximately 73 per cent of the agricultural area is under food crops, while non-food crops account for 27 per cent in terms of aerial acreage. While such a distribution almost holds true for the regions of coastal Andhra and Telengana, in Rayalaseema the acreage difference between food and non-food crop is only 7 percentage points. This is largely because paddy, a wet crop and a dominant crop, is not grown on a large scale in Rayalaseema due to prevalent dry conditions. Therefore, a larger extent of dry crop (both food and non-food) is noted in this region.

The major crops are: paddy, jowar, maize, red gram, green gram, groundnut, chillies, cotton, tobacco and sugarcane. The programme of modernisation of agriculture in Andhra Pradesh - increasing application of HYV seeds, chemical fertilisers and the use of improved agricultural implements - has led to an increase in total output as well as per acre yield of the major crops grown in the state. However, such changes are more noticeable in respect of large holdings owned by bigger farmers. A perusal of the village surveys highlights the fact that the use of modern implements and new technology in paddy cultivation has benefited mainly the big farmers, rather than the small and marginal farmers.

Rice occupies almost 28.6 per cent of the net sown area in the state. However, significant variation among regions is noted. In coastal Andhra, almost 46 per cent of the net sown area is under rice, while it is 20.6 per cent and 10.5 per cent in Telengana and Rayalaseema, respectively.

Jowar, the crop least affected by technological changes from the point of growth of yield per acre, is the most dominant crop in the villages of Telengana. It occupies almost 27 per cent of net sown area, as compared to the state figure of 15.2 per cent. In coastal Andhra and Rayalaseema the area under Jowar is 4.2 per cent and 14 per cent respectively.

Among the non-food crops, groundnut leads in terms of area under cultivation and accounts for 13.7 per cent of the net sown area. The other major non-food crops are pulses, cotton, tobacco and chillies. Again a significant regional variation is observed while analysing the dominance of different non-food crops. Groundnut is found to be the dominant non-food crop in Rayalaseema, while pulses are the chief non-food crops in the villages of coastal Andhra and Telengana. With food crops being more dominant in the latter two regions, it is quite understandable that the extent of non-food crops in these regions would be considerably lower when compared to Rayalaseema region. Cotton and tobacco are grown more extensively in coastal Andhra, as compared to Rayalaseema and Telengana, although the acreage under these crops is quite low (Reddy, 1991). Sugarcane is another crop which is seemingly on the rise, especially in the coastal Andhra region.

As per the surveys, the crops are essentially grown under two cropping seasons, i.e. *kharif* (June to November) and *rabi* (December to March). During the summer, i.e. March to May, most of the land is left fallow except in some areas with better irrigation facilities, where some vegetables and, at times, even paddy is grown. In the surveyed villages of coastal Andhra region, paddy is the most popular crop. Some of the other crops that are frequently mentioned are pulses, jowar, bajra, chillies, sugarcane and tobacco. There is also mention of cotton (in Ponnalur), gingili (in Pachipenta, Vemulapudi) etc. Among the surveyed villages in the Rayalaseema region, the most popular crops reported are paddy and groundnut, while fruits (especially of the citrus variety) are also common. Cultivation of sugarcane (in Iruvaram and Moram), and sunflower (in Chinna Tumbalam) are also reported. In respect of Kadithota it has been recorded that the cropping pattern has significantly changed over the years with the proportion of food crops declining from two-third to one-sixth. For Telengana, the surveyed villages report paddy as the major crop, followed by groundnut, green gram, castor, maize, jowar and sugarcane. A couple of villages (Repakagommu and Chennipadu) report cultivation of cotton, tobacco and chilli. Sunflower is also reportedly grown in Chennipadu and Sangam. A mango garden has been extolled in the report on Mandalapally.

Land Revenue

The local demand for the *Fasli* 1392 was Rs. 6874.05 lakh, with coastal Andhra accounting for 62 per cent of the demand, followed by Rayalaseema 24 per cent. Only 14 per cent of the demand is shown against Telengana. While coastal Andhra and Telengana paid 22 per cent of their demand, Rayalaseema collected only 1.5 per cent of its demand (which included arrears). This clearly indicates a slackness in the collection of land revenue which, if collected systematically, would go someway in supporting developmental expenditure (Table 1.8).

Table 1.8: Demand, Collection and Balance (DCB) of Land Revenue Across Regions (upto 84-85)

(Rs. in lakhs)

Region	Demand	Collection	Written off	Balance
Coastal Andhra	4265.44	977.72	5.27	3282.45
Rayalaseema	1632.23	25.84	—	1606.39
Telengana	976.38	221.51	25.02	729.85
Andhra Pradesh	6874.05	1225.07	30.29	5618.69

Source : Bureau of Economics and Statistics, AP (1984-85).

4. AGRONOMICS

Agronomics essentially encompasses the production processes involved in agricultural operations. It analyses the inputs and outputs involved in the production of a particular crop. The inputs are basically some form of land, labour and capital, while the output constitutes the total produce in monetary terms or in physical quantity terms. An analysis of this nature brings out the dimensions of productivity and efficiency of a particular agricultural practice or a crop. In the following section the agronomics of three villages are presented. These three villages are selected from each of the three regions, namely, coastal Andhra, Rayalaseema and Telengana. The present section is being presented in the form of case studies culled from the surveys. Given their disparate presentation, it was not possible to quantify the available information to arrive at an overview or generalisation.

Atmakur village, Guntur district, Coastal Andhra

The major crops here are irrigated paddy, black gram, red gram and sugarcane. Sugarcane is seen to be the most profitable crop in this village followed by paddy, red gram and black gram. A shift towards sugarcane, a phenomenon which has been observed in the recent surveys, is obviously on account of the fact that sugarcane, has a higher profit margin (Table 1.9).

Table 1.9 : Agronomics of Atmakur Village, 1991

Crop	Average yield per acre	Total Cost (in Rs.)	Gross Income (in Rs.)	Net Income (in Rs.)
Paddy	19 Qtls	2000	6270	4270
Black gram	4 Qtls	700	3200	2500
Red gram	4 Qtls	1200	3200	2000
Sugarcane	35 tonnes	3500	10150	6650

Source : Socio-Economic Survey of Atmakur Village, Guntur District, 1991.

The major supply inputs include the following :

(i) *Seeds* : Improved seeds are obtained by the cultivators from the depots of AP State Seed Development Corporation at Guntur and Vijayawada and Agriculture depot at Mangalagiri. Most of the improved seed is procured from local farms and from their own sources.

(ii) *Fertiliser* : There are four sources for obtaining fertiliser — private dealers; agricultural depot (Mangalagiri); Primary Agricultural Co-operative Society (PACS), outlets of Agro-industries Corporation and MARKFED (Mangalagiri); and directly from the manufacturers.

(iii) *Insecticides* : Insecticides are procured from three sources — private dealers; Guntur District Co-operative Marketing Society Ltd. (Mangalagiri); PACS, outlets of Agro-industries Corporation and MARKFED (Mangalagiri).

(iv) *Agricultural Implements* : Agricultural implements are procured through agriculture department and from private industries at Chilakaluripeta, Tadikonda and Sattenpalli.

(v) *Agricultural Credit* : Both short-term and long-term credit is available from the Bank of India, Pedavadlapudi, and

> the PACS at Mangalagiri. But these are mostly availed of by the rich farmers, who are in a position to provide securities required for getting a loan. The small and marginal farmers, normally borrow from the rich *ryots* paying an interest of 2 per cent per month.

The farm produce is marketed in three ways: (i) sold directly to rice millers in the village itself, (ii) sold to mills through middle men, (iii) sold at the Agriculture Marketing Centres.

The agricultural wages prevailing in the village for planting, harvesting etc. are Rs. 20 to 25 per day for men and Rs. 10 to 15 per day for women. They are paid in cash. Recently a new system has come into vogue. The landholders give wages on contract basis to a group of labourers. For plantation of seedlings and harvesting, the wages are Rs. 150 to 200 per acre.

The economy being largely dependent on agriculture, there is a seasonal variation in the availability of employment. Near complete employment is achieved usually in the months of July through February, with December being the peak month for employment when harvesting of paddy takes place. Agricultural operations are almost absent from March to June.

Kalagatur village, Chittoor district, Rayalaseema

The main crops in this village are paddy, groundnut, sugarcane and mulberry. The cost of labour is taken as Rs. 20 per day for males and Rs. 15 per day for females. It is clear from the analysis of the information as presented in the surveys, that groundnut under rainfed conditions, emerges as the least profitable crop followed by paddy, groundnut under irrigated conditions, sugarcane and lastly mulberry.

If we consider the risk factor, mulberry is the most risky crop, because during the rearing stage, if any infection strikes, the entire crop of silkworms dies. On the positive side, the price of cocoons in 1991 was as high as Rs. 200 per kg, almost three times the 1992 market rate (Table 1.10).

Table 1.10 : Agronomics of Kalagatur Village, 1992

Crops	Yield per acre (in kg.)	Total Cost (in Rs.)	Gross Income (in Rs.)	Net Income (in Rs.)
Paddy	2,250	4,100	6,750	2650
Sugarcane	40,000	4,850	18,000	13,150
Groundnut (Rainfed)	400	1,950	2,800	850
Groundnut (Irrigated)	800	2,550	5,600	3,050
Mulberry	300	7,400	24,000	16,600

Source: Socio-Economic Survey of Kalagatur village, Chittoor District, 1992.

It is evident from the surveys that the risk averting type of farmers prefer groundnut and paddy, under irrigated conditions. But the best bet, under irrigated conditions is sugarcane. Mulberry is the enterprising farmer's crop. It is noted that the various risk-profitability options are open to a farmer having irrigation facilities only. For a farmer with only dry lands, his options are limited and so is his profit.

Kothur village, Adilabad district, Telengana region

In Kothur the major crops of economic importance are paddy, maize, jowar, turmeric, red gram, green gram, sesame, sunflower and groundnut. In general 50 per cent of the total income from agriculture is invested in production, while 50 per cent of the gross return accrues as net income to the cultivators (Table 1.11).

In this village sunflower fetches the maximum income followed by paddy, maize, and red gram. The least profitable crops are jowar, and green gram. Marketable surplus in this village is not much as most of the farmers belong to the category of small and marginal peasantry. Approximately around 60-70 per cent of the agricultural produce is consumed domestically, which leaves only about 30-40 per cent for marketing. Coupled with this are the institutional problems of markets and credits.

Table 1.11: Agronomics of Kothur Village, 1993

Crop	Yield per acre (in kgs)	Total Cost (in Rs.)	Gross Income (in Rs.)	Net Income (in Rs.)
Paddy	1,540	2,200	5,390	3,190
Maize	1,100	1,500	2,915	1,415
Jowar	450	1000	1,170	170
Groundnut	350	2,500	2,800	300
Sunflower	750	1,600	5,625	4,025
Red gram	180	600	1,800	1,200
Green gram	160	600	1,240	640

Source : Socio-Economic Survey of Kothur village, Adilabad District, 1993.

5. ECONOMY

Macro Features

Andhra Pradesh, which ranks fifth in the country in terms of area and population, witnessed an acceleration in its overall economic growth in the post-independence period. Compared to a low growth rate of 1.9 per cent in the 1960s, the state domestic product grew at 3.3 per cent in the 1970s and 4.4 per cent during 1980-86. The acceleration has been mainly due to the performance of the secondary and tertiary sectors. The share of the secondary sector increased from 13 per cent in 1960-61 to 21 per cent in 1986-87 and of the tertiary sector from 28 per cent to 40 per cent during the same period.

The phases of industrial growth of Andhra Pradesh differ from that of the other southern states. For instance, Tamil Nadu experienced rapid industrial progress between 1950-75 followed by deceleration, and Karnataka gained momentum in the 1960s, but was unable to sustain it after 1975 when deceleration set in. On the other hand, Andhra Pradesh entered the rapid growth phase in the mid-seventies and has shown no signs of deceleration as yet. The share of the manufacturing sector in the state domestic product increased from 8 per cent in 1960-61 to 13 per cent in 1985-86.

State expenditure, which formed 12 per cent of the net state domestic product in 1960-61, had increased to 13 per cent in 1970-71, further to 19.5 per cent in 1980-81 and to 26.8 per cent in 1986-87. In per capita terms, governmental expenditure had increased from Rs. 33 in 1960-61 to Rs. 76 in 1970-71, to Rs. 266 in 1980-81 and to Rs. 625 in 1986-87 at current prices. Of this, per capita plan expenditure had increased from Rs. 14 in 1960-61 to Rs. 206 in 1986-87.

Food grain production had increased from 64.93 lakh tonnes in 1960-61 to 99 lakh tonnes in 1987-88, with a peak of 118.8 lakh tonnes in 1983-84.

The state consumer price index for industrial workers recorded an increase of 125 per cent during the period 1975-76 to 1987-88, while at the all-India level it had increased by 135.1 per cent during this period. The consumer price index for agricultural workers during this period increased by 66.6 per cent in the state as compared to 85 per cent at the all-India level.

Poverty

Ahluwalia (1978) has examined the trends in the incidence of rural poverty in Andhra Pradesh from 1957-58 to 1973-74 using the poverty line of Rs. 15 per capita per month at 1960-61 prices, and adjusting it for various years with consumer price index for agricultural labourers. His estimates reveal that the early sixties were marked by a fall in the incidence of poverty, followed by a rising phase in the late sixties. Subsequent studies have indicated a sharp decline in the incidence of poverty in both rural and urban areas in the late seventies and early eighties.

Radhakrishna *et al.* (1985) computed the incidence of poverty across rural and urban classes for the developed and backward regions of Andhra Pradesh, using Rs. 101.80 per capita per month as the poverty line for rural areas [as given by the Planning Commission for the year 1983-84 based on the state sample of 38th round of National Sample Survey (NSS) data]. The poor have been further classified into two groups, namely, very poor and moderately poor by treating the households whose per capita expenditure was less than 75 per cent of the poverty line, i.e. Rs. 76.35, as very poor.

In the rural areas of the developed region which comprises East Godavari, West Godavari and Krishna districts, only 19 per cent of the households were very poor and 29 per cent were moderately poor. In the backward region, comprising Anantapur, Kurnool and Mahabubnagar, as many as 50 per cent of the households were very poor and 30 per cent were moderately poor.

In the developed region agricultural labourers accounted for 67 per cent of the very poor while in the backward region they account for 57 per cent of the very poor. In the developed region, the incidence of poverty among the cultivator class is very low, whereas in the backward region, a sizeable proportion of the poor are cultivators. These facts are further corroborated by the village surveys. The cultivators account for 24 per cent of the very poor and 41 per cent of the moderately poor households in the backward regions of Andhra Pradesh.

The major conclusions regarding the status of poverty, based on a review of literature as well as the village surveys, are:

(a) There has been a declining trend in the incidence of poverty, particularly in the seventies and eighties;
(b) Poverty is concentrated among the agricultural labourers is almost all the districts as well as the cultivators and self-employed class in the districts of Srikakulam, Anantapur, Mahabubnagar, Medak, Adilabad, Karimnagar and Warangal;
(c) Inter-district comparisons reveal that agricultural development in general reduces the incidence of poverty among cultivators and self-employed class, but it does not improve the lot of the agricultural labourers who constitute the core of the poor;
(d) With agricultural development the absolute numbers of poor agricultural labour households increases, although the poverty level declines, since the number of agricultural labour households expands significantly; and
(e) It is seen that Rayalaseema and Telengana have a larger percentage of their population below the poverty line (60 per cent) as compared to coastal Andhra (49 per cent).

In the 42nd round of NSS surveys (1986-87), 47.57 per cent of the population and 41.85 per cent of the households were below the poverty line in rural areas. The corresponding figures for urban areas were 40.74 per cent and 35.31 per cent. This works out to 21.23 million persons in rural areas and 6.39 million persons in urban areas living below the poverty line. In terms of poor households, the figures are 4.27 million in rural areas and 1.24 million in urban areas of Andhra Pradesh. Thus, poverty is clearly pervasive and is likely to remain so, unless more positive and permanent strategies to remove it are undertaken.

Profile of the Poorest of the Poor

A profile of the last man/woman in one village from each of the three regions is presented. Their characteristics have been extracted after a careful review of the surveys on hand.

Mellika Rajaiyya in North Mopur village is a Yanadi Scheduled Caste. He lives all alone in a *kuchha* house. His wife died long ago. He has no sons/daughters to look after him. He is illiterate and has no land or livestock. He used to survive by doing agricultural labour work in his younger days but is now starving and ekes out his living by begging in the village temple. He wears clothes given to him by villagers and generally puts some leaves on his head to avoid the heat. He also receives a monthly old age pension of Rs. 30. He has never received any support from the government nor has he ever approached it, for he has no faith in the government. The old age pension he is receiving is too paltry. For him, life is left with no meaning and he eagerly awaits death. He felt delighted when we photographed him and talked to him, for he felt at last somebody was giving him importance (North Mopur village, district Nellore, coastal Andhra).

Kummari Buddanna, 65, is a potter by profession. He had to give up his traditional occupation about 10 years ago when he developed cataract. His wife died seven years ago and his two daughters are married and settled in Kosigi Mandal. Talking about the old days, Buddanna said that he used to be the only potter in Chinna Tumbalam and the neighbouring four villages. The main articles that he used to make were pots for storing water (*kunda*), pots for cooking (*madike*), drainage pipes (*dooni*) and small earthen lamps (*pramedalu*). For preparing these articles he used to get black clay from Mucchigiri and red earth from Basaldoddi villages. He used to mix them in a 50:50 ratio. For firing the pots he used paddy straw and fuel wood. He was helped in his work by his wife. There was high demand for his products on account of his monopoly. Earlier, the payment used to be in kind and he used to get one-fourth *seer* to two *seers* of paddy depending on the size of the pots. Later people started paying him in cash. By tradition he was expected to provide a few pots free during certain village festivals such as the Gangamma festival. Pot making used to provide him employment for nine months a year. During the months of July, August and September he used to work as an agricultural labourer. Buddanna has no land of his own. He said that the introduction of plastic pots for storing water has drastically cut down on the demand for his products. Now living a lonely dark life in one corner of the village, Buddanna survives on the benevolence of his neighbours who feed him twice a day. His potter's wheel lies disused in one corner of his house (Chinna Tumbalam village, district Kurnool, Rayalaseema, 1993).

Kothur village has a total population of 1,334, out of which 658 are males and 676 are females. Pallerla Butchamma belongs to the *vysya* community and was married to a palmist who divorced her. About 20 years ago she was married once again to Ramanaiah. Ramanaiah used to sell salt and other things in the surrounding villages. About 10 years ago he too died leaving a small one-room house with broken tiles. She does not have any land nor does she know any trade or service. If one enters her so-called house one does not see anything except a small mat, three or four utensils and a few torn items of clothing. She used to work in the local school which paid her a paltry sum of Rs. 60 per month. Even this work was not continuous. Presently she does household work in two or three houses, cleaning utensils, sweeping etc. If the people are kind enough they feed her, otherwise for three or four days of service they give her Rs. 3 as wages. She is about 60 years old and even doing such work is difficult for her. On an average she gets Rs. 20 per week. The Andhra Pradesh government has a social security scheme under which widows, landless agricultural workers, and old people are provided monthly pensions. She applied for the old age pension three years ago but there was no response from the authorities. She has applied once again. Disowned by her community, neglected by society and cold shouldered by government officials, she is now waiting for some divine help (Kothur village, district Adilabad, Telengana, 1993).

It would be clear from the above extracts that one of the characteristics common to these people, besides, of course, their being poorest of the poor, is age. This would be an indication that certain groups of people like senior citizens (irrespective of gender), small children, mothers, girl children and widows constitute the most vulnerable sections of rural society. The extracts also throw light on the process of alienation operating on such groups from both the society and the government.

Rural Credit

The Government of Andhra Pradesh has been assisting the co-operative movement through progressive budgetary allocations under successive state plans. *Inter alia* the following types of co-operatives have been promoted: credit co-operatives, warehousing and marketing co-operatives, process co-operatives, consumers' co-operatives, weaker sections co-operatives (farming, labour etc.), sugar co-operatives, handloom and powerloom co-operatives, sericulture co-operatives, village industrial co-operatives, co-operative spinning mills, and fishermen co-operatives.

The surveys reveal that co-operative establishments in the villages are increasing, though at a slow rate. An analysis of the surveys indicates that in a majority of the villages, there are no co-operatives. Further the establishment of co-operatives is limited to sectors like dairy, weaving, toddy-tapping etc., although absence of milk co-operatives has been reported in several surveys (Ammapalem, Pachipenta, Chollangi Peta, Rellivalasa, Mamidipalli etc.). Of late, co-operative thrust is also being extended to sectors like fisheries (in Sangam) and sericulture. It is also observed that there is a need to enhance the delivery mechanism of the co-operative societies, as from most of the surveys one can deduce that several co-operative societies have become defunct.

The main objective of a credit policy/institution in a developing economy is to provide a large number of small farmers with credit. The banks are not interested in doing business with small farmers as they find it uneconomical. In this context the co-operative credit movement has to take root and flourish in rural areas. Going by its success in some other parts of the country, it has proved to be an important channel of rural credit.

In Andhra Pradesh, the government has initiated a new experiment in co-operative credit through the 'single window system'. This was first introduced in 1985 in three districts; and after the successful implementation in those districts, it has been agreed in principle to implement the system in the entire state. The main objective of the single window system is to co-ordinate the activities of different credit and institutional agencies so that the farmer has to approach only one agency for any form of help which he/she needs. At the village level this objective is being achieved through the Primary Agricultural Co-operative Credit Societies. From the surveys, it is clear that such schemes are still in a nascent stage as far as their spatial distribution is concerned. The absence of agricultural credit facilities has been reported in several villages (e.g. in Kothur, Elurupadu, Vemulapudi, etc.). There are also instances of Primary Agricultural Co-operative Credit Societies becoming dysfunctional (Madepalli).

The Andhra Pradesh State Co-operatives Bank has been very active and it is noted that Andhra Pradesh leads the country in agricultural development banking, though it lags behind in loan recovery. Decentralisation has also been brought about in rural credit delivery with the introduction of the service area concept. Under this, each rural or semi-urban branch will operate in a limited service area of not more than 25 villages for the purpose of lending to priority sectors. Such schemes have led to improvement in the delivery system.

Village Industries

The development of industries in rural areas has been an integral part of industrial policy and programmes for rural development in India, though the degree of priority given to it has varied over the years. In the early years, development of industries in rural areas was viewed primarily as a programme for the preservation and revitalisation of traditional rural industries but not as a programme for rural industrialisation. As a result, rural industries did not play an effective role in providing a reasonable level of income to those engaged in them or in integrating the rural areas into the overall process of industrialisation in the country.

From a review of the village surveys it is noted that modern small-scale industries are yet to find a foothold in these villages. In more than 75 per cent of the villages surveyed, it is found that there is conspicuous absence of modern small and cottage industries, and the ones available are largely rice and flour mills and that too mostly in the coastal Andhra region. Nevertheless traditional village industries prevalent in the rural areas of Andhra Pradesh are spinning and weaving, basket-making, palm fibre extraction, toddy tapping, *beedi* making, oil pressing, pottery, carpentry, black-smithy, brick-kilns etc. It is quite clear that spinning and weaving are the only truly industrial activities of the villages. A regional flavour is provided by fibre-based industries in the coastal Andhra region, by sericulture in Rayalaseema, and by *beedi*-making and toddy-tapping in Telengana. It is interesting to note that in several reports, particularly those relating to coastal Andhra region, absence of major or significant village industries has been recorded despite the existence of rice mills (which perhaps are so common that they are not considered significant). In Korrapadu village which was surveyed in 1984 and again in 1986, the earlier survey records the absence of village industries while the later one mentions rice and flour mills and pottery. In Lakshmipuram (1983) a shift from weaving to agricultural labour has been recorded. In Madepalli (1986) processing of human hair is mentioned as an important industrial activity. In Venkatapuram (1991) there are powerlooms.

It is imperative that industries in villages should be developed on the basis of the skills of the people and resources of the region. Agriculture being the most dominant activity in all the villages reported, it is necessary that agro-based industries are encouraged. Examples may be sericulture, pisciculture, palm-oil extraction, etc.

The state has intervened by establishing primary industrial

societies for taluks and villages; nevertheless, rural industrialisation is still to come of age in a manner in which it can bring about a change in the economic landscape of the villages.

6. GOVERNMENT INTERVENTIONS

Any state intervention in rural areas has to essentially address issues pertaining to employment generation, poverty alleviation, provision of social infrastructure (like education, health and family welfare, drinking water facilities, public distribution system etc.), and provision of infrastructure to enhance the organisational abilities of the villagers, among others. It may further be noted that more than the sectoral intervention, it is equally significant to understand the mechanics of such intervention. For instance, it would be inappropriate if the state or even the district unilaterally decided on the nature of public investment in the villages. In this context the present national agenda of political decentralisation, with increased participation from the under-privileged sections of society through the gram panchayats, is a right step in the direction of empowering the people.

Most of the interventions listed earlier largely fall under the rubric of rural development. The interventions in the sectors falling within the domain of rural development have essentially been addressed by the Five-year Plans. Since the initiation of the planning process, a major thrust has been given to rural development in general. The Eighth Plan document of Andhra Pradesh clearly emphasises the importance of provision of social infrastructure. Herein, the sectors which are being given priority are population control, eradication of illiteracy, universalisation of elementary education, provision of safe drinking water and primary health facilities. It may be noted that although the intentions of the state in improving the standard of living of the rural population are sincere, nevertheless it would perhaps be a Herculean task to provide such facilities to one and all given the social milieu of our villages. It remains to be seen how the government intervenes in the wake of liberalisation, wherein the role of the state will be considerably reduced and may be limited to that of a facilitator.

To achieve the objective of alleviating poverty by generating employment, the major programmes being implemented include Integrated Rural Development Programme (IRDP), Training of Rural Youth for Self-Employment (TRYSEM), National Rural Employment Programme (NREP), Jawahar Rozgar Yojana (JRY), among others. Despite the conceptual shortcomings of IRDP, it continues to be one of most popular programmes of the Central government. The programme is being implemented in almost all the villages surveyed. It is also evident from the surveys that the beneficiaries of this programme are largely the Backward Castes, followed by Scheduled Castes and Tribes. A perusal of the surveys further indicates a bias in identifying the beneficiaries. The major shortcomings of this programme revealed by the surveys are:

(a) It is not in conformity with the natural and human resource base of the area;

(b) The thrust on supply of milch cattle as an asset to the poor is clearly evident which, in course of time, becomes a burden on them, as there is no fodder available to feed the cattle;

(c) The poor often find it extremely difficult to pay off the loan as the returns from the asset are not adequate;

(d) The delivery mechanism of this programme is not transparent enough so as to provide the limited resources to a wider and more deserving section of the poor; and

(e) The identification of the poor in most the surveys deviates significantly from the desirable.

It may be added that such programmes directed towards the poor do not sufficiently take into consideration the fact that the poor are not a homogeneous group. Studies indicate that it would be worthwhile to arrive at a typology of the poor based on their varying levels of deprivation. This would perhaps be most useful in reaching the poorest of the poor.

On the education front, in the villages surveyed, the progress is far from the objectives laid down by the state. As noted earlier, in less than 10 per cent of the villages (e.g. Repakagommu and Sangam) any kind of intervention in the form of Total Literacy

Campaign or adult literacy exists. Even the institutional support to the education sector is inadequate.

Interventions in the rural health sector are almost non-existent, at least in the villages surveyed. Even the primary health centres are not adequately equipped to improve the health conditions of the rural masses. Surveys reflect the poor state of the dispensaries and inefficiency on part of the visiting medical professionals. Consequently, the family welfare programme has also got diluted, which in turn adversely affects the objectives of limiting population growth.

Provision of protected drinking water is seen to exist in only 25 per cent of the villages surveyed. Intervention in rural sanitation is almost absent except in one or two villages where some community initiatives are being taken for better rural hygiene.

Rural housing is one area where Andhra Pradesh can be held up as an example. Several survey reports mention implementation of weaker section housing programme in the villages. The acquisition and distribution of house sites to the weaker sections of the society is being done in a systematic way. The government, through its agency, the Andhra Pradesh State Housing Corporation Limited, has been adopting a two-pronged approach: (i) sites and services programme; and (ii) permanent housing programme. Under the former, basic infrastructure like community wells, roads etc. are provided. The permanent housing programme consists of three components — rural semi-permanent, rural permanent and urban permanent. Government subsidy, loan and beneficiaries' contribution taken together provide the finances for this scheme. The cornerstone of this programme is self-help. The state ranked first in the country in its achievement in providing housing to the poor. More than 15 lakh houses have been constructed since its inception in 1979. During 1992-93, 2,03,574 houses have been constructed, which is an all-time record.

Another achievement has been in the organisation of the public distribution system. Although the strategy of supplying rice at Rs. 2 per kg, on a sustainable basis, might be highly uneconomical, nevertheless it is also a pointer to the fact that there exists a section which finds it hard to afford rice at other than subsidised rates. Coupled with this is the differentiated ration card system, which determines the eligibility of a person to avail of subsidised food grains. An analysis of the surveys indicates a mixed response to this strategy. The public distribution system or the fair price shop is seen to exist in only 50 per cent of the villages surveyed. The behavioural responses of the target group to the functioning of the fair price shops are also not very positive.

The ban on arrack is another popular scheme implemented by the state. This scheme is perhaps next only to the Rs. 2 per kg rice scheme in popularity. However, it remains to be seen how effectively such a scheme can be implemented. In this regard a more positive intervention would be to change the attitude of the people, which may not be possible only through legislation.

In general, interventions by the state government are much less both in terms of their nature and magnitude. The state government's intervention is noted in the areas of subsidised food grains, rural housing, pension schemes and upliftment of the scavenging class. Therefore, the schemes pertaining to generation of employment, perhaps the most crucial one in the present context, are largely those sponsored by the Central Government. It is quite clear from the surveys that a more participatory approach should be adopted for any intervention by the state, otherwise a clear divergence in the viewpoints of the villagers and those of the decision makers is inevitable, which will lead to the failure of those schemes.

GLOSSARY

Beedi	Indian cigarette (tobacco rolled in tendu leaves)
Benami	Ostensible change in the name of the owner of property to circumvent the law
Brahmin	One of the highest or priestly caste in the Hindu social system
Deepawali/ Diwali	Hindu festival celebrated to commemorate the return of an Indian God Ram from exile
Dussehra	Hindu festival to celebrate the defeat of Ravan (evil) by Ram
Fasli	Agricultural Year
Inam	Grant of land free of land revenue or at a favourable rate of land revenue, made during the British rule
Inamdari	The system of Inam
Jagir	Service lands, a tenure common under the native Government in which the public revenues of a tract of land are made over to a servant of the state
Jamun	A type of tropical fruit
Jatras	A religious procession to honour local deities
Kammas	The name of a Telugu lower caste
Kapus/Balijas	Backward caste groups
Khadi	Hand woven cloth made of hand-spun yarn
Kharif	Crop sown in rainy season (June-July) and harvested in September-October
Konda	The Indian tree-pie
Mahalwari	An intermediate tenurial system wherein the village is treated as "Mahal" (body) and the cultivators are responsible for payment of revenue
Makarsankranti	Festival celebrated by Hindus in the month of January

Mokhansadari	A system wherein the village is held on service tenure. It is granted on a favourable assessment or no assessment to any person for past or expected service
Mustadari	Rentier of the villages
Muttadari	Old tract in hilly or forest areas
Nizams	A dynasty of princes/kings of the erstwhile state of Hyderabad
Panchayat	Rural local self-governing body at the village level
Poramboke	A term used to denote lands which are at the disposal of the Government and generally set apart for community use, such as forest, tank bed, grazing, road etc.
Rabi	Crop sown in Autumn (October-November) and harvested in Summer (March-April)
Reddis	An intermediate Hindu caste in Andhra Pradesh
Ryot	Cultivator/Peasant
Ryotwari	According to or with ryots, applied to revenue settlements
Sarf-e-khas	Land owned and controlled by Nizams
Tangedu	*Cassia augustifolia*, the wild floral species used in tanning
Telugu	Vernacular language of Andhra Pradesh
Ugadi	Telugu New Year
Yanadi	A scheduled caste group
Yerakarra	A red corn
Zamindar	A landlord or a proprietor directly responsible to the state for payment of revenue for the land he possesses
Zamindari	The office and right of a zamindar; the tract of land constituting the possession of a zamindar

LIST OF VILLAGE SOCIO-ECONOMIC SURVEYS CONDUCTED BY OFFICER TRAINEES

S.No.	Village	District	Year	Officer Trainee
COASTAL ANDHRA				
1.	G. Mamidada	E. Godavari	1983	L. Panigrahi
2.	Penuguduru	E. Godavari	1985	J. Ragmond Peter
3.	Chollangi Peta	E. Godavari	1986	S. Bhattacharya
4.	Routhulapadi	E. Godavari	1987	S. Narsing Rao
5.	Polavaram	Krishna	1983	Rajiv Sharma
6.	Rangapuram	Krishna	1987	Abhay Tripathi
7.	Seethanapalli	Krishna	1989	Ms. Y. Sri Lakshmi
8.	Pedapatnam	Krishna	1992	Sumita Dawra
9.	Pedur	Nellore	1983	N. Ramesh Kumar
10.	Gandipalem	Nellore	1985	S.K. Joshi
11.	Patur	Nellore	1986	J.C. Sharma
12.	Kothur	Nellore	1987	Bhambal R. Meena
13.	Gonupalli	Nellore	1992	Ajay Jain
14.	North Mopur	Nellore	1993	Sanjay Jaju
15.	Chethupalli	Visakhapatnam	1983	CBS Venkataramana
16.	Vemulapudi	Visakhapatnam	1985	A.C. Punetha
17.	Komira	Visakhapatnam	1987	Rajeshwar Tiwari
18.	Iruvada	Visakhapatnam	1991	Sunil Sharma
19.	Pachipenta	Vizianagaram	1984	Bhanwar Lal
20.	Mamidipalli	Vizianagaram	1988	Aditya N. Das
21.	Rellivalasa	Vizianagaram	1989	Shalini Misra
22.	Sathivada	Vizianagaram	1989	Adhar Sinha
23.	Gudem	Srikakulam	1984	Dinesh Kumar
24.	Lingalavalasa	Srikakulam	1985	Ajay Misra
25.	Elurupadu	W. Godavari	1984	Randeep Sudan
26.	Madepalli	W. Godavari	1986	Kumari Veena
27.	Kumardevam	W. Godavari	1988	N.K. Prasad
28.	Yerragunta Palli	W. Godavari	1990	R. Karikal Valaven

(Contd.)

S.No.	Village	District	Year	Officer Trainee
29.	Poduru	W. Godavari	1992	R.P. Sisodia
30.	Pothunuru	W. Godavari	1993	Vikas Raj
31.	Ponnalur	Prakasam	1984	V.K. Agarwal
32.	Koppolu	Prakasam	1986	H.L. Samariya
33.	Dharmavaram	Prakasam	1988	R.R. Mishra
34.	Nandivelagu	Guntur	1987	Harish Kumar
35.	Ganeshuni Palem	Guntur	1989	A. Giridhar
36.	Atmakur	Guntur	1991	Shashank Goel
TELENGANA				
37.	Dharmapuri	Karimnagar	1983	K.P. Chandra
38.	Konapur	Karimnagar	1985	A.V. Sagar
39.	Sabitam	Karimnagar	1988	D. Sreenivasulu
40.	Irukulla	Karimnagar	1990	A. Shanthi Kumari
41.	Kothapalli	Karimnagar	1993	Budithi Rajashekar
42.	Kamalapuram	Warangal	1983	M. Nagarjuna
43.	Chinnaboinapalli	Warangal	1987	Dr. D. Sambasivarao
44.	Yashwantapur	Warangal	1989	Poonam Singh
45.	Namiligonda	Warangal	1992	G. Sai Prasad
46.	S. Itikyal	Medak	1984	T. Vijay Kumar
47.	Venkatapuram	Medak	1991	Rajat Bhargava
48.	Bhagepally	Nizamabad	1984	M.G. Gopal
49.	Sangam	Nizamabad	1992	Harpreet Singh
50.	Sangam	Nizamabad	1993	Ms. Mythili Yerra
51.	Bhoodan Pochampalli	Nalgonda	1984	L.V. Subramanyam
52.	Ammapalem	Khammam	1984	T. Radha
53.	Mandalapally	Khammam	1986	R. Subramanyam
54.	Mustibanda	Khammam	1988	J.S.V. Prasad
55.	Repakagommu	Khammam	1991	K. Praveen Kumar
56.	Laxmapur (B.K.)	Mahabubnagar	1984	P. Subramanyam
57.	Venkateswarlabavi	Mahabubnagar	1986	Dr. P.V. Ramesh

(Contd.)

Appendix-A : *(Contd.)*

S.No.	Village	District	Year	Officer Trainee
58.	Chennipadu	Mahabubnagar	1991	K.S. Jawahar Reddy
59.	Gangaram	Rangareddy	1989	Mrs. I.R. Kumudini
60.	Kothur	Adilabad	1993	K. Vijayanand
RAYALASEEMA				
61.	Lakshmipuram	Kurnool	1983	Latha Rao
62.	G. Singavaram	Kurnool	1985	V. Nagi Reddy
63.	Bychegiri	Kurnool	1987	Satish Chandra
64.	Kadithota	Kurnool	1989	Dr. Vijay Kumar
65.	Chinna Tumbalam	Kurnool	1993	S.S. Rawat
66.	Duskuppam	Chittoor	1983	Kamal Kr. B. Pargi
67.	Palluru	Chittoor	1984	B.P. Acharya
68.	Iruvaram	Chittoor	1986	Dr. Manmohan Singh
69.	Moram	Chittoor	1988	Debabrata Kantha
70.	Kalagatur	Chittoor	1992	K.R. Rao
71.	Korrapadu	Anantapur	1984	S.P. Singh
72.	Korrapadu	Anantapur	1986	Suresh Chand
73.	Guttur	Anantapur	1990	Somesh Kumar
74.	Kanuparthi	Cuddapah	1984	Binoy Kumar
75.	Palampalli	Cuddapah	1985	A.R. Sukumar
76.	Poli	Cuddapah	1993	Jayesh Ranjan

BIBLIOGRAPHY

Ahluwalia, M.S. (1978) 'Rural Poverty and Agricultural Performance in India', *The Journal of Development Studies,* 14: 3.

A.P. Scheduled Caste Co-operative Finance Corporation Ltd. (1984) Scheduled Caste Action Plan (1984-85) Government of Andhra Pradesh, Hyderabad.

A.P. Scheduled Caste Co-operative Finance Corporation Ltd. (1990) Minor Irrigation Projects for Economic Development of Scheduled Castes in Andhra Pradesh (1991-92 to 1994-95). Government of Andhra Pradesh, Hyderabad.

Bhadouria, B.P.S. and V.B. Dubey (1989) Panchayati Raj and Rural Development: A Study in Rural Local Finances in Uttar Pradesh and Andhra Pradesh. Commonwealth, New Delhi.

Bureau of Economics and Statistics (1986) *Report on Second Economic census 1980.* Government of Andhra Pradesh, Hyderabad.

Bureau of Economics and Statistics (1987) An Outline of Agricultural Situation in Andhra Pradesh (1985-86). Government of Andhra Pradesh, Hyderabad.

Development Commissioner, SSI and Commissioner of Industries, Government of AP (1992) Report on the Second All-India Census of Small Scale Industrial Units (regd. upto 31st March 1988). Ministry of Industry, GOI, New Delhi.

Finance and Planning (Plg. Wing) Department (1980) Sixth Five-Year Plan 1980-85, Andhra Pradesh (Vols. 1&2). Government of Andhra Pradesh, Hyderabad.

Finance and Planning (Plg. Wing) Department (1985) Seventh Five-Year Plan 1985-90, Andhra Pradesh (Vols. 1&2). Government of Andhra Pradesh, Hyderabad.

Finance and Planning (Plg. Wing) Department (1990) Eighth Five-Year Plan (1990-95), Andhra Pradesh (Vols. 1&2). Government of Andhra Pradesh, Hyderabad.

Innaiah, N. (1986) State Government and Politics : A Study of Andhra Pradesh Politics 1985-86. Scientific Services, Hyderabad.

Klaus, Mading (1988) *Peasants in South India - A Study of Social Values in Telengana.* Panchsheel Publishers, New Delhi.

Lakshaman Rao, V. (1985) *Economic Development of Andhra Pradesh.* B.R. Publishing Corp., Delhi.

Lakshaman Rao, V. (1988) *Economic Growth of Andhra Pradesh.* Chugh Publication, Allahabad.

Land Reforms Unit, (1995) *Land Reforms.* Lal Bahadur Shastri National Academy of Administration, Mussoorie.

Mangalam, S.J. (1986) *Historical Geography and Toponomy of Andhra Pradesh.* Sundeep Prakashan, New Delhi.

Mahendra Reddy, J., Yadava Reddy, M., Upadhyay, K.S., and Raghuram, (1989) *Industrial Development of Andhra Pradesh.* Sterling Publishers,

New Delhi.

Mukund, Kanakalatha (*ed.*) (1990) *Andhra Pradesh Economy in Transition.* Centre for Economic and Social Studies and Booklinks Corporation, Hyderabad.

Narasimhamurthy, K.L. (1986) *Planning for Integrated Area Development: A Case Study from Andhra Pradesh.* B.R. Publishing Corp., Delhi.

Prakasam Institute of Development Studies (1988) *Issues in Co-operative Movement in Andhra Pradesh.* PIDS, Hyderabad.

Radhakrishna, R., Sastry, S.A.R., Sudhakar Reddy, S., and Mitra, F.K. (1988) *Levels of Living in a State Setting.* Centre for Economic and Social Studies, Hyderabad and Concept Publishing Company, New Delhi.

Rajasekhar, D. (1988) *Land Transfers and Family Partitioning - A Historical Study of Andhra Village.* Oxford and IBH, New Delhi.

Ramakrishna, V. (1993) *Social Reforms in Andhra Pradesh (1848-1919).* Vikas Publishing House, Delhi.

Rama Mohan Rao, K. (1990) *Development of Handloom Industry: A Study of Andhra Pradesh.* Discovery Publishing House, New Delhi.

Rama Raju, B. (1983) *Folk Tales of Andhra Pradesh.* Sterling, New Delhi.

Rao, E.N. (1986) *Strategy for Integrated Rural Development: A Case Study of a Region in Coastal Andhra.* B.R. Publishing Corp., Delhi.

Rao, P.R. (1988) *History of Modern Andhra Pradesh.* Sterling, New Delhi.

Rathnaiah, K. (1991) *Social Change Among Malas: An Ex-Untouchable Caste in South India.* Discovery Publishing House, New Delhi.

Rayadu, C.S. (1991) *Rural Credit in India - A Study of Andhra Pradesh.* Mittal Publications, New Delhi.

Reddy, A.V. (1991) *Modernisation of Indian Agriculture (with special reference to Andhra Pradesh).* Mittal Publications, New Delhi.

Reddy Ram, G and Harigopal, G. (1985) *Public Policy and the Rural poor in India - A Study of SFDA in Andhra Pradesh.* CESS Research Studies and Concept, New Delhi.

Reddy, Y.V. and Kosalram, K. (*eds.*) (1988) *Study of Planning in Andhra Pradesh.* CESS and Booklinks, Hyderabad.

Society for Promotion of Wastelands Development (1990) *Common Lands of Andhra Pradesh: An Analysis of the Grazing Problem.* SPWD, New Delhi.

Srinivasan, K.V. (*ed.*) (1986) *State Administration in Andhra Pradesh: Selected Aspects.* Creative Education Systems Society, Hyderabad.

Subramanyam Reddy, D. (1990) *Agrarian Relations and Peasant in Modern Andhra: A Study of Kalahasti Zamindari.* Daya Publishing House, Delhi.

Tilak, J.B.G. (1987) *The Economics of Inequality in Education.* Sage, New Delhi.

Upender, M. (1990) *Marketable and Marketed Surplus in Agriculture.* Mittal Publications, New Delhi.

Venkateswarlu, D. (1990) *Harijan-Upper Class Conflict: A Study in Andhra Pradesh*. Discovery Publishing House, New Delhi.

Wade, Robert (1988) *Village Republics: Economic Conditions for Collective Action in South India*. Cambridge University Press, Cambridge.

2

TAMIL NADU

S. Irudaya Rajan and U.S. Mishra*

A PROFILE

Tamil Nadu is one of the four southern states of the Indian sub-continent. It lies in the shape of a rhomboid between the Deccan Plateau and the Bay of Bengal stretching from Kanyakumari at latitude 8° N to the Pulicat lake at 11° N. The Western Ghats in the west, the Bay of Bengal in the east and the Gulf of Mannar which separates India from Sri Lanka in the south constitute natural boundaries of the state on three sides. Tamil Nadu covers a little over 1,30,000 sq. km. representing about four per cent of the country's geographical area.

The plateaus and plains of Tamil Nadu can be conveniently described in terms of four broad natural regions.

(1) The northern coramandal coastal plane (Cholamandalam),
(2) The western plateau around Coimbatore (Kongunad) and Salem (Baramahal),
(3) The Cauvery delta, and
(4) The south-eastern plains.

* We are grateful for the following persons for their help during the preparation of the paper: Dr. Michael Raj, Dr. A. Shantapparaj and Dr. K.S. James.

The northern plains include Madras, Chengalpattu, eastern North Arcot and the northern parts of South Arcot, and Tiruchirapalli. Lying to the west and south of the northern plains between the Cauvery and the Palghat gap, Coimbatore and Periyar districts and reaching upto Dindigul the Cauvery delta is the most fertile region of the state and along with the northern plains is the home of its early settlements and civilisation. The delta mainly consists of Thanjavur district with adjacent areas of Tiruchirapalli and South Arcot. The rivers Cauvery, Coleroon (Kollidam) and Vennar intensively irrigate this tract through their deltaic branches. Finally, the south-eastern plains of Tamil Nadu comprise the districts of Madurai, Ramanathapuram and Tirunelveli. Parts of these plains are irrigated by the rivers Periyar, Vaigai and the Tamaraparani but by and large these districts depend largely on rainfall impounded in extensive tanks along the coastal regions of Ramanathapuram and Tirunelveli and on the tank systems linked to the Periyar-Vaigai supplemented to some extent by well irrigation in western Ramanathapuram. Kanyakumari which is the southernmost district of Tamil Nadu is however favourably endowed with rains from both the south-west and north-east monsoons.

Presented below is some basic information about the state (For more details, refer Appendix I). As of 1991, the state comprised of 21 districts with a population of 55.6 million. The state ranks seventh among the states of the Indian union according to the size of its population. It has a population density of 429 persons per sq. km. as against the all-India figure of 273 persons per sq. km. The state accounts for 6.7 per cent of the country's Scheduled Caste and Scheduled Tribe population.

As per the 1991 census, 43.3 per cent of its population were classified as workers and of the total working population 24.84 per cent were cultivators, 34.63 per cent were agricultural labourers, 34.42 per cent industrial and other workers and 6.11 per cent were marginal workers.

The administrative set-up of the state is in terms of 22 revenue districts, 60 revenue divisions, 172 taluks, 1,101 revenue firkas and 17,275 villages. During 1989-90 the state had three corporations, 98 municipalities, eight township committees (under the municipal act), 16 townships (under the panchayat act), 384 panchayat unions, 632 town panchayats, 12,612 village panchayats (Table 2.1).

Table 2.1 : Panchayat Unions, Village Panchayat, Town Panchayats and Townships by Districts, 1990-91

Name of the District	Development District	Panchayat Unions	Village Panchayats	Town Panchayats	Townships
1. Chengalpattu	2	27	1,188	43	4
2. South Arcot	2	34	1,766	31	1
3. North Arcot	1	20	1,618	27	
4. Thiruvanmalai	1	18	11		
5. Salem	2	36	729	55	1
6. Dharmapuri	1	18	588	18	
7. Periyar	1	20	342	61	
8. Coimbatore	1	21	388	58	2
9. Nilgiris	1	4	27	21	
10. Tiruchirapalli	2	32	888	46	1
11. Thanjavur	2	34	1,451	40	1
12. Pudukottai	1	13	498	8	
13. Madurai	1	21	560	37	2
14. Anna (Dindigul)	1	14	304	24	
15. Ramanathapuram	1	11	444	8	1
16. Kamarajar	1	11	453	10	
17. Pasumpon	1	11	438	12	
18. Tirunelveli	1	19	435	36	2
19. Chidambaram	1	12	408	20	
20. Kanyakumari	1	9	88	66	1
Tamil Nadu	25	384	12,612	632	16

Source : Statistical Handbook of Tamil Nadu, 1991.

The state has 17 per cent forest land as against 19.5 per cent for the country as a whole. The major forest produce are: timber, fuel wood, sandal wood, pulp wood and poles of various sizes. Tea, rubber, wattle bark and cashew are some of the minor forest products of the state. There is also an abundance of minerals like lignite, limestone, granite, clay, and gypsum.

The state has 33 river basins with some large ones like Cauvery, Pennaiaru, Vaigai and Tambaraparani. As of 1989-90 the gross irrigated area in the state stood at 3.04 million hectares and the net irrigated area at 2.49 million hectares. Of the net irrigated area 45 per cent was irrigated through wells and tubewells followed by 34 per cent through canals and 20 per cent by tanks.

The net sown area is 44 per cent of the total area of the state. The principal crops are paddy, cholam (jowar), cumbu (bajra), maize and ragi. Among pulses black gram, red gram, green gram, and horse gram are widely grown, while the major types of oilseeds are groundnut, gingili, castor and coconut. Of late sunflower is also becoming popular. Coconut, sugarcane, tobacco and chillies are considered to be the commercial crops of the state.

The state has shown remarkable recovery on its demographic front during the decade 1981-91. Registering a decennial growth rate of 14.94 per cent, Tamil Nadu had the second lowest population growth rate across the country. But on the social and development front the state does not present an impressive picture as the development indicators are in no way different from that of other pronounced backward regions of the country. However, the state has certain advantage in the pace of development as its CMIE index of relative development of infrastructure based on selected indicators is 139 in contrast with the national index of 100.

Considering the percentage of urban population as a proxy for development, the state can be considered marginally urbanised with one-third of its population living in urban areas. In fact, evidence from literature shows that there has been a more even urban growth in the state compared to other regions of the country, as its different class size towns have shown growth over decades unlike the exceptional growth of higher class size towns alone at the cost of restricting the growth of small class size towns and new urban centres. However, the state exhibits a large disparity in urban growth across its districts. There are districts, namely, Chengai MGR, Nilgiris, Coimbatore, Madurai and Chidambaram which have almost 50 per cent of the population living in urban areas while in five out of 21 districts only 15 per cent of the population live in urban areas. This indirectly depicts developmental disparity across the districts. Other available developmental/infrastructural indicators available for the districts show large variation confirming a wider imbalance in development across different districts.

The state of Tamil Nadu appears to be pioneer in implementing many development programmes, besides those sponsored by the Government of India for the socio-economic betterment of the people. One such well-known programme is the nutrition meal programme which is termed as noon-meal scheme in schools or otherwise nutrition meal centres in the social welfare sector. This programme seems to have benefited a lot of people and consequently has resulted in lesser number of school dropouts. This programme happens to be popular in the state as a whole.

The Integrated Rural Development Programme has succeeded to some extent in the state but there remains large discrepancies in the number of beneficiaries. Districts which are largely rural do not seem to be having greater number of beneficiaries compared with those which are more urban.

The benefits of the public distribution system through fair price outlets reaches few needy people. In fact, in certain districts these outlets are more in urban places than in rural areas. In general, rural areas have a greater number of fair price shops though not in tune with the population to be catered to.

However, a comparison of the state with the national scene in terms of few socio-economic indicators shows the state in a favourable light (Table 2.2).

REVIEW OF LITERATURE

The state of Tamil Nadu with its two-thirds rural population has been an agrarian state all through. Till date more than 60 per cent of its main workers are engaged in agriculture and allied activities. Historically, the state has the claim of being a rice growing state and over time its agrarian scene has witnessed several reforms and changes. A brief recent review of works on the agrarian scene of Tamil Nadu is given below to have a better understanding of the issues involved.

Table 2.2 : Tamil Nadu at a Glance: Major Socio-Economic Indicators

Items	Year	Tamil Nadu	India
Area ('000 sq. km.)	1993	130	3287
Population (in million)	1991	55.6	846.3
Density (Persons per sq. km.)	1991	429	257
Sex Ratio (Females per 1000 Males)	1991	974	927
Urbanisation (Per cent of urban population to total population)	1991	34.2	25.7
Net Domestic Product (in Rs. crores)	1990	24,841	3,62,316
Per capita income at current prices	1990	4,428	5,015
People below poverty line (%)	1987	32.8	29.9
Net irrigated area (lakh hectares)	1989	24.97	451.44
Fertiliser Consumption ('000 tonnes)	1991	839	12,728
Food grain Production ('000 tonnes)	1991	7,692	1,71,497
Villages electrified (%)	1993	100	84.2
CMIE Index of relative development of infrastructure	1989	139	100
Infant Mortality Rate (per 1000 live births)	1991	57	80
Total Literacy Rate (%)	1991	54.6	52.1

A note on myth and facts behind agrarian unrest in the state by *Economic and Political Weekly* (1981) finds the socio-economic features of rural Tamil Nadu being responsible for the wide growth of rural discontent and consequent militant social and political protests. On this line of argument, Harriss (1982) claims that the economic, ideological and political conditions in the state have been associated with the development of capitalism and 'peasant' agriculture in parts of south India. This study was based on the eastern North Arcot district.

Whenever issues related to agriculture are addressed, the question of rainfall and irrigation occupy a place of prominence, and in a scenario, where agriculture is largely rain fed, the extent of poverty needs to be assessed based on the extent of rainfall. Considering a random sample of 261 producers practising dry land agriculture in Andhra Pradesh, Karnataka and Tamil Nadu (all classified as drought prone), Harriss (1983) examines the production and exchange relations of rain fed agriculture to assess the nature of poverty. The rise in paddy prices has been attributed to the failing monsoons in the state and also to the unprecedented situation on the power front (Moses, 1983).

During drought, farmers in the state follow a strategy of protecting crop yield at the expense of shrinkage in irrigated acreage, especially of crops needing summer irrigation. This often results in instability in the farm output. On the other hand, in years of above normal rainfall, farmers are known to maximise production to utilise extra water availability by expanding acreage under irrigation (Dhawan, 1983).

The study of the importance of irrigation in agriculture is important in the case of Kanyakumari district in Tamil Nadu which has frequent instances of crop failure as a result of water scarcity. Hence, Narayana *et al.* (1982) make an assessment of the physical techno-economic, organisational and institutional aspects of the irrigation system in Kanyakumari district. Another study by Thamodaran *et al.* (1982) examines the water management system in southern Tamil Nadu through production function programming. Its findings are that both concrete and silt system is more profitable within the analysed agro-climatic situation. The technological change in production relationships for paddy and banana is neutral.

The drought situation in the state because of the failure in irrigation management has multi-pronged implications. A view on the drought situation based on a village in the state by Moses (1993) opines that agricultural labourers and small cultivators are forced to take loans from money lenders in trying circumstances and the interest rate charged on such loans varies between 36 to 120 per cent per annum.

In agriculture, labour is a sensitive component, and often the output price (price of the produce) has some linkages with the wages associated with the labour for such produce. While examining input demand and output supply in case of cotton farming in

Tamil Nadu, Subramaniam and Nirmala (1988) find the demand for labour being more sensitive to changes in the price of cotton than to changes in real wages. This may be attributed to the fact that higher cotton prices typically raise the demand for labour in crop management and the demand for other inputs positively associated with labour.

In an earlier study, Subramaniam (1986) also examined labour demand and supply responsiveness in cotton farming and estimated cotton supply and input demand elasticities using a profit function. In the wake of new farm technology, Rajagopalan and Varadarajan (1983) designate the state to be having a labour surplus economy. Hence they recommend labour intensive technology to solve the problem of unemployment through large absorption of labour in agriculture assuming a reduction in the high transaction cost of labour.

Regarding productivity variation in farms, a study by Randhir and Krishnamoorthy (1990) urges for the creation of employment opportunities due to low level of labour use. Credit facilities need to be made available to the farmers in the form of short-term credit since capital has a scope to improve productivity.

To understand the unemployment scene in the state with particular reference to Kanyakumari district, Nair *et al.* (1984) examined education, employment and land holding pattern in Kadathuchery village of Kanyakumari district to elaborate on the genesis of its present socio-economic condition. Another study by Rajagopalan and Anuradha (1987) exclusively examines the structural changes in land holdings in Thanjavur district of Tamil Nadu and its associated reasons. The main conclusions reveal a reduction in the size of land holdings and a decline in the number of tenants. However, tenants are better placed than before.

In an attempt to assess sustainable agricultural development through watershed management in dry areas of the state, it is argued that sustainable agricultural development requires management of renewable resources such as soil, water, vegetation, livestock and not mere increase in productivity. In Tamil Nadu, agricultural development has meant irrigated agriculture with little importance given to dry lands.

In the above context, a study on agro-climatic planning and

regional development in the state by Arputharaj *et al.* (1990) recommends several strategies for increasing agricultural production in the state. These strategies include (i) land re-distribution, (ii) afforestation, (iii) reclamation of saline soils, (iv) social forestry, (v) rehabilitation of canal irrigation system, (vi) waste land development programme, (vii) ground water recharging, and (viii) drainage and irrigation management. These strategies have been chalked out on the basis of previous experience and are recommended to be implemented at the panchayat level.

Government intervention in the management of food grain prices is being implemented since 1965-66 and an evaluation to this effect made by Prabha (1983b) concludes that it was satisfactory. Under conditions of short supply of food grains, government intervention has taken the form of price control, acquisition of food grains through compulsory levies on producers/traders/millers at prices fixed by government and ancillary measures such as movement restrictions, imports to augment government supplies and the controlled distribution of rice and wheat through rationing.

Harriss (1982) examines the marketed surplus of paddy through price and non-price factors conditioning the marketed surplus. The two broad findings of this study are: the major contribution by the cultivators with small families towards marketed surplus compared to those with large families; and the contribution of tenants to marketed surplus is far lower than that of owners/occupiers.

While addressing the dynamics of rural transformation in the state, Kurien (1981) discusses several dimensions of rural economy comprising land and assets, agricultural growth in its various dimensions such as agricultural transformation, size of land holdings, scale factor, rural poverty, prices, wages and consumption patterns.

Another work of Harriss (1981) on transitional trade and rural development explores the myth of perfect competition using a case study of a district in Tamil Nadu. This study analytically covers different functions performed by trade and the circuit of trading capital from its origin to accumulation.

Studies relating to various industries in the state are ample in literature, but the recent ones are match stick industry, tannery and textiles. A study on the match stick industry by Kothari (1983) considers a sample of 45,000 child workers in Sivakasi to establish socio-economic reasons for perpetuation of child labour in this region. Further, the study analyses the effect of government policy on Sivakasi match industry, the extent of violation of laws prohibiting the employment of children and laws relating to child labour in general.

Stressing on the need for a comprehensive approach to rural industrialisation, Srinivasan (1984) argues against the cheap exploitation of labour in the match stick and *beedi* rolling industry and suggests the use of this labour in some modern industries too for the benefit of both the villagers and entrepreneurs. Factors influencing industrial entrepreneurship was examined based on a study of tanners of North Arcot district by Ramaswami (1984).

A lot of studies have taken account of labour unrest in the industrial sector of the state. For instance, Mani and Shenbagavalli (1985) have noted the strike by two lakh textile workers which led to the setting up of a special tribunal for settling the dispute. This particular issue of labour problem was analysed from the perspective of mechanisation and labour utilisation in tanneries in North Arcot district by Usha (1985). This study further examined the factors influencing industrial entrepreneurship in the tannery industry.

While analysing the labour market in the state, Harriss (1982) describes the character of an urban economy in relation to small-scale production and labour markets considering the case of small-scale units in Coimbatore district. Conclusions are drawn on the process of reproduction of different forms of small-scale production and it is argued that while they are subordinated in various ways to big capital production their persistence is ensured by the interest of big capital itself and by the structure of markets in particular.

On taking note of the dynamics of capitalist labour process in the case of the knitting industry, Krishnaswami (1989) analyses the nature of capitalist labour process, its dynamics and the division of labour in the hosiery industry in Tirupur. He finds that the organisation of production is not uniform as it is organised according to the availability of capital, market demand, and nature of the work force in order to facilitate profit maximisation. Another study by Kalpagam (1981) on similar lines focuses on the structure of export garment industry in Madras to examine the structure and composition of the labour force and account for the attempts at unionising the workers in this industry.

AN EXAMINATION OF VILLAGE STUDIES

Over the last 10 years, the village studies carried out by the officer-trainees have covered 17 out of 24 districts of the state. A total of 78 village studies are distributed over these districts according to the size of the districts (Table 2.3). Districts with larger number of villages are represented with more number of village studies. The state has 12612 villages with a fairly skewed distribution across districts – some districts have thousand or more than thousand villages. The coverage of villages across districts is more or less in tune with the frequency of villages in each of the districts. Thus the 78 studies together can provide a proper reflection of the rural scene in the state.

We present below a district-wise description of villages based on the studies conducted. However, the description is limited to 13 out of the 17 districts covered, as four of these districts are represented by just one or two villages each (For more details on each village, see Appendix II).

Periyar

Four villages were covered in Periyar district. Two of them were large villages with population of more than 5,000 and the other two were smaller villages comprising of 3,000 and less than 2,000 persons respectively. The sex ratio in the villages seems balanced, of course with a male domination. With regard to Scheduled Caste (SC) population, only one village was reported to be having no SCs, two had less than 10 per cent SCs and one village had slightly more than 10 per cent. In terms of population density, one village had as high as 2,253 persons per sq. km. against another one with just 226 persons per sq. km.

Table 2.3 : Distribution of the Selected Village Studies Across Districts (1980-81 to 1992-93)

No.	Districts	1980-85	1985-90	1990-93	Total
1.	North Arcot	2	2	3	7
2.	Salem	2	2	3	7
3.	Tiruchirapalli	3	2	2	7
4.	Tirunelveli	2	2	3	7
5.	Chidambaram	1		1	
6.	Thanjavur	4	2		6
7.	Coimbatore	2	3	2	7
8.	Madurai	2	4	2	8
9.	Chengalpattu	1	4	1	6
10.	South Arcot	3	2	3	5
11.	Ramanathapuram	1	2		3
12.	Periyar	2	1		3
13.	Pudukottai	1	1	1	3
14.	Dharmapuri	2			2
15.	Kamarajar	2	1		3
16.	Anna (Dindigul)	1			1
17.	Pasumpon Muthuramalingam	2		2	
	Total	16	39	23	78

The age composition across the villages was similar as the distribution in broad age groups revealed less than 25 per cent children (below age 14), between 60 to 70 per cent in the working age group (age 15 to 59) and the rest elderly (above age 60). The percentage of working population stands at around 50 per cent in all villages which accommodates a greater degree of differential between sex as around one-third of females are reported as workers while more than 60 per cent of their counterparts were workers in three of the study villages. Mukasi Hanumanpalli village is distinct in this regard where 67 per cent of the female population is in the work force. Among workers a large percentage are agricultural labourers except in Puthur Puthupalayam where 46.4 per cent are cultivators.

With regard to land holdings and its use, majority have less than one hectare; and more than 5 hectare land holdings are rare. Two of the villages had almost 100 per cent dry land and the other two had more than 60 per cent dry land. The extent of irrigation is highest, i.e. 80 per cent in Doddampalayam with 100 per cent dry land followed by Mukasi Hanumanpalli. The net sown area is more than 70 per cent in two villages and the other two have less than 50 per cent area under crops. Two of the villages seem rich in livestock too.

The four villages have varied number of households, with the biggest having around 2,000 households against the smaller one with 400 households. Average household size varies between 3.7 to 4.8. Most of the villagers are Hindus except one village which has a Christian and Muslim population (less than 10 per cent). The socio-economic scene of these villages based on broad indicators such as literacy, infrastructure and medical facilities presents a gloomy picture. The overall literacy level in all villages is less than 50 per cent with a great degree of disparity between the sexes.

Tiruchirapalli

Seven villages out of 888 villages were studied in the district. They have population sizes varying between 2,000 and 4,000. Five of the seven villages have a sex ratio in favour of males. The population density ranges between 279 persons per sq. km. and 502 persons per sq. km. Four villages accounted for a major share of SC population with one village having a 70 per cent SC population.

Information on the age composition of the population is available for five villages, of which three have a common age structure with one-third of the population as children, roughly 60 per cent in the working age group and the rest elderly. The other two villages have a greater share of child population reflecting the high fertility levels and indicating the fact that they are lagging behind in the process of demographic transition.

The number of households ranges between 405 and 936 with an average household size between 4 and 5 persons per household. In all the villages except one, one-fourth are SC households. All these villages are Hindu villages except one where 3 per cent of the population are Christians. The percentage of workers to the total population is 62 per cent in Srinivasallur and around 50 per cent in the other villages. Three-fourth of the workers are classified as agricultural labourers.

The land holding pattern in the village was skewed with a majority holding less than one hectare of land and a few households with more than 5 hectares. There is a greater balance between dry and wet land. Also, the net sown area across the villages ranges between 52 per cent and 94 per cent. The proportion of irrigated area is substantially high in these villages as in Vadiyam where it is as high as 85.3 per cent of the total agricultural area. All the villages are more or less rich in livestock.

In terms of infrastructure facilities like education, health, sanitation, drinking water, etc., these villages present a very poor picture. In fact, none of these villages even have a health sub-centre. With regard to sanitation, there seems to be no drainage facility or proper toilet facility in the village. Wells and hand pumps are the major source of drinking water and they are few in number. The only indicator which seems impressive is the extent of electrification as most of the villages are partially electrified. Transport facility is quite satisfactory in two of the seven study villages but communication facilities like post and telegraph are poor.

Chengai MGR

This district is represented by six villages with population sizes varying between 1,000 and 3,000. Except one village having a population size of nearly 3,000, all the other study villages have a population below 2,000. Five villages have sex ratios in favour of males barring one which has a sex ratio of 1,015 females per thousand males. Four villages have a good proportion of SC households and the other two also have some share of SC households. The population density across these villages varies in a large range between 124 persons per sq. km. and 620 persons per sq. km.

The population age structure reveals that one village has more than 70 per cent of the population in the working age group while the other villages have around 60 per cent. The average household size in four villages is between 5 and 6 persons per household while the other two villages have an average household size of 3.7 and 4.4 persons per household. The religious composition shows all the villages dominated by Hindus with a small proportion of Christians.

The percentage of workers is less than 50 per cent in two of the villages revealing a greater degree of dependence in these two villages. In one village this ratio is as high as 68 per cent. A peculiarity observed in the category of workers is that very few are engaged in agricultural activities in three of the six villages where more than two-third of the workers are categorised as other workers. Among the workers in the agricultural sector, most of them are classified as agricultural labourers. These villages have a greater share of dry land and hence most of them have at most 50 per cent of the area under cultivation. The landholding pattern is no different in villages of this district too. The selected villages in this district seem to be least dependent on agriculture which is clear from the work force structure.

The level of literacy in these villages is quite high with not much difference between sexes. Except one village, all other villages have literacy rates of more than 50 per cent with one village having a literacy rate of 71 per cent. This is an encouraging trend despite rudimentary educational facilities in the villages. The noon meal scheme is very popular in these villages with a record number of beneficiaries. These villages have poor access to medical facilities as only one village has a primary health centre and three of them have only a sub-centre within the village. Further, these villages fare poorly in terms of sanitation arrangements and wells seem to be the main source of drinking water. Though, transport facilities are more or less good in these villages, communication facilities need improvement.

Coimbatore

The seven villages surveyed have a population size varying between 1,500 and nearly 7,000. Four villages have a population size more than 4,500 and other three have a population size more than 1,500.

All villages have a sex ratio in favour of males except Thenamanallur where the sex ratio is in favour of females. Almost all the villages are less densely populated except Angalakurichi which has a population density of 866 persons per sq. km. All the villages have a share of SCs and, in fact, four of them have one-fifth SC households.

The average household size ranges between 4 and 5 persons per household. Almost all the study villages have a smaller proportion of children together with a substantial share of elderly ranging between 7 to 15 per cent of the total population. The percentage of workers in all the villages amounts to less than 50 per cent except in one village where it is more than 60 per cent.

A large proportion of the workers are agricultural labourers. However, in four villages more than one-third of the workers are cultivators. Around 60 per cent of the land area is dry land except in one village where there is a perfect balance between dry land and wet land. The net sown area ranges between 60 to 90 per cent though the extent of irrigation is limited to one-third of the net sown area.

The literacy level in these villages varies between 45 to 50 per cent with the exception of two villages which have 25 and 35 per cent literacy rates. There is a wide gap between the sexes. In terms of general amenities, these villages need further attention as the drinking water situation is yet to be improved.

North Arcot

In this district seven villages were studied. They have a population size varying from less than 1,500 to more than 4,000. Three of these villages have a sex ratio in favour of females and the other four have a sex ratio ranging between 925 and 984 females per thousand males. Population density in half of the villages is quite high as compared to the rest which are sparsely populated. All the villages have some proportion of SC households except Kandaneri. In fact, Perumugai has a 50 per cent SC population followed by Kilkuvalaivedu with 34.8 per cent.

The age composition of the population in these villages seems normal except in a few villages where the child population is around 40 per cent. The average household size in all the villages is between 5 and 5.6 persons per household. The worker population ratio was very poor reflecting on the dependency burden of these villages. With regard to the composition of workers, there is a balance between agricultural labourers and cultivators in some villages and in the rest, agricultural labourers were prominent.

Of the total land area in all the villages two-third is dry land. There is a large variation in the net sown area which varies between 49 per cent and 87 per cent. Irrigation facilities are very poor in all villages except one where the net irrigated area is around 50 per cent.

These villages seem to have good literacy levels though there is a wide differential between the sexes. In terms of education and health facilities, these villages lag behind as there are hardly any schools nor are any health facilities available. With regard to sanitation, these villages have no public sanitary arrangement. In the case of drinking water, wells seem to be the most popular source among the villagers. Transport and communication facilities are reasonably good. Two villages have reported the practice of child labour in tannery industries. Government development programmes have hardly reached these villages.

Salem

In Salem seven large villages with a minimum population size of 3,300 were studied. The population size ranges between 3,300 and 15,717. All the villages have a sex ratio in favour of males with three of the villages having very low number of females. The number of households varies between 302 and 3,000 and the average household size ranges between 4.1 and 5.6 persons per household. Four villages have a good share of SC population.

All the study villages depict an age structure agreeing with declining fertility levels except one where the child population is approximately 43 per cent. The percentage of workers is less than 50 per cent. One village where there is widespread prevalence of child labour has a ratio above 80 per cent. A large proportion of workers are categorised as agricultural labourers.

In half of these villages, the dry land and wet land is distributed in a ratio of three is to one and in the other villages they are equal in proportion. In many of these villages around 50 per cent of the area is cultivated. Of the net sown area 50 per cent is irrigated. The villages have reasonable numbers of livestock. Three of the villages have milk co-operatives and all of them have one primary agricultural co-operative each.

All the villages have good transport facilities but in terms of communication facilities two of the villages has no post office; while one large village has three post offices. On the whole, villages in Salem have better transport and communication compared to villages in other districts. On the contrary, medical facilities and sanitary arrangements in these villages are not satisfactory.

Thanjavur

Thanjavur was represented by six villages with population sizes between 951 and 2,671. All villages except one have a population of more than 1,500. Three of these villages have a sex ratio in favour of males. The number of households ranges between 201 and 537. The average household size ranges between 4.5 and 5 persons per household. All the villages have one-third SC households.

The age composition of the population across all the villages shows an age structure with 60-65 per cent in the working age group, 30 to 35 per cent children and the rest above age 60. The percentage of workers is less than 50 per cent indicating a high degree of dependency. Majority of the workers are agricultural labourers though in these villages a substantial number of workers were categorised as cultivators too.

In three villages, three-fourth of the land is classified as wet land and one-fourth as dry land and in the other three villages it is the other way round. Irrigation is more widespread with the percentage of irrigated land varying between 40 to 80 per cent. The land holding pattern shows that 70 to 85 per cent of holdings are less than one hectare and less than 5 per cent of the holdings are above 3 hectares.

On the health and sanitation front, these villages seem to be very poor as none of the villages have any medical facility or sanitary arrangements. The main sources of drinking water are wells or hand pumps. Only one village has piped water supply with nine public taps within the village. Educational infrastructure in terms of school is present in four villages which have elementary schools and two have a high school within the village. Transport facilities are more or less satisfactory but the communication facilities are extremely poor as none of these villages have any telegraph and telephone facility and two of them even do not have a sub-post office.

South Arcot

In South Arcot, five villages with a population size varying between 1,330 and 3,681 were studied. All the villages have a sex ratio favouring males, except one with a sex ratio of 1,111 females per thousand males. The share of SC population is significant in two of the villages while the rest have some proportion of SCs. Population density across the villages varies from 336 persons per sq. km. to 1,184 persons per sq. km.

In one village the age composition shows 25 per cent children and 10 per cent in the age group above 60. Another village had 35 per cent of the population as children and 7 per cent elderly. Average household size ranges between 3.3 and 6 persons per household. In fact, except one village, the average household size varies between 5 and 6 persons per household. All the villages have a majority of Hindus except in two villages where Muslims account for 14 and 30 per cent of population respectively.

The percentage of workers was impressive in one village where it was 70 per cent and in the case of other villages it was less than 50 per cent depicting a greater degree of dependency. Male workers are more than female workers in all the villages. Like in other villages, most of the workers are agricultural labourers. In one village, 40 per cent of the workers are cultivators while 18.4 per cent are engaged in other activities.

In four of the five villages a major proportion of the land is dry land. Only in Adivarangonallur, the proportions of dry and wet land are balanced. Villages in South Arcot have a better proportion of land area under crops. The percentage of area under crops is more than 60 per cent in each village. The proportion of irrigated area is good in two of the villages where it covers more than 70 per cent of the net sown area. In the case of other villages, one-third of the area is irrigated. Land holding pattern is more or less homogeneous across all the villages, i.e. small land holdings (below one hectare) being in larger proportion compared to large land holdings. The availability of livestock is not impressive.

The literacy level, including female literacy level is very high. This may perhaps be due to the availability of elementary schools in all the villages though there are no middle or high school. In terms of medical facilities and sanitation, these villages present a very poor scene. However, all the villages have a satisfactory level of electrification. With regard to drinking water, hand pumps seem to be the main source of drinking water. Transport facilities are satisfactory in four villages but communication in terms of post and telegraph facilities lag behind substantially.

Madurai

In Madurai district eight villages were studied. These villages have large populations varying between 3,000 and 8,000, except one village with a population below 1,000. All the villages have SC households. Five of the villages have sex ratios in favour of females. The population density varies between 290 persons per sq. km. and 1,180 persons per sq. km.

The age composition of these villages is more or less homogeneous except the largest village which has an elderly population of 27 per cent. This village has an average household size of 7.5 persons per household against other villages with an average household size between 4.1 and 5.6 persons per household. Roughly around 10 to 25 per cent of the households are SC households. The villages have a predominant Hindu population.

The percentage of workers for one village is around 70 per cent whereas in others it is less than or equal to 50 per cent. In one village there is a large proportion of workers in non-agricultural activities and in others most workers are categorised as agricultural workers. In most of the villages two-third is wet land except one which has 100 per cent dry land.

Kamarajar

Kamarajar district is represented by three villages of small, medium and large population sizes; one has a population of around 1,500, another has around 3,000 and the biggest village has a population above 5,000. Two of the villages have a marginal proportion of SCs. Two of the villages have a sex ratio favouring males while in the third one females outnumber males. Population density is the lowest in the smallest village and the highest (738 persons per sq. km.) in Kanniseripudur.

The three villages have substantial differences in age distribution in terms of differential share of child and elderly population. The share of working age population in all the three villages is above 60 per cent. The average household size across the three villages ranges between 4 and 5.5 persons per household. With regard to religious composition, two of them were Hindu villages while one has 25 per cent Christians.

The percentage of workers in all the villages is around 50 per cent. Among the workers, a majority are agricultural labourers. These villages have a large proportion of dry land and at the same time irrigation seem to be entirely absent. The land holding pattern shows a larger proportion of smaller holdings. These villages do not have enough numbers of livestock.

The total literacy levels in all the villages is less than 50 per cent with a substantial difference between the sexes to such an extent that the level of literacy among females is half that of males. All the villages have an elementary school within the village though not any middle school or high school.

Unfortunately, none of these villages are covered by the popular noon meal programme. Two villages have a primary health centre and a sub-centre within them except the small village where no such facility is available. The villages have no public sanitary facilities at all. The most common source of drinking water is wells followed by hand pumps. Village industry is apparently absent in these villages. Transport and communication seems to be the poorest in all these villages.

Tirunelveli

Tirunelveli is represented by seven villages with a population size ranging between 1,500 and 5,800. Three of them are small villages and have a population size around 2,000 and the rest have a population of more than 3,000. Three villages have sex ratios favouring males while the other four have sex ratios favouring females. Population density in five villages is between 400 to 500 persons per sq. km. while the other two villages have a population density of more than 800 persons per sq. km. Five of the villages have a marginal SC population.

The population age structure shows that in three villages 60 to 70 per cent of the population is in the working age group and in the other four villages they account for 50 per cent of the population. The elderly population ranges between 2.9 and 7.9 per cent. The average household size varies between 3 to 5 persons per household. Also, five of the villages have a substantial proportion of SC households. All the villages are Hindu dominant with one or two having one-fourth of the population as Christians and Muslims.

A large number of houses were tiled with 25 per cent of them being in the category of *pucca* or thatched. The percentage of workers is less than 50 per cent except in one village where it is 58 per cent. There seems to be a greater balance in the category of workers with an equal distribution in the category of cultivators, agricultural workers and other workers.

These villages have two-third of the cultivable land as dry land and the rest as wet land. Except one, all the villages have less than 50 per cent of the land under cultivation. The extent of irrigation is quite high in four villages. With regard to the distribution of land holding, the pattern is the same like other districts of the state with a larger proportion of small land holdings. These villages have a better numbers of livestock.

The literacy levels are well above 50 per cent though there remains a sex differential. This is despite the availability of ample number of schools in these villages. All the villages have a noon meal centre except one and they are mostly in schools. In terms of medical facilities these villages present a very poor scene as none of them even have a sub-centre, including the village which has a population of more than 5,000. On the infrastructure and sanitation front, these villages are no different apart from having a greater degree of electrification. However, two of the villages are not electrified.

Drinking water facilities are comparatively better in the villages of Tirunelveli compared to villages in other districts of Tamil Nadu. Well irrigation also seems popular among the villagers. Transport facilities are ranked good in four of the seven villages but in terms of communication some of the villages do not have even a sub-post office. In relation to other infrastructure indicators, it is striking that all the villages have one fair price shop each. The number of government programme beneficiaries are not too many.

Pudukottai

This district is represented by two large villages with population sizes of around 5,000 each. One of the two villages has a 20 per cent SC population and the other one has less than 5 per cent SCs. In both the villages, the sex ratio is in favour of males but in one of them it is as low as 885 females per thousand males. In terms of population density, one village has 256 persons per sq. km. while the other one has 642 persons per sq. km.

The population age structure is more or less same in both the villages with roughly 45 per cent of the population below the age of 14 years. The working age group population is well below 50 per cent. The village with greater density of population has a higher average household size of 6.2 persons per household while the other one has 5.4 persons per household. Both the villages are predominantly Hindu with one having a few Christian and Muslim households.

The percentage of working population is well above 50 per cent though the working age population is below 50 per cent indicating that children below age 14 years or persons above 60 years are working. Two-third of the workers in one village are categorised as agricultural workers but in the other a majority are in the category of cultivators. Female worker proportion seems to be visibly different in the two villages. Both the villages are mostly having dry land with less than 20 per cent of the land being classified as wet land. The land holding pattern is more or less like any other district of the state. The number of livestock is quite impressive.

Literacy levels are low in both the villages. With regard to medical facilities both the villages have a primary health centre and a sub-centre. On the sanitation front, there is absolutely no visible effort. Electrification is satisfactory to a certain extent and in one of the village there are smokeless *chullas* and bio-gas plants. One villager has overhead tanks and public taps for drinking water whereas in the other village wells and hand pumps are the most popular source of drinking water. Though the transport facilities are good in both the villages they have poor communication faciiities.

Ramanathapuram

Ramanathapuram is represented by two villages with population sizes of 2,600 and 2,800. One of the villages has nearly one-third of its population in the SC category and the other one has less than 10 per cent of its population as SC. In both these villages the sex ratio is in favour of females. The population density is 425 persons per sq. km. in one village while the other one has 258 persons per sq. km.

The population age structure in the two villages is very different. In one village children account for 50 per cent of the population while in the other it is 23.3 per cent. The village with lesser proportion of child population has more than 70 per cent of its population in the working age group. The average household size in the two villages is 5.3 and 4.6 persons per household. The religious composition of these two villages reveal that one of them is an entirely Hindu village while the other one has less than 10 per cent of non-Hindu community.

The percentage of working population is well below 50 per cent in both the villages. There seems to be a large proportion of cultivators in the category of workers. The land in both the villages is predominantly dry land and the net cropped area is around 80 per cent. Twenty to 25 per cent of the cropped area is under irrigation. The land holding pattern is more or less the same as in other districts of the state.

The literacy level is less than 40 per cent and there is a wide difference between the sexes. But surprisingly, these villages have two elementary schools each, along with a middle school in one village and a high school in the other. One village has two noon meal centres in the schools while the other village has one in a *balwadi*. Both the villages do not have any medical facility within easy access as there is no health centre within the village. Sanitary arrangements are minimal. Though both the villages are electrified, in one of the villages there is no electricity in two-third of the houses. Wells are the major source of drinking water for both the villages.

Broad findings and Recommendations for Further Research

Though Tamil Nadu's macro indicators such as literacy, urbanisation, fertility and other socio-economic and infrastructural indicators look impressive, the village studies paint a dismal picture of the ground-level situation.

The state of Tamil Nadu merits distinction today because of its demographic achievement during the last decade. Though the demographic success story is attributed mainly to governmental efforts in energising the family welfare programme and strong political commitment within the state, the role of changing socio-economic scene in the state is no less important.

No doubt, the state is pretty advanced in areas of urbanisation, industrialisation, education, employment etc., based on macro indicators at the district level. But the micro-level investigation based on village studies seem contrary to expectations. The agricultural practices are still traditional in nature and mechanisation has had the least impact in remote villages. There is little evidence of commercialisation of agriculture in remote villages. This may however be due to lack of stress on irrigation in the dry land region and paucity of the reach of government programmes to promote agricultural productivity to a great extent.

The state has a large number of social welfare schemes and

incentive schemes for improving socio-economic conditions of the poor. But these were not being implemented in the study villages. A survey of social welfare schemes of the state and its reach could be assessed through such micro investigation. But unfortunately, almost all the studies have limited themselves to enquiring about IRDP, village health schemes and the well known noon meal scheme. An effective evaluation of these programmes cannot be made in terms of the number of beneficiaries but by making a comparison between the socio-economic conditions of its beneficiaries and others.

Some areas for further research in Tamil Nadu could be as follows: the role of public distribution system in maintaining food supply in rural areas, the reasons for the high infant and child mortality, impact of noon meal scheme on primary education among weaker sections and the impact of various social security and assistance schemes on the poor, particularly the eldery, disadvantaged widows in the rural society.

DISTRICTS OF TAMIL NADU AT A GLANCE

Districts	Population	Sex ratio	Density per sq.km.	Decenial Growth rate 1981-91(%)	Proportion of Urban	% of Literate Population Population (1991)		
(1)	(2)	(3)	(4)	(5)	(6)	(7)	(8)	(9)
1. Madras	3795028	930	21811	15.82	100.00	87.9	74.9	87.6
2. Chengai MGR	4620967	957	588	27.77	44.83	77.1	55.2	66.4
3. North Arcot	3000208	987	494	14.14	31.76	72.9	48.6	60.9
4. Dharmapuri	2395606	944	249	19.96	9.41	57.2	34.2	46.0
5. Thiruvanmalai	1997458	982	323	11.85	12.10			
6. South Arcot	4870871	968	447	15.92	15.76	65.6	39.7	52.9
7. Salem	3914239	932	453	13.73	28.86	64.6	41.5	53.3
8. Periyar	2322851	960	283	12.30	24.77	65.5	41.6	53.8
9. Nilgiri	704827	987	277	11.85	49.81	81.8	61.5	71.7
10. Coimbatore	3531078	910	473	15.39	53.20	76.5	55.7	66.4
11. Dindigul	1768679	973	292	13.05	21.28	69.2	43.9	56.7
12. Tiruchirapa	4114323	983	371	13.90	26.73	73.4	48.9	61.2

(Contd.)

(1)	(2)	(3)	(4)	(5)	(6)	(7)	(8)	(9)
13. Thanjavur	4526709	996	547	11.40	22.94	77.2	54.8	66.0
14. Pudukkotai	1322494	1006	284	14.32	14.27	71.8	43.6	57.6
15. Pasumpon	1074989	1029	263	10.57	26.78	76.9	49.7	63.0
16. Madurai	3447595	972	525	16.02	44.99	77.7	54.7	66.4
17. Kamaraj	1554350	995	363	15.92	37.55	75.7	54.7	66.4
18 Ramanathpur	1135887	1020	268	11.11	21.98	74.8	48.7	61.6
19. Chidambaram	1455796	1047	315	7.79	41.39	82.0	64.6	73.0
20. Tirunelveli	2493189	036	366	12.15	31.72	77.5	54.2	65.6
21. Kanniyakumari	1591174	994	945	11.79	16.92	85.7	78.4	82.1
State	55638318	972	428	14.94	34.20	73.8	51.3	62.7

LIST OF SOCIO-ECONOMIC REPORTS

S.No.	Officer Trainee	Year	District & Village
1.	B. Anand	1988	Thenthiruperai Village Socio-Economic Survey.
2.	Anil Kumar	1992	A Socio-Economic Survey of Vadiyam Village, Kulithalai Taluk, Tiruchirapalli District.
3.	Anshu Prakash	1987	Socio-Economic Survey Report - Veppanganeri Village, North Arcot District.
4.	K. Arulmozhi	1986	Socio-Economic Report of 51-Tamaraikulam Village, Palani Taluk, Anna District.
5.	Jasbir Singh Bajaj	1985	A Socio-Economic Study of Pandrakottai Village in South Arcot District.
6.	Ruolkhumlien Buhril	1985	A Socio-Economic Survey of Melkavarapattu Village, Panruti Taluk, South Arcot District.
7.	C. Chandramouli	1986	Socio-Economic Report of Doddampalayam Village, Sathy Taluk, Periyar District.
8.	Jitendra Kumar Dadoo	1985	Socio-Economic Report of Keelacheruvoi Village in Tittagudi Taluk, South Arcot District.
9.	Dai Otem	1989	Socio-Economic Study of Pudukudi Village, Tirunelveli, Kattaboman District.
10.	Dai Otem	1988	Socio-Economic Study of Pudukudi Village, Tirunelveli, Kattaboman District.
11.	Satyanarayan Das	1987	Socio-Economic Survey Report of Nannayam Village, Cannanore District.

(Contd.)

S.No.	Officer Trainee	Year	District & Village
12.	P.W.C. Davidar	1987	A Socio-Economic Study on Sarfojirajapuram.
13.	K. Deenabandhu	1983	Peria Gollapatti - A Socio-Economic Survey.
14.	Ashok Dongre	1988	Neerethan Village, Vadipatti Taluk, A Report on Socio-Economic Survey.
15.	Shanthani Feodore	1985	Socio-Economic Report of Ikkarai Boluvampatti Village, Alandurai Firka, Coimbatore District.
16.	K. Gnanadesikan	1984	Socio-Economic Survey of Puliambakkam Village.
17.	S. Gopal Krishnan	1991	Socio-Economic Study - A Report on Kudumianmalai Village in Pudukottai District.
18.	V. Iraianbu	1989	A Socio-Economic Survey on Iswarankoil Pattu Village, Thanjavur District.
19.	T. Jacob	1985	Socio-Economic Survey of Kilkuvalaivedu Village, Vandavasi Taluk, North Arcot District.
20.	T.S. Jawahar	1991	Socio-Economic Survey of Singadivakkam Village.
21.	V.K. Jeykodi	1985	Socio-Economic Survey of Annimangalam Village in Ariyalur Taluk, Tiruchirapalli District.
22.	B. Chandrakant Kamble	1993	Socio-Economic Survey of Palavoor Village in Tirunelveli District
23.	Meenakshi Kanwar	1985	Socio-Economic Report of Mallur in Salem District.
24.	Vikram Kapur	1989	A Socio-economic Report on Ayan Thenkarai Village.
25.	Dayanand Kataria	1990	Socio-Economic Study of Mannarkoil Village.

(Contd.)

S.No.	Officer Trainee	Year	District & Village
26.	Ramesh Kaumar Khannan	1983	Socio-Economic Survey of Karuvappanaickenpettai Village in Kulithalai Taluk of Tiruchirapalli District.
27.	S. Krishnan	1990	Socio-Economic Survey of Kodangi Palayam Village, Palladam Taluk, Coimbatore District.
28.	L. Krishnan	1984	Socio-Economic Survey of Kumarmangalam Village in Kulithalai Taluk, Tiruchirapalli District.
29.	Praveen Kumar	1989	Socio-Economic Report of Karaikurichi Village.
30.	M. Madhavan Kutty	1986	Socio-Economic Survey of Podumbu, Madurai North Taluk.
31.	S. Abhilaksh Likhi	1993	Puthur Pudupalayam Village - A Study.
32.	Niranjan Mardi	1987	Socio-Economic Survey of Srinivasallur, Musiri Taluk, Tiruchirapalli District.
33.	Md. Nasimuddin	1990	Pannaikiudi A Socio-Economic Report.
34.	Babulal Meena	1992	Socio-Economic report on Mechcheri Village, Salem District.
35.	Ashok Ranjan Mohanty	1986	The Story of Erichanatham-report on the Socio-Economic Survey of Erichanatham Village, Kamarajar District.
36.	N. Muruganandan	1992	A Socio-Economic Survey on Thottakadu Village, Thanjavur District.
37.	Smitha Nagaraj	1987	Athu Pollachi Village: A Socio-Economic Report.
38.	Jiwesh Nandan	1989	Kothamangalam Viilage: A Socio-Economic Report.
39.	Rina Ojha	1985	Thirumohur, Madurai North

(Contd.)

S.No.	Officer Trainee	Year	District & Village
			Taluk, An Enquiry into its Society and Economy.
40.	N.S. Palaniappan	1984	Socio-Economic Survey of Somayanallur Village.
41.	Uma Kant Panwar	1992	Socio-Economic Study of Village Seemanuthu.
42.	Girija Shankar Patnaik	1981	A Socio-Economic Survey of Karipatti Village, Salem District.
43.	Gurnihal Singh Pirzada	1983	Sithalangudi, Nilakottai Taluk, An Enquiry into its Society and Economy.
44.	S.K. Prabhakar	1990	A Socio-Economic Survey, Sathanur Village in Thiruvaiyaru Taluk.
45.	Anshu Prakash	1987	Socio-Economic Survey Report Veppanganeri Village, North Arcot District.
46.	Braj Kishore Prasad	1985	Socio-Economic Report on Ananthalai Village, Wallajah Taluk, North Arcot District of Tamil Nadu.
47.	Pyare Mohan	1986	Socio-Economic Study of Pudukottai Village Perungalur.
48.	K. Raja Raman	1990	A Socio-Economic Report of Gunabeelam, Tiruchirapalli.
49.	R. Rajagopal	1985	Socio-Economic Study of Perur Village, Tirunelveli District.
50.	Jagmohan Singh Raju	1986	A Socio-Economic Report of Pethanaickenur Village, Pollachi Taluk, Coimbatore District.
51.	T.K. Ramachandran	1992	A Socio-Economic Survey of Kanniseripuddur Village, Kamarajar District.
52.	Ramesh Chand Meena	1992	Socio-Economic Survey Report Ussoor Village, Vellore Taluk, North Arcot Ambedkar District.

(Contd.)

S.No.	Officer Trainee	Year	District & Village
53.	Rajiv Ranjan	1986	A Socio-Economic Study of Thimmapuram Village in Krishnagiri Taluk of Dharmapuri District.
54.	T. Rao Prabhakaran	1983	Socio-Economic report on Vittilapuram Village.
55.	Varaprasad Rao	1985	Melakottaiyur, Chengalpattu Taluk, An Inquiry into its Society and Economy.
56.	P. Ram Mohan Rao	1986	Rameswaram: A Socio-Economic Study.
57.	M. Saikumar	1991	Continuity and Change in a Tamil Nadu Village: A Socio-Economic Profile of Yethapur.
58.	K. Phanindra Reddy	1988	Socio Economic Report on Vairavikulam Village.
59.	D. Sabitha	1990	Socio-Economic Report, Orikai Village, Kanchipuram Taluk, Chengai Anna District.
60.	V. Sankaran	1983	Socio-Economic Survey of Pudukkotai Village, Arasarkulam Keezhapatti.
61.	Satya Gopal Korlapati	1988	Socio-Economic Survey of Inam Kasireddiapatti.
62.	Sandeep Saxena	1990	Socio-Economic Report on Periakrishnapuram Village in Salem District.
63.	K. Shanmugam	1986	A Socio-Economic Survey on Milathur IVth Sethi Village.
64.	Ambuja Sharma	1985	A Report on the Socio-Economic Survey of Ayothipattanam (A village in Salem Taluk), Salem District Tamil Nadu.
65.	A. Shegaonkar Viswanath	1986	A Socio-Economic Survey of Salur Village, Sivaganga Taluk, Pasumpon Muthuramaliyam Dist.

(Contd.)

S.No.	Officer Trainee	Year	District & Village
66.	K. Ashok Vardhan Shetty	1984	Socio-Economic Survey of Karungulam Village, Tirunelveli District.
67.	Shiv Das Meena	1989	A Socio-Economic Survey Report of the Village Injambakkam.
68.	Paramjeet Singh	1987	A Socio-Economic Report on Thennamanallur Village, Coimbatore South Taluk, Coimbatore District.
69.	Harmander Singh	1985	Socio-Economic Report of Kandaneri Village.
70.	Swaran Singh	1987	Socio-Economic Report of Kavanoor Village.
71.	H.K. Sinha	1984	Socio-Economic Survey Report of Pillandipattu Village, Gudiyatham Taluk.
72.	Shakti Sinha	1980	A Socio-Economic Survey of Amoor.
73.	P. Sivasankaran		The Socio-Economic Study of Vagaiyur Village.
74.	T.V. Somanathan	1989	Tirukkarugavut : A Scoio-Economic Survey.
75.	C. Umashankar	1991	Socio-Economic Survey Report of Perumugai Village, Vellore Taluk.
76.	Salini Vasisth	1989	A Socio-Economic Report on Ayyangarkulam Village of Kancheepuram Taluk, Chengai Anna District.
77.	H.R. Verma	1987	Socio-Economic Survey Mukasi Hanumanpalli Village-A Study.
78.	H.R. Verma	1988	Socio-Economic Report of Mukasi Hanumanpalli Village, Erode Taluk, Periyar District.
79.	Apurva Verma	1988	Socio-Economic Survey of Dhalavaihalli Village,

(Contd.)

S.No.	Officer Trainee	Year	District & Village
			Dharmapuri District.
80.	B. Vijayan	1983-84	Socio-Economic Survey Report on Alandurai Village, Coimbatore District.
81.	Pradeep Kumar Vyas	1989	Socio-Economic Study of Village B. Adivarganallur.
82.	Rakesh Kumar Yadav	1991	Socio-Economic Report on Angalakurichi Village.

BIBLIOGRAPHY

Annadurai, C. (1988) 'The Public Distribution System in Tamil Nadu: An Interim Assessment' *Bulletin Madras Development Seminar Series,* Vol.18(1), pp.25.

Arputharaj, C., Sheila E. Jane and V. Saraswathi. (1990) 'Agro-Climatic Planning and Regional Development in Tamil Nadu' *Indian Journal of Agricultural Economics,* Vol. 45(3), pp.320.

Athreya, Venkatesh, B. (1990) *Barriers Broken: Production Relations and Agrarian Change in Tamil Nadu,* Sage Publishing House, New Delhi.

Dahanasekharan, K. and Thangarajan, K.A. (1988) 'A Study of the Impact of Tree Cultivation Incentive Programme on Rural Poor in Gobi-Chettipalayam Forestry Range of Periyar District'. *Indian Journal of Agricultural Economics,* Vol.43(3), pp.323.

Dhawan, B.D. (1983) 'Impact of Irrigation on Instability in Farm Output: A Case Study of Tamil Nadu State'. *Economic and Political Weekly,* Vol.18(39), pp.A109.

Economic and Political Weekly (1981) 'Tamil Nadu: Myths and Facts Behind Agrarian Unrest'. Vol.16(50), pp.2027.

George, Ivy. (1990) *Child Labour and Child Work,* Ashish Publishing House, New Delhi.

Harriss, Barbara (1984) *State and Market: State Intervention in Agricultural Exchange in a Dry region in Tamil Nadu, South India,* Concept Publishing Company, New Delhi.

Harriss, Barbara. (1983) 'Relations of Production and Exchange and Poverty in Rainfed Agricultural Regions'. *Economic and Political Weekly,* Vol. 18(39), pp.A82.

Harriss, Barbara. (1982) 'The Marketed Surplus of Paddy in North Arcot District, Tamil Nadu: A Micro Level Causal Model'. *Indian Journal of Agricultural Economics,* Vol.37(2), pp. 145.

Helen, G.J, Sekar, R., and Pinto. (1992) *Situation of Working Children in Tamil Nadu,* Workshop Report, National Labour Institute, India.

Irudaya Rajan, S. (1994) 'India's Population: Heading Towards a Billion'. *Economic and Political Weekly*. Vol. XXIX, Nos. 51-52, pp. 3201-3205.

Irudaya Rajan, S. *et al.* (1991) 'Decline in Sex Ratio: An Alternative Explanation?' *Economic and Political Weekly,* Vol. XXVI, No. 51, pp. 2963-64.

Irudaya Rajan, S. *et al.* (1992) 'Decline in Sex Ratio: Alternative Explanation Revisited.' *Economic and Political Weekly,* Vol. XXVII, No. 46.

Irudaya Rajan, S. (1986) 'Levels and Trends of Urbanization in India: A Comparative Study of Tamil Nadu.' *Nagarlok,* Vol. XVIII, No. 3, pp. 21-35.

Irudaya Rajan, S. and Arulraj, M.R. (1987) 'Literacy Profile: A District-wise Analysis of Tamil Nadu' *Yojana* (Tamil), Vol. 18, No. 16.

Irudaya Rajan, S. and Jayaramachandran, S. (1986) 'Water Supply Management in Tamil Nadu', *Yojana*, (Tamil), Vol. 18, 1-15 November.

Irudaya Rajan, S. and Jayakumar, A. (1992) 'Impact of Noon Meal Programme on Primary Education: An Exploratory Study in Tamil Nadu' *Economic and Political Weekly,* Vol XXVII, Nos. 43 and 44, pp.2372-80.

Irudaya Rajan, S. *et al.* (1993) 'Two-Child Family in India: Is it Realistic?' *International Family Planning Perspectives* Vol. 19, No. 4, pp. 125-128 & 154.

Irudaya Rajan, S. *et al.* (1993) 'Demographic Transition and Labour Supply in India', *Productivity,* Vol. 34, No. 1, pp. 11-21.

Irudaya Rajan, S. (1989) 'Aging in Kerala: One More Population Problem?' *Asia-Pacific Population Journal,* Vol. 4, No. 2, pp.19-48.

Iyyampillai, S. (1988) 'Social Forestry in Tamil Nadu: Prospects and Problems' *Indian Journal of Agricultural Economics,* Vol.43(3), pp.315.

Jayaraj, D. (1987) *Marketing of Groundnut in North and South Arcot District of Tamil Nadu,* Unpublished Ph.D. Dissertation, University of Madras.

Kalpagam, U. (1981) 'Labour in Small Industry: Case of Export Garment Industry in Madras', *Economic and Political Weekly,* Vol.16(48), pp.1957.

Karkal, M. and Irudaya Rajan, S., (1991) 'Progress in the Provision of Basic Human Needs, India, 1961-1981. *Economic and Political Weekly,* Vol. XXVI, No 8, pp. 443-451.

Kothari, S. (1983) 'There is Blood on those Matchsticks: Child Labour in Sivakasi', *Economic and Political Weekly,* Vol.18(27), pp.1191.

Krishnaswami, C. (1989) 'Dynamics of Capitalist Labour Process: Knitting Industry in Tamil Nadu', *Economic and Political Weekly,* Vol. 24(24), pp.1353.

Maghalingam, S. (1990) *Role of Co-operative Organisations in Developing Tribal Economy (A Study of LAMP Tribal Cooperatives).* Mittal Publishing House, New Delhi.

Mari Bhat, P.N. and Irudaya Rajan, S. (1992) 'Demographic Transition in Kerala: A Reply' *Economic and Political Weekly,* Vol. XXVII, No. 23.

Mari Bhat, P.N. and Irudaya Rajan, S. (1990) 'Demographic Transition in Kerala Revisited. *Economic and Political Weekly,* Vol. XXV, Nos. 35 & 36, pp. 1957-1980.

Mishra, U.S. *et al.* (1995) '1981-91: A Decade of Urban Explosion!' *Urban India,* Vol. 13, No.2.

Mohan, T.C., Veerasamy, T., and Sivaraman, S. (1985) 'Bayesian Analysis of Crop Loan Overdues in Co-operative Societies in Thanjavur District, Tamil Nadu', *Indian Journal of Agricultural Economics*, Vol.39(4), pp.549.

Mohan, T.C., Elango R., Namasivayam, D. and Manoharan, K. (1982). 'The Role of Subsidy in Risktaking by Farmers - A Study in a South Arcot Village', *Indian Journal of Agricultural Economics,* Vol.37(3), pp.247.

Moses, B.C. (1983) 'Tamil Nadu: Waiting for the Rains', *Economic and Political Weekly,* Vol.18(10), pp. 334.

Nair, Narayanan K., Sivanandan P., and Ratnam V.C.V. (1984) 'Education, Employment and Land Holding Pattern in a Tamil Village', *Economic and Political Weekly,* Vol.19(24&25), pp.948.

Narayana, D., Ratnam V.C.V. and Narayan N. N. (1982) 'An Approach to Study of Irrigation: A Case of Kanyakumari District', *Economic and Political Weekly,* Vol.17(39), pp. A.85.

Narayanamoorthy, A. (1990) 'Case Study of a Successful Paddy Cultivator of Pudukkotai District of Tamil Nadu', *Indian Journal of Agricultural Economics,* Vol.45(3), pp.374.

Palanippan, R.M. and Chockalingam V. (1988) 'Profitability of Social Forestry in Rainfed Areas of Ramanathpuram District in Tamil Nadu', *Indian Journal of Agricultural Economics*, Vol.43(3), pp.319.

Pandian, M.S.S. (1987) 'Peasants, Natural Resource Use and State Intervention in Nanchilnadu, 1850-1940', *Economic and Political Weekly,* Vol.22(26), pp.1032.

Poduval, R.N. (1987) *Food grain Economy of Tamil Nadu: Problems and Prospects*. Emerald Publishers, Madras.

Prabha, T. (1983a) 'Movement Restrictions, Procurement and Market Price - A Case Study of Tamil Nadu', *Economic and Political Weekly,* Vol.18 (26), pp.A53.

Prabha, T. (1983b) 'Government Operations in Rice: A Case Study of Tamil Nadu', *Indian Journal of Agricultural Economics,* Vol.37(1), pp.27.

Rajagopalan, R. and Anuradha B. (1987) 'Structural Changes in Land Holdings of Thanjavur District of Tamil Nadu', *Indian Journal of Agricultural Economics,* Vol.42(3), pp.307.

Rajagopalan, V. and Varadarajan S. (1983) 'Nature of New Farm Technologies and its Implications for Factor Shares - A Case Study in Tamil Nadu', *Indian Journal of Agricultural Economics,* Vol. 38(3), pp.424.

Ramaswami, K.S. (1984) 'Factors Influencing Industrial Entrepreneurship: A Study of Tanners of North Arcot District in Tamil Nadu', *Economic and Political Weekly,* Vol.21 (20&21), pp.PM61.

Sampath, R.K. and Jayalakshmi, Ganesan. (1972) *Economics of Dry Farming in Tamil Nadu*, Sangam Publishers, Madras.

Saradamoni, K. (1987) 'Labour, Land and Rice Production: Women's Involvement in Three States', *Economic and Political Weekly,* Vol.22(17), pp.WS2.

Sivarajasingham, S. (1990) 'Sustainable Agriculture Development through Watershed Management in Dry Areas of Tamil Nadu', *Bulletin of Madras Development Seminar Series,* Vol.20(11), pp.515.

Srinivasan, S. (1988) 'Long Term Rural Credit in Anna District, Tamil Nadu: A Case Study', *Indian Journal of Agricultural Economics.* Vol.43(3), pp.419.

Srinivasan. (1987) 'Economics of Grape Cultivation in Dindigul Taluk, Anna District, Tamil Nadu', *Indian Journal of Agricultural Economics,* Vol.42(3), pp.467.

Srinivasan, S. (1984) 'A Primary Health Centre in Tamil Nadu: Some Observations', *Kurukshetra,* Vol.33(2), pp.15.

Srivastava, A.P. (1983) 'Agricultural Production and Increasing Fertiliser Application', *Economic and Political Weekly,* Vol.18(13), pp.A17.

Stanislaus, Sebastian, M. (1985) *Farmer's Response to Price Changes in a Developing Economy,* Ashish Publishing Company, New Delhi.

Subramaniam, G. (1987) *Cotton in Madurai District: An Econometric Analysis,* Northern Book Centre, New Delhi.

Subramaniam, G. and Nirmala, V. (1988) 'Input Demand and Output Supply Response of Cotton Farmers in Tamil Nadu' *Indian Journal of Agricultural Economics,* Vol.42(3), pp.521.

Subramaniam, G. (1986) 'Labour Demand and Supply Responsiveness of Cotton in Madurai District, Tamil Nadu', *Indian Journal of Agricultural Economics,* Vol. 40(2), pp.155.

Sundari, T.K. (1985) *Caste and the Agrarian Structure: A Study of Chengalpattu District,* Ph.D. Dissertation, Centre for Development Studies, Trivandrum.

Swaminathan, M. (1990) 'Village Level Implementation of IRDP: Comparison of West Bengal and Tamil Nadu', *Economic and Political Weekly,* Vol.25(13), pp.A.17.

Thamodaran, R., Shashanka, Bhide and Earl O. Heady. (1982) An Economic Analysis of Water Management System in Southern Tamil Nadu - A Production Function Programming', *Indian Journal of Agricultural Economics,* Vol. 37(1) pp.43.

Timothy Randhir, O. and Krishnamoorthy, S. (1990) 'Productivity Variations and Water Use in Farms of Madurantakam Tankfed Area of Chengalpattu District, Tamil Nadu', *Indian Journal of Agricultural Economics*, Vol.45(1), pp.56.

Udaya Kumar, M. (1986) *Irrigation and Croping Intensity in Tamil Nadu: A Districtwise Analysis*, Unpublished M.Phil Dissertation, Centre for Development Studies, Trivandrum.

Uduman, Mohideen, K.S.S. (1991) *Institutional Credit and Agricultural Development: A Study of Annur Block of Coimbatore District*, Mittal Publications, New Delhi.

Venkataraman, S. (1987) *Agricultural Wages in Tamil Nadu 1950-51 to 1980-81,* Unpublished M.Phil Dissertation, Centre for Development Studies, Trivandrum.

Venkataramani, G. (1973) *Land Reforms in Tamil Nadu,* Sangam Publishers, Madras Institute of Development Studies, Madras.

Venkataramani, G. (1987) *Minor Irrigation in Tamil Nadu,* Sangam Publishers, Madras Institute of Development Studies, Madras.

Zachariah, K.C. *et al.* (1994) *Demographic Transition in Kerala in the 1980s.* Centre for Development Studies Monograph Series, Trivandrum.

3

KERALA

P. Michael V. Siromony

1. INTRODUCTION

If paradise is green, Kerala is truly Eden. It is very appropriate to call it God's own country, for reasons like Nature's bountiness, evergreen land with two monsoons, sangamom of various cultures and land where there is a confluence of many religions. It became a landing base for the foreigners then, in search of pepper, cardamom and other spices. The people of Kerala throng for learning; people are aware of the benefits of education, health, sanitation and people respect other religions; a place where people are politically very conscious and make use of the democratic values. Everything is questioned, debated and discussed.

Nature has been bountiful to this narrow strip of the country sandwiched between the Arabian sea and the Western Ghats. Kerala, a tropical paradise, is a land of colours and contrasts, where yesterday, today and tomorrow blend in graceful harmony.

State Formation and Division

The state of Kerala was formed on 1st November, 1956 by merging the princely states of Travancore, Cochin and the Malabar part under the Madras presidency. Currently there are 14 districts. It has a total area of 38,864 sq. kms. and with a coastline of 580 kms. It is a narrow stretch of land with maximum width of 72 kms.

On the basis of physical features the land is divided into lowland, with a long and narrow coastal belt with extensive sand and backwaters. Paddy and coconut plantations dominate this area and is quite densely populated. Kuttanad which is the 'rice bowl' is in this area is below the sea level. The midland is between the lowland and highland, the soil is lateritic. The major crops are paddy, tapioca, pepper, rubber and cashew. The higher regions of this area have plantations of cardamom, coffee, tea etc. The highland, known as the Western Ghats, is largely covered with thick forests punctuated by plantations. The highest peak in the Western Ghats, the Anamudi peak touching 2,817 metres, is located in the Idukky District near Munnac.

Natural Assets

There are 44 rivers of which three are east flowing. Bharathapuzha is the longest river. As the number of rivers are quite high, canal irrigation is the major source of irrigation and also the source for hydro-electric power projects.

The state has a long chain of backwaters and lakes along the coastal belt. The state is blessed with fresh-water lakes like Sasthamcottah lake, Vellayani lake, Periyar lake etc. There are many islands too like Vaipeen, Wellington, Bolghatti etc. Due to hilly terrains there are many waterfalls also. The state is blessed with two monsoons and fertile soil. The major plantation crops are cardamom, coffee, tea, pepper, rubber, cashew, cocoa, coconut, arecanut, cloves, etc. Other crops like tapioca, sweet potato and yam also occupy considerable area. In horticultural crops jackfruit occupies a prominent place though other fruits like banana (long variety) is predominant. Pineapple, guava, papaya, sapota etc. are grown. A lot of medicinal plants are also found and hence Ayurveda is very popular. Kerala is known for its teak and rosewood. Fisheries play an important role in the economy as well as in the daily food.

Administrative Machinery

The administrative machinery has a tremendous bearing on the development of the people. The peoples representatives, namely, the MPs, MLAs and members of the Panchayat Raj Institutions play very prominent role in the development of the state. The Panchayats are very active. There are around 1,000 panchayats, and three Municipal Corporations. Elections to these institutions are conducted very regularly. The District Council was introduced in 1991 and gradually allowed to weaken.

Currently there are 14 districts, 61 taluks, 1,452 Revenue villages, and 152 development blocks. The three-tier Panchayat Raj Institution will improve the administration by involving the people as considerable powers under 29 subjects have been given to the panchayats. The officials and people's representatives are quite accessible and sensitive to the problems. Being people literates participative, media alert and active, the administration is also responsive and committed to the welfare of the people.

The Economy

Kerala occupies a pre-eminent portion among the states in India because of her achievements in the social sectors like education, health, public distribution system, infrastructural facilities in rural areas, and radical land reforms which abolished tenancy and provided housesites to the hutment dwellers. The improvements in the field of health have led to a drastic reduction in infant mortality which is 17 per 1000 live birth and the life expectancy at birth for female children exceeds 70 years which could be compared with any developed countries. These improvements have reduced the birth rate to about 21 per 1000 population. The migration of the unemployed and their remittances amounts to around Rs. 5000 (approximate) crore per annum. There is no abject poverty or starvation. Beggary is conspicuously absent.

Areas of Concern

The areas of concern are unemployment, stagnant agricultural growth, very limited industries without trade unionism which pushes up the cost of production and hence makes industries non-competitive.The problem of drinking and high suicidal rates is very alarming. These problems are to be addressed urgently.

Scope of the Study

The study attempts to bring out the trends and current status in the socio-economic scenario in the rural Kerala, covering the last 12 years of study (1982-1992) solely depending on the micro-level socio-economic surveys conducted by the officer trainees.

The broad areas covered are:

— Agriculture
— Land Holdings
— Rural Industries
— Health
— Education
— Housing
— Wage Structure
— Government interventions and the Impact
— Village Life
— Conclusion : Development Experience of Kerala

The study would also highlight the imbalances and the correction measures. The shortcomings are due to the fact that the study has to rely mostly on the socio-economic survey reports of the officer trainees.

The sample size of the surveys vary from 50 to 100 households. Thus they are not truly representative. Villages in extremely interior rural areas where some backwardness or problems were selected so give the trainees a good exposure to the problems of rural areas. Hence a generalisation for a district could be made based on few reports but in some districts there are only one or two reports. On the basis of these, generalisation for the entire state will have some shortcomings.

2. AGRICULTURE

Agriculture is the predominant economic activity in Kerala specially in rural areas. Agriculture follows a multi-tier, multi-cropping and mixed cropping pattern. Barring paddy which is sown in about 5.5 lakhs hectares as a single crop, the remaining area supports mixed crops. The Kalpadaru (coconut) is almost natural to Kerala barring the hill districts and thus has monopolised the land. The scenario is that paddy cultivation becoming uneconomic the area under paddy is gradually shrinking and food sufficiency is becoming a major problem. All-out efforts by enforcing the Kerala Land Utilisation Act and various incentives like group farming, providing various inputs etc. is showing a only downward inclination of productivity. The area under paddy is getting converted to coconut, banana even rubber etc.

Kerala's Agro-climatic Condition also Suits the Various Plantation Crops

	Area in lakh hectares as on 1992
Paddy	5.5
Coconut	8.7
Pepper	1.8
Cardamum	.45
Arecanut	.63
Plantain (Banana)	.67
Cashew Nut	1.1
Tapioca	1.3
Tea	.35
Coffee	.85
Rubber	4.5

Only the major crops have been highlighted in the table in addition tubers, millets, wheat and potato also grown in certain pockets. The flat land, valley and the hills all are contiguous and creps grown according to the agro-climatic situation.

For food, vegetables and fruits (other than banana) and for cereals the state is heavily dependent on other neighbouring states. The Public Distribution System is the only source of food grains and by and large they are efficient. The surplus items which are exported out of Kerala are spices (pepper, cardamom, ginger and coconut oil).

The land is very productive, and per hectare productivity in terms of money value Kerala tops the country. Kerala receives two monsoons, dams and canal irrigation is the major source of irrigation.

The climatic variations over the past two decades have led to a change in the cropping pattern in the plantation crops. Cardamom which needs heavy shade and is sensitive to climatic change is decreasing in area. This has led to expansion of pepper — which is a strong light demander — and has led to a lot of denudation. Coffee which is heavily dependent on the blossom showers, sometimes fail to flower as that critical blossom shower is missing and pepper which is pollinated by rain water dripping through its spikes occasionally fails.

Kerala is the only state where at the Panchayat level a Krishi Bhavan is functioning with a qualified agricultural officer and other staff for technical guidance. The farmers are also very progressive and quite fast in trying new crop varieties and very innovative. The Government through its schemes and *Malayala Manorama* through its annual award for the best farmer in the last half decade has made the farmers progressive and innovative. While interacting with farmers one could understand the rich experience they have and their suggestions are worthy in terms of application.

Some survey reports are discussed below.

Trivandrum

Sathyavathy in 1982 reports from Kottukal village. Agriculture and productivity is constrained by irrigation, and crop failure due to monsoon failure is a common occurrence. There is either too much water or too less water. Tank irrigation is common in the village. Paddy is the major crop. Two crops raised subjected to water availability. High use of fertiliser and pesticides are reported. Local varieties are also under use. Other crops like tapioca, coconut, rubber are the major economic crops. Agricultural implements are of traditional types. Tubers, vegetables, banana, pineapple and fodder are also grown.

Quilon

In Clappana village Kiran Soni in 1986 reports that 83 per cent of the village area is under cultivation. The predominant crop is paddy. A local variety of rice, Orumundakam, is also grown. The other major crops are coconut, tapioca, seasamum, banana, arecanut and pepper. High-yielding varieties of tapioca like H-97 are grown. Banana cultivation is also very economic and heavy application of fertilisers are very common. Cocoa is also grown. Minikit schemes, farmers training programmes are common. Local outlets are available for fertilisers and pesticides at the Panchayat level.

Pathanamthitta

From Iravon village Ajay Kumar in 1985 reports, all crops are grown as it is a base of the Western Ghats. Small farms and people living in the farmsteads are common. Paddy is the major crop. There is very heavy conversion of paddy to other crops. One farmer, converted 24 acres out of 50 acres to rubber and coconut. No modern technology in tilling could be applied due to small size and terraced area. Land pressure is felt. Tapioca - 831 acres; coconut - 315 acres; rubber - 667 acres; sugarcane and others - 300 acres. The wage rates for sowing in 1985 were Rs. 25 for men and Rs. 15 for women, while currently it is Rs. 60 and Rs. 50. Coconut is affected by root wilt and the yield is declining. Coconut is profitable and income is double than that of Paddy. The profit from banana is equal to that from coconut.

There is preference for rubber planted in the hilly area where irrigation facilities are absent. Three fertiliser depots are there in the village where pesticides are also available. Minor irrigation schemes are under implementation. A cooperative society in the village provides marketing facilities for produce like rubber and spices. The soil conservation demonstration plots at Eravon has created a good impact in the area.

Allappuzha

Ramesh Negi reports from Purakkad village in 1984 that heavy demand from the farmers to convert the wet land to garden land. For the last 15 years paddy cultivation is not being carried out. Only one crop is possible here. Fertiliser consumption is low. Nutrient loss through leaching and soil erosion is reported. Organic farming by promoting blue green algae is recommended. Manure application is poor. Here monocrop is the rule and intercropping trial had not succeeded. Pulses and vegetables cultivation is possible and is being tried through extension but is yet to take root. In Allappuzha, Kuttanad area is the 'rice bowl' of Kerala where the land is below the sea level.

Kottayam

Panachikad village surveyed by V.S. Chauhan reveals: Paddy 580 ha, coconut 576 ha, tapioca 200 ha, banana 60 ha, and pepper 30 ha in the village. High yielding varieties are used in paddy. Certain areas under paddy cultivation are below sea level and hence water has to be pumped out. No tractor is used. Agricultural workers' wage is Rs. 40. There is a heavy pressure to convert to coconut plantation. In tapioca as well as coconut HYVs are used. Banana is intercropped with Dioscorea and pepper is common. Vegetable cultivation is being taken up. Rubber is under expansion, coffee, cocoa, and pineapple also reported. Fertiliser and pesticide application is quite common. The slackness of the official machinery is also highlighted. There is lack of market support for the produce. All agricultural produce other than tapioca is sent outside.

Ernakulam

R.K. Singh in his survey of Valakom village in 1984 reports the cropping pattern: paddy, rubber and coconut. Other crops like banana, tapioca and pepper are common. Paddy is irrigated through pumps as there is a heavy concentration of wells. Traditional water wells and manually operated water wheels are very common. The area under paddy crop is being reduced. Ploughing with bullocks is predominant. Yield of paddy is 2,500 kg per hectare, and of banana is 1.2 tonnes per hectare. The farmers are well aware of the improved seeds, fertilisers and pesticides and supplied by the cooperative societies and private traders. Wage rate is Rs. 50 for male and Rs. 35 for female workers. Krishi Bhavan's role and its various schemes is highlighted.

Palghat

K. Shivaji reports from Muthalamada village in 1986 that the major crops are: Paddy 2,046 ha, cotton 600 ha, groundnut 3,800 ha, pulses 350 ha, tapioca 6,504 ha and coconut 392 ha. The area is covered under the Gayathri Irrigation Project. Sinking of wells and bore-wells are very common. Agricultural pattern is of both dry and wet land crops like cotton, groundnut and sugarcane over large areas is unique to this area. Migrant labourers from Tamil Nadu are abundantly available. Tractors and tillers are very common. The area is a rain deficit area. Palghat district is called the granary of Kerala.

Thrissur

V. Ramakrishnan reports in 1993 from Pananchery village that paddy is the major crop followed by coconut, banana, pepper arecanut and cashewnut. Since 1986 the area under all crops except arecanut is on the increase. Group farming is under implementation (where inputs over an area are shared). The year 1992-93 was declared as paddy year by government of Kerala. The farmers sell the paddy to the local middleman. Storage house for paddy could increase the income of the farmer. Regulated markets can play an important role. The Krishi Bhawan is active and also the Agricultural Developmental Committee which focuses on local problems, identifies suitable farmers, disseminates knowledge through seminars and reviews the work of the Krishi Bhavan effectively.

Kozhikode

Prakash Kumar in 1986 reports from Pudupady village that rubber is the major crop while crops like coconut, pepper, banana, tapioca are also reported. Paddy is very less. Traditional ploughing with bullock is very common. High yielding varieties are used. Tapioca quickly exhausts the soil and also promotes soil erosion. There is a rubber factory run by a cooperative society. Rubber has increased in area from 1,575 hectares to 2,100 hectares over the period 1980 to 1986. Power tillers are privately available for hire at the rate of Rs. 30 per hour and implements like sprayers, dusters etc. are quite common. Many Agro facility centres are available. Source of water are available in plenty and minor irrigation schemes have a lot of potential.

Kasargode

Tenzing reports from Koipady in 1987 as follows. Arecanut with 677 acres is the major crop followed by paddy 308 acres, coconut 257 acres and cashew 124 acres. The district is known for arecanut and cashew. Bose plough is common while tractors and power tillers are appearing. Tools and implements need to be modernised. Farm yard manure is not used much but green manure application is followed. Schemes like intensive pulse development, oil seed development and soil testing facilities have been introduced. Cocoa is the major inter crop cultivated. Arecanut is the most profitable crop. Well irrigation and pumpsets are the common mode of irrigation.

Plantation Crops

Kerala is the home of all plantation crops. The state accounts for 46 per cent of the area under plantation crops of the country. The major crops are tea, coffee, rubber and cardamom. Barring tea most of the plantation holders are small holders. The plantations are mostly in rural areas and they take care of the local development, induces local skills, provides opportunity for entrepreneurs, earns or saves foreign exchange and prevents migration of people towards the urban areas. Climatic changes have lead to an increase in the area under rubber and considerable reduction in the area under cardamom.

All the socio-economic reports cover the plantation crops or cash crops including pepper, arecanut, coconut, cocao, cashew and rubber.

Rubber

Rubber is the major plantation crop accounting for 85 per cent of the area in the country and accounting for more than 90 per cent of the rubber produced in the country. Both the area and per hectare productivity has been on the rise, thanks to the efforts of the Rubber Board, progressiveness of the small farmers and the powerful farmers lobby. From 3.5 lakh hectares in 1987-88 it touched 4.37 lakh hectares in 1993-94 and productivity also went up by 30 per cent in the same period. The achievements to be highlighted are introduction of good clones, replacing the old with new crops, application of technology and an effective extension work by the Rubber Board. Only 10 per cent of the rubber produced is consumed in the state. Kottayam district tops with more than 25 per cent of the total planted area followed by Ernakulam and Pathanamthitta. All the districts have some area under rubber plantation.

Coffee

Coffee is predominantly grown in the hilly areas mainly in the districts of Wayanad and Idukky. Most of the coffee growers are small farmers. The total area under coffee is 84,000 ha which is 31 per cent of the area in the country. This commodity which was under severe crisis regained its position in the international market due to Brazilian frost. The productivity is around 330 kg per hectare and on an average it fetches around Rs. 275 crores of foreign exchange per year. In order to enhance production, irrigation, specially sprinkler irrigation has been taken up. Coffee is a good crop for soil conservation on slopes. The species coffea robusta is preferred. New varieties are also released from time to time.

Coconut

Coconut is the mainstay of the rural economy of Kerala - in terms of employment and income. The distribution of coconut is from

Trivandrum to Kasargode in all districts. The crop covers around 8.8 lakh hectares and 39 per cent of the cropped area. It provides employment to nearly ten lakh people and the coir industry provides employment to 5 lakh people mostly women. Farmers prefer coconut because of high returns and since it needs less labour and attention.

Pepper

Pepper is one of the major export oriented crops with 98 per cent of the country's production, has the monopoly. Currently the area under pepper is 1.8 lakh ha. Pepper is concentrated in Kannur, Wayanad and Idukki districts. Diversification into white pepper and green pepper is common. Organic farming of pepper can add to the value. Productivity is almost stagnant at around 275 kg. per hectare.

Cashew

Cashew is another important plantation crop cultivated in low hilly terrain and along the coast predominantly in Kannur, Calicut, Mallapuram and Kasargode. There are 690 processing units employing about 3 lakh workers mostly women. A massive replanting scheme is being taken up for producting better quality kernel with better clone. There is monopoly procurement of cashew by Kerala State Cashew Development Corporation. There are 196 factories in private sector and 70 owned by Kerala State Cashew Development Corporation. Still there is short supply of cashew hence raw nuts are imported and processed. It is a good foreign exchange earner.

Tea

Tea covers nearly 35,000 hectares which is 8 per cent of the area planted all over the country. Both in terms of area and production it is concentrated in Idukky, Wayanad and Palghat districts. There are 132 estates, 90 per cent of which are above 50 hectares. Tea plantation and processing industry provides continuous employment and income. In Wayanad under the bonded labour rehabilitation project, Priyadarshi Tea Plantation and factory was set up. It is doing well and has entered the market. This is an exclusive tribal project, and is a success story.

Cardamom

The small cardamom is unique to Kerala and is grown predominantly in the hill districts of Idukky, Palghat, Wayanad and also in parts of other districts. The cardamom crop area is under reduction and currently is 43,459 ha. Due to micro-climatic changes the productivity is also decreasing. Idukky district under the cardamom hill reserve has switched over to pepper. The fluctuation of price of cardamom also had affected the crop area adversely. Kerala accounts 70 per cent of the production of the country.

Arecanut

Arecanut plantation is common in areas where there is water source. The first oil palm plantation including a processing plant also started in Kerala. The plantation has the benefit of locally developing the area, make the labourers settled, provides employment and prevents rural migration. The above mentioned plantation crops have been covered in one form or other by the micro-studies.

On analyzing the various reports the general issues, problems and trends are highlighted.

— Agriculture and mixed farming is the mainstay in the village.
— Major diseases affect crops like banana, coconut, pepper, cardamom, coffee etc.
— Despite all schemes the productivity of paddy is on the decline and paddy is considered non-profitable.
— There is large-scale conversion of land under paddy to banana, coconut and rubber.
— The cost of production is very high.
— In many areas technological upgradation had been done.
— Marketing needs attention specially in paddy.
— Group farming efforts are better and it is participative and

economical.

- — Low farm yard manure application and heavy fertiliser and pesticide application is the trend. Fertilisers and pesticides are locally available.
- — Per unit productivity can be increased and there is potential.
- — High yielding varieties in all crops are preferred by the farmers.
- — Agricultural labour wages is quite high.
- — Intensified efforts to be made to make agricultural activities profitable.
- — Value addition in agricultural produce is less.
- — There is a preference for plantation crops like rubber while pepper and coconut is also catching up.
- — Despite the Kerala Land Utilisation Order conversion of paddy to other crops is going on and lands are kept fallow.
- — Coconut is grown all over the state and also in the rural areas.
- — Holdings are small and gradually mechanisation is being introduced all over the state.

3. LAND HOLDINGS

The Kerala land reforms implementation was a watershed. Due to the effecive implementation of the land reforms the land holding patterns are very socialistic. The process of land reforms is almost complete.

Land holdings are mostly small in size. The fact that land holding less than one acre is nearly 50 per cent is also reflected in the surveys. V. J. Kurian, 1983, reports the land holding patterns in Kattakampal village, Thrissur district as follows :

Size	Area (acres)
Less than 1 acre	1,584
1 - 5 acre	762
5 - 10 acre	13
10 - 20 acre	Nil
20 acre and above	Nil
Total	2,359

Sudhakharan reports in 1982 in Arattupuzha village of Alleppy district.

Size	Area (acres)
Below 1 Acre	9673
1 - 5 acres	214
5 - 10 acres	5
10 - 20 acres	1
Total	9893

Further analysis shows that :

Below 5 cents	2709 nos.
Between 5 cents to 10 cents	1965 nos.
Between 10 cents to 50 cents	4311 nos.
Between 50 cents and 1 Acre	674 nos.

In Alleppy District in the village nearly 50 per cent of the land holders are having less than 10 cents of land.

Sathiavathy reports in 1982 in Kottukal village, Trivandrum district as follows :

Below 0.04 hectares	4567
0.04 - 0.25	6886
0.25 - 0.50	2767
0.50 - 1	1721
1 - 2	794
2 - 3	185
3 - 4	63
4 - 5	23
5 - 10	2
10 - 20	Nil
20 and above	1
Total	17009

Paul Antony in 1983 reports in Kattappana Village of Iddukky district (Plantation District).

Landless	4
Upto 5 cents	14
6 - 10 cents	20
11 - 50 cents	49
51 - 100 cents	22
101 - 150 cents	14
151 - 200 cents	11
201 - 300 cents	7
301 and above	9
Total	150

Thus more than 75 per cent of the land holdings are less than 1 acre.

In Arcacode village, Malappuram district, T.K. Manoj Kumar's report of 1987 reveals that :

0 - 2 Acres	450
2 - 5 Acres	10
5 - 10 Acres	0
10 Acres and above	1

More than 95 per cent of the land holdings are below 2 acres.

All the study reports reveal that nearly 90 per cent land holders are below 1 acre and hence are marginal farmers. This covers nearly 50 per cent of the land.

Land Holding Pattern of Scheduled Castes

The Scheduled Castes (SCs) constitute 10.26 per cent of the total population. They are spread all over the state but more concentrated in Quilon, Thiruvananthapuram, Palghat, Thrissur and Ernakulam.

Analysing the holdings and area, the general population holds an average of 0.33 hectares, the SCs hold an average of only 0.10 hectares. The land holding pattern is as per the density of the population. The districts of Thiruvananthapuram, Kollam, Allappuha, Kottayam, Ernakulam and Thrissur are holding much less. In Wayanad and Kasargod the land holding is to that of the general category. Quite a large number of people under the SC category are landless, and efforts are continuously made to distribute lands under land assignment scheme or under the houseless scheme, site for house.

Tribal Land Holdings

Land and its improvement is important resource for economic development, to provide stability, to increase incomes, and as an insurance against poverty. For tribal people forest and land are the assets for their survival. Though considerable amounts of land belonging to the tribals have been lost by land alienation due to heavy pressure on land, by cheating, forcibly taking and creating false records, etc. yet land as a resource is available with the tribal people. Though the Restoration of Tribal Land Alienation Act is in force it is not being properly implemented except for registering the cases. The average land holding works out to 0.52 hectares and in the plain districts like Allappuzha 0.04 hectares, Ernakulam 0.13 hectares and Thrissur is 0.10 hectares. The population of tribal people in these districts are less than 5000 people. In major districts like Palghat, Idukky, Malappuram, Thiruvananthapuram and Kasargode land holding is high. Most of the tribal lands are without title. Tribal people numbering 35 groups constitute 1.1 per cent of the total population.

Michael in 1982 in the study of Malappuzha-I village reports out of the 152 families there were 51 tribal families. More than 30 per cent tribal families are landless and very many have only 5 to 10 cents and their huts.

Land reforms were effectively implemented and the following benefits accrued :

- — There are no landlords and tenants now.
- — Small land holders have been given adequate protection and loan facilities for the development of land.
- — Security of tenure given to the tenant and no eviction.
- — Tenants given the right to pay the purchase price in 16 instalments or as a lump sum.
- — Absentee landlordism prevalent in certain areas (due to other occupation or migration) is negligible.

— Landlords who have surrendered land are entitled for compensation and these have been given.
— A family of 5 members could retain 15 acres.

Once again for three years government has ordered that any land ceiling case can be opened in case of complaint. The only criticism about the land reforms is that there are lot of exemptions for plantations. Through land reforms nearly 10 lakh tenants have been given hutment rights.

The socio-economic reports have not brought forward any cases of further sale of land assigned, though in a vast number of cases it is difficult to detect.

As a recommendation the tribal people should be given title to their land and should be made non-transitable. The alienated land of tribals should be restored. When the tribals or SCs sell land in distress situations, such land could be purchased by SC/ST corporation to be distributed back to the landless SC/ST or the land kept under mortgage and finance be given. Some tribal lands are under joint ownership, which is an impediment for their development.

Land related statistics are as follows as on 30-9-1993.

Total no. of ceiling cases	—71101
Cases disposed	—70059
Net extent of land ordered for surrender	—131870 hectares
Extent taken over	—92542 hectares
Extent distributed	—62467 hectares
Extent reserved for public purposes	—20247 hectares
No. of SC beneficiaries	—56889
Extent of land distributed for SC beneficiaries	—24442 hectares
No. of ST beneficiaries	—7043
Extent of land distributed to ST beneficiaries	—5049 hectares
Other beneficiaries	—69371
Extent of land distributed to other beneficiaries	—32976 hectares

On analysis the total number of land holdings in Kerala in 1990-91 was 54,19,189 covering 18,01,823 hectares. The average size of the holdings is 0.33 hectares. The following seven districts having land holding less than the state average : Thiruvananthapuram 0.17 hectares, Kollam 0.17 hectares, Allappuzha 0.21 hectares, Ernakulam 0.24 hectares, Thrissur 0.24 hectares, Malappuram 0.30 hectares and Kozikode 0.29 hectares. The districts, namely, Pathanamthitta 0.36 hectares, Kottayam 0.42 hectares, Pallakkad 0.43 hectares, Kannur 0.45 hectares, Kasargode 0.60 hectares, Wayanad 0.77 hectares and Iddukki with 0.83 hectares have land holding higher than the state average (Agriculture Census 1990-91).

The trend of land holding over a period of five years show that marginal land (below 1 hectare) has increased from 46.02 per cent to 48.83 per cent over the period 1985-86 to 1990-91. The other categories, namely: small 1 to 2 hectare, semi-medium 2-4 hectares, medium 4-10 hectares, large 10 hectares and above in terms of number of people and area is diminishing.

4. RURAL INDUSTRIES

As all the socio-economic surveys were in the rural areas, the studies have focused only to the rural industrial scene. In general, industrialization in Kerala has not happened in a big way both in terms of investment by Government of India and by the state. Most of the industries are concentrated in Ernakulam - Cochin, Alwaye, Trivandrum, Palghat and Cannoore.

The traditional industries are coir, cashew, handloom and fisheries, and they are the major rural industries spread all over Kerala. The other rural industries are saw mills/rice mills etc. Districts like Idukky and Wayanad are hilly and eco-fragile districts where only agro-based or plantation based activities like tea, coffee, pepper, cardamom, cocoa, etc. plantation and processing are common.

In Vellanad village, Trivandrum district, Tara Kodiyan in 1984 reported that the village has mostly cottage industries. Few communities are working and they are traditional weavers of reed/ bamboo mats. Among the traditional handicrafts the art of weaving bamboo mats is the simplest in form and adapted. Reed/bamboo mat weaving, agricultural operations and fisheries are interdependent. For manuring, storing, drying and for partition of housing and as side walls they are used. The craft is popular wherever bamboo and reeds are available. Most of the bamboo/ reed mats are utilitarian. Women do the mat weaving while the men collect the raw material and market the finished product. Tara reports that the Forest Department's restrictions, lengthy procedures, lack of financial support and exploitation in markets is affecting this industry. In few places weavers have formed cooperatives with support from NGOs, like Mitraniketan, and government agencies like KVIB (Khadi and Village Industries Board). Among the rural industries manual quarrying is very common. As construction is one of the major activities, this supports the quarrying.

Fisheries

Rajan in his survey of Neendakara village of Quilon district says that Neendakara is a fishing village. The fishing season starts with the onset of the monsoon and continues till December. In summer the catch is poor. Mechanised and traditional fisherman co-exist, and fish processing industries are well developed. Motorised fishing vessels outnumbered country crafts and catamarans. There are good infrastructural facilities for boat landing, shore based facilities, processing factories and insulated vans for collection in Neendakara. A shark liver oil factory has also been started. Ice plants, cold storages, boat/trawler repairing centres, specially under the private sector, have come up. The Indo-Norwegian project made a good impact in the area. The use of mechanised boats and gill nets given through the Project have enhanced the fish catch. It is observed that the Indo-Norwegian Project has been oriented towards the elite fisherman and the traditional fisherman has been left out. Neendakara and Shaktikulangara are the twin coastal villages which are the centre of fisheries in Kerala. Depending on the season and catch, the fisherman migrate to other parts of the state.

No. of catamarans in Neendakara	—	10
No. of country canoes	—	300
No. of mechanized country crafts	—	200
No. of mechanized boats for gill nets	—	10
No. of mechanized boats for travelling	—	3000

The inland fisheries in Asthamudi waterway has been very badly affected due to pollution. The shrimps fisheries is on the decline.

In trawlers the sharing of the income is as follows :

Boat owner	65 per cent (upto 75 per cent)
Crew	32 per cent
Auctioner	3 per cent

Sixty per cent of the catch is transported to inland markets, 20 per cent is locally consumed and 20 per cent is cured. In many parts of Kerala the fishermen are still in the clutches of the middlemen.

There are many private export companies. The State Cooperative Apex Federation (MATSYAFED) started in 1984 for the welfare of the fishermen. The Kerala Fishermen Welfare Societies Act, 1980, looks after the welfare of the fishermen who are living in nearly 400 villages.

The on-going schemes benefiting the fishermen are housing scheme, educational concession, Vanitha banks (which give loans at low interest), supply of kerosene for outboard motors, Vanitha bus service, community peeling centres, MATSYAFED input schemes, NCDC schemes, production centres, Vyasa stores (sales of fishing implements and other accessories).

There is a steady decline of catch due to over-fishing in certain areas. A ban on trawlling for a distance of 7 km. From the shore is being enforced through a marine protection force. The per capita fish consumption has also declined from 10 kg. to 9 kg. and Kerala which topped came second to Maharashtra.

Overall development of the fisheries sector has resulted in the traditional fishermen not being able to compete due to technological backwardness, lack of good transportation system. The introduction of trawling and purse-seines and its harmful effect have threatened the very survival of the traditional fishermen. The trawlling and purse-seines actually scrapes the sea bed and thus brings up juvenile fish and fish eggs while simultaneously destroying natural formations which facilitated the fish breeding.

All this has resulted in the decline and non-availability of many varieties of fish. The threat to the survival of the traditional sector has lead to major clashes and violence. Father Albert had organised the traditional fishermen under the Kerala Swatantra Matsya Thozilali Federation. Trawlers are now banned in June, July and August and the fish catch by the traditional fishermen has improved.

The state is blessed with 3,60,535 ha of brackish water which is a potential area for inland fisheries development. Inland fisheries have much potential for development and this is being made possible through FFDA (Fish Farmers Development Agency).

Prawn is a major foreign exchange earner earns 86 per cent of the total foreign exchange. A separate agency (ADTACH) has been created for promoting prawn culture. This is an area where the state has rich potential to create rural employment specially for the fishermen.

Copra Industry

In Ambalapuzha village, Allappuzha district, D.K. Singh in 1989 has covered the copra unit as a rural industry. During processing the white kernel is removed, sun dried, in some places by hot air, and the oil is extracted in a ordinary ghani or rotary ghani. Around 65% of the oil is extracted, and the oil cakes are used for feeding cattle. There is heavy competition. KERAFED is the oil federation cooperative dealing with extraction and marketing of coconut oil. Copra industries are common in rural Kerala.

Rubber based and Other Miscellaneous Village Industries

E.K. Majhi in 1989 from Puthupally village, Kottayam, highlights in his survey that most of the tiny industries have started since 1985 with the support of the government and banking institutions. Some of the successful units are :

— Wood based - (Furniture and house building materials)
— Coffee - Coffee processing units
— Engineering units - making gates, grills, shutters, steel furniture etc.
— Garment making

— Plastics - Making polythene bags.
— Rubber based - Production of rubber bands, chappals, latex goods, elastic threads, balloons, gloves, rubber mating etc.

Gayanesh Kumar in 1988 reports in his survey from Mulavucad village, Ernakulam, that household industry seems to be the only solution to generate employment. Furniture making is doing well.

Khadi Industry Working Sheds

The khadi shed for spinning of threads is a big investment on infrastructure but wages per head (for women) is meagre at Rs. 5. Because of the poor income women don't prefer these units. But there is scope for using this infrastructure for some other activities like weaving etc. which will create employment and income. Cycle hiring shops have an average income of Rs. 30 to Rs. 35 per day.

Beedi Manufacture

The private entrepreneurs rely on unemployed girls for beedi rolling. They supplying leaf and the tobacco to the girls pay them Rs. 15 for 1000 beedis rolled.

Wooden Boat Repairing

There is expertise available in rural areas to make and repair boats.

From Malampuzha-I village, Palghat, Michael 1982 and Asha reports in 1988 as follows.

Weaving

A weaver's cooperative society is functioning providing employment to six households. These families are traditionally weavers. Men weave and the women do the curing of yarn, threading, winding etc. The average earning is Rs. 15 per dhoti.

Pottery

The community which is traditionally doing pottery has taken to agricultural operations. Now they do pottery only during the agricultural lean season. This denotes that agricultural wages are higher and better. The use of earthen items is also on the decline. There is also the difficulty in getting clay-pit lease from private land owners. Not much technological improvement in this sector has happened.

Brick Making

This is done with a dual purpose by the land owners of leasing out the land and of bringing down the level of paddy cultivation. The entrepreneur faces the problem of threat from the rains, lack of storage places, not being able to invest enough and high cost of fuelwood for the kiln.

Cane or Reed Weaving

The Kavara caste people supplement their income from agriculture by reed or cane weaving. Forest restrictions make it difficult to get canes or reeds. Transporting to distant places is one of the constraints. The daily income is reported to be Rs. 15.

Knife Making and Leather Work

Two families are engaged in this work. Competitiveness and price is the problem.

Rice Mills

As Palghat is the rice bowl, in this village itself there are five rice mills. The rice mills are a profitable venture.

Cattle Feed Factory

There is a cattle feed factory with a capacity of 100 M.T. per day.

It sells to the milk cooperatives, government schemes of the DRDA and the Animal Husbandry department. Around 100 people are employed (technical personnel, skilled and unskilled labour). This is one of the factories of the Kerala Cooperative Milk Marketing Federation (Milma).

In Anjur village, Thrissur, Subrato Biswas covers a diamond cutting unit.

Diamond Cutting

A diamond cutting unit has been established and the skilled labourers are from Tamil Nadu. Power supply is available.The diamond waste is used for cutting tools. It is reported that there is no problem in the marketing and it is a well run unit with heavy capital investment. The total employees are less than 10 in number.

Aerated Water Making

A plant has been set up for production of soft drinks and soda water. The market is the rural area where branded products have not made any impact. Raw materials are only water, carbon dioxide, essence and sweeteners. It employs four people.

This particular village because of good entrepreneurship capabilities have taken up these projects.

A.K. Dubey from Calicut in his study in 1982 reports about :

Coir Industry

Coconut husks are left in pits dug in the shallow seashore area and covered by mud and rocks for a period of nine to twelve months. Each pit may contain 500-1500 husks. After that they are cleaned and beaten with a wooden hammer in order to separate the outermost cover from the fibres. Then the fibres are spun manually. Mostly women are engaged in this industry. In a small village like Ebothun about 200 families are engaged in this.

The economic position of the weavers in the village is very deplorable. They need consumption loans and are unable to guarantee repayment of any institutional loan which they might take.

He has also reported modern industries like flour mills, timber mills, ice factory and battery units.

Under the tertiary sector there are general merchants, tailoring shops, restaurants, shops selling household items, cinema halls, photography studio etc. The production-cum-training centre run by the Harijan Welfare Department imparts training in carpentry, weaving and ratten weaving. It provides stipends, loan and subsidy facilities for setting up new units.

In Mallapuram T.K. Manoj Kumar reports in 1987 the following :

— Wooden furniture and wood sawing employing nine people
— Oil extraction and grain grinding employing 3 people
— Rubber chappel units employing three people
— Printing job works employing nine people
— Leather wastes employing four people
— Candle units employing six people

Invariably in all sectors the number of people employed are less than 10 to avoid the Factories Act.

Transport and Communication

Buses are operating well as there is a bus-station and 12 privately owned jeeps are operating as well. The village has STD facilities.

P.G. Tenzing in his micro-study of the village Koipady in Kasargode also highlights saw mills, oil mills, beedi rolling and a plastic company. Among cottage industries he lists basket weaving and blacksmithy.

The Department of Industries through the District Industries Centre and Kerala Financial Corporation and the KSDIC supports lot of schemes. The major attractions are :

1. Ten per cent investment subsidy is provided on fixed assets, viz., land, building and equipment if registered after 1-4-1979.

2. Sales tax exemption is given for a period of 5 years for 90 per cent of the fixed capital investment.
3. EDP - Entrepreneurial Development Programme: It provides interest free loans upto Rs. 10,000 for starting industries.
4. SEEUY : Self-Employment for Educated Unemployed Youth. Loans to the extent of Rs. 35,000 are provided.

In addition there are schemes for women entrepreneurs and for weaker sections, namely Scheduled Castes and Scheduled Tribes.

Conclusion

The soico-economic surveys bring out the following:

— Rural areas are not able to attract industries.
— Traditional industries are getting weakened.
— Raw material supply problems exists. Adequate raw materials like coir husk, Cashew Bernd is not available.
— Adequate unconditional finance not available.
— The risk taking habit is very less among the population.
— The gulf returnees are reluctant to invest in industries. Their funds instead get invested in housing and construction activities.
— Fear of labour problems and trade unions.
— There are no major industries even in major cities which could spin off ancillary industries.
— High labour wages and input costs make the ventures less economic.
— There is no techological upgradation of traditional industries.

Thus the overall village industry scenario is not a very happy one. Though the Khadi and Village Industries Board has been assisting the copra industry, oil crushing, match factories, weaving, food processing and have introduced sericulture, reeling etc., it has no major impact.

In view of the existence of basic infrastructure like roads, communication, telephones, water, electricity adequate technical manpower, the alarming unemployment scenario has to be critically analysed and steps taken to shift to non-polluting industries like electronics, tourism and in the tertiary sectors.

5. HEALTH

Kerala's achievement in the health sector is commendable and can be compared with that of any developed countries. The health sector development took the direction of institutional development, manpower development and adequate resource allocation. Kerala has successfully tackled the first generation problems like infant mortality rate, maternal mortality rate and death rate. The decadal growth rate of population in Kerala between 1981 to 1991 is 13.98 whereas the all-India figure is 23.5.

	Kerala	All India
Birth Rate	17.1	29
Mortality rate	6	10
Infant Mortality rate	13	79
Life Expectancy	69 & 72	59
Immunization coverage	91	
Polio coverage (percentage)	100	
Anti Measles	99%	
BCG & Polio	88%	60
Deliveries	90% (In hospitals/Institutions)	
No. of Beds per Lakh Population	400 (including Govt. and Private)	

All the survey reports reveal the presence of allopathy or ayurvedic or homeopathic institutions and the services rendered by these institutions. Even private hospitals are common in rural areas. Many of the grassroots level institutions like health sub-centres are managed by para-medical staff.

All the reports highlighted that the family welfare programme is successfully covered and the two-child norm is accepted even among the tribal people. People are very much aware of the immunization programmes. Drinking boiled water is a common habit, which prevents many water-borne diseases.

There is an inadequate number of doctors in the PHCs and

due to budgetary limitations medicines are in short supply. Hospital development committees are formed in all hospitals, whose members are both officials and peoples representatives. They look after the development of the hospitals, and wherever the committee is active, the hospital is in a good condition.

6. EDUCATION

Kerala is made up of former princely states who had always given importance to education. The trend has continued and from the First Five-Year Plan onwards adequate allocation is made for education. The literacy rate is quite high touching 90 per cent. The female literacy is 86 per cent and for the Scheduled Tribes it is 51 per cent.

All the studies have highlighted the presence of two to three lower primary schools either Government run or privately run, and having good enrolment. The minority run schools have played an important role in providing education. From the study reports it is evident that for 95 per cent of the rural population a school is available within 1 km. This has greatly helped the education of girls. The teacher-pupil ratio is 1:30 whereas the all-India average is 1:35.

The schools are provided with all basic facilities. Mid-day meals are provided and the Parent-Teachers Associations are active. The Anganwadis under the ICDS scheme also play a crucial role in preparing the child for school. In most of the survey reports the role of the Anganwadi and the active role of the Anganwadi teachers has been highlighted. The need for an Anganwadi is always felt in the villages. Child labour is minimal or nil in rural areas, as there is a conducive environment to go to school.

The government spends 24 per cent of its plan expenditure for the social sector and education takes a large share. It is estimated that Rs. 1319 is spent per pupil during the primary stage and Rs. 2168 at the secondary stage. About 47 per cent of the education budget is spent for primary education and 30 per cent for secondary education.

The survey reports of R.K. Sharma (1987) in Muvattupuzha village in Ernakulam district talks about a college with post-graduate courses. The teacher-student ratio of 1:30 is confirmed in the socio-economic report. Schools for physically and mentally handicapped children is also reported. Government schools lack infrastructural facilities. There are many innovative schemes like Total Primary Education Programme being implemented in Trichur district (D.K. Dhodawat, 1993). It is a very common sight to see large numbers of well-dressed children going to school. Not sending a child to school is a stigma. The transport concession given also encourage the parents to send their children to school even to far away places. Through the schools various health, sports and cultural activities at school, district and state level are also organised.

7. HOUSING

One of the biggest activities in Kerala is construction of houses both sponsored by government and individuals, and also by gulf returnees. The housing oriented industries are developing fast.

Due to escalation of cost, cost effective housing technology innovated by Laurie Baker, and the various institutions, building centres etc. sponsored by NIRMITHY have made a good impact even in remote areas. There are various schemes in operation as there is lot of demand.

The major schemes are:

1. Rehabilitation Housing Phase-I and II.
2. LIG Housing Scheme (Eligible own land, house loan Rs. 7,200). MIG Housing Scheme (Income Rs. 7200 to Rs. 18,000. Loan amount Rs. 27,500).
3. SC Welfare Department Housing Scheme.
4. ST Welfare Department Housing Scheme.
5. Kerala State Development Corporation for SC & ST provides loan.
6. JRY - IAY Housing Schemes.
7. Village Housing Scheme
   (i) Rehabilitation Housing Phase-I
   (ii) Rehabilitation Housing Phase-II
   (iii) Rehabilitation Housing Phase-III.

8. Kairali Housing Scheme.

In addition private finance companies like HFDC are also financing housing activities but for the high income category.

The survey reports show that well constructed houses employing modern architecture is to be seen even in rural areas. The housing sector provides lot of employment both to skilled and non-skilled persons.

The traditional architecture which is cost effective is also very common. Some of the study reports have photographically covered small thatched houses, tiled houses, plastered and non-plastered houses, houses constructed of burnt and unburnt bricks and palatial houses with modern architecture.

8. WAGE STRUCTURE

The wage rates prevailing in the state are almost double than the minimum wages and this is true in both rural and urban areas.

Unskilled labour on an average gets Rs. 60 for non-agricultural work and Rs. 50 to Rs. 60 for agricultural work. Women are paid Rs. 10 less than men.

Manoj Joshi in his report (1989) from Cheruturuthy village, Trichur, says that the prevalent wage rate for unskilled labour for men is Rs. 45 and for women Rs. 30 whereas the minimum wage declared was Rs. 28 and Rs. 21 for unskilled labour.

Rajasekharan from Mulavana village, Quilon, reports in 1983 that agricultural labourers wages were Rs. 25. The current wages are Rs. 60.

Tara Kodiyan in 1984 reports that the agricultural wage rate is Rs. 30 for men and Rs. 25 for women. The current rate is Rs. 60 for men.

From Katteppana village, Idukky, Paul Antony (1983) reports that the wage rate is Rs. 35 for men.

Similarly all the reports have highlighted the high wage standard, much above the minimum wages.

Unemployment among unskilled labourers is quite high. During the season one gets maximum 20 days of employment (cultivation and harvest). In the lean season it may be as low as 10 days depending on the monsoon. Rainy days are the lean season.

The wage rates have been rising every year and are due to:

1. Strong trade unions which never allow the rate to come down as they have good bargaining power.
2. Reluctance of people to do manual labour after their education.
3. Opportunities available for migration.
4. Support provided by Government to unions and labourers help in strengthening their bargaining power.
5. Most of the people have some land around their huts to grow coconut, banana, tapioca, vegetables, rubber, jackfruit etc. which sustains them.

Impact

Due to the high wage rate there is no absolute poverty but unemployment is certainly there. The purchasing power of the working class is quite high.

The high wage rates makes the agricultural sector uneconomic and non-competitive. Land after cultivation could be put under pulses or other crops but since it is uneconomic the land is left fallow.Though land and irrigation facilities are available yet vegetable cultivation and other operations are uneconomic due to high labour cost. Hence, many of the agricultural produce specially vegetables come from other states. Kerala has become a consumer state.

The high wage rate in all sectors including the unorganised sector attracts a lot of workers from the neighbouring states of Tamil Nadu and Karnataka. Construction workers, both skilled and unskilled, from the state migrate to Bombay and Gulf countries. Kerala is the workers' paradise in terms of wages, rights and concessions.

In the long-term interest of the economy wages should be optimal and productivity oriented. Trade unions in sectors like coir industry, quarrying, loading/unloading, do not allow mechanisation and this makes the sector non-competitive. Most of the raw materials are transported from other states. The cost of living is quite high even in the rural areas. Due to this high cost of living the wage rates are also high.

9. GOVERNMENT INTERVENTIONS AND THEIR IMPACT

There are many government interventions to improve the quality of life of the individual and the community. The schemes for individuals are IRDP, TRYSEM, Plan schemes, self-employment schemes etc. The community oriented schemes are NREP/JRY, drinking water schemes, rural water supply scheme, soil conservation programmes, group farming etc.

The IRDP scheme was launched in 1978 and extended to all blocks by 1981. The criteria was fixed on a minimum calorie level of 2400. In 1989 the annual income cut-off level was fixed at Rs. 6400 per family. The maximum quantum of subsidy is Rs. 3000 for all and for STs it is Rs. 5000. The IRDP beneficiaries should be 30 per cent SC/STs and 33.33 per cent women.

The beneficiaries are selected by the village extension officer, who forwards the list of beneficiaries to the IRDP extension officer, who forwards it to the BDO who in turn forwards it to the bank, and DRDA. The DRDA releases the subsidy to the bank.

In Iringal village in Kozhikode district T.K. Jose reports 27 per cent of the families (1279 nos.) are below poverty line of which 58 are SC families. In the 7th Plan 249 families were assisted after physical verification. The observation is :

No assets partially	— 6 cases
No assets fully	— 12 cases
Repayment irregular	— 28 cases
Not paid a single instalment	— 4 cases

The general observation is that the assets are of poor quality in spite of purchase committees. The reasons are as follows:

- — Ignorance of beneficiary
- — Overemphasis on primary sector
- — Understanding between the asset owners and implementing agencies
- — Poor service facilities in the village

— Shortage of forward and backward linkages

Under the area oriented scheme for Iringal village the fisheries scheme is more successful. According to T.K. Jose: "Voluntary organisations are to be associated in the implementation, as they will create awareness which in turn will reduce the malpractices. IRDP has created an impact and ripples at the grass root level."

The basic objective of IRDP is to assist families below the poverty line in rural areas by enabling them to take up self-employment which would lead to permanent asset creation. This is achieved by giving financial assistance as loans from financial institutions, subsidy from Government, training for self-employment, technical advice from Government departments etc.

Schemes under IRDP during the 7th Plan in Iringal

Year	Primary Sector	Secondary Sector	Tertiary Sector	Total
1985-86	22	17	18	57
1986-87	21	16	23	60
1987-88	23	15	24	62
1988-89	8	6	8	22
1989-90	11	16	21	48
Total	85	70	94	249

Another study in Villiappally village, Kozikode, in 1983 has the following observations:

1. The emphasis on physical and financial target fulfilment should be dropped. The performance of every block should be measured not in terms of the number of families they have been able to assist, but in terms of the number of people they have been able to lift above the poverty line.
2. There should be no fixed quantum of assistance for all sections of the poor.
3. Household surveys should be undertaken with more precision and the aptitude, main occupation and assets of the families should properly be recorded. The survey should be conducted by trained staff.

4. More emphasis should be given to the secondary and tertiary sectors.
5. Cattle farms should be opened by the Government in all the districts so that good quality cattle can be provided.
6. Industrial estates should be started exclusively for the TRYSEM beneficiaries.
7. More emphasis should be put on infrastructural facilities and assistance should only be rendered in the fields where marketing facilities are actually available.
8. The staff in the Block Development Office should be strengthened and additional Village Extension Officers appointed. Some of them should be exclusively entrusted with IRDP programme.
9. Monitoring is another field on which special emphasis should be laid. Follow-up action and constant monitoring of the progress of a beneficiary after assistance is of crucial importance.
10. The Block Development Officer should have more autonomy in the implementation of the schemes. He should be allowed to set up infrastructural facilities without having to wait for years for sanction from the higher-ups as is the case at present.
11. Most importantly, NREP (National Rural Employment Programme) and IRDP should be linked. The majority of the NREP works undertaken should be with an eye to augment the infrastructural facilities required for IRDP.

The above suggestions are by no means exhaustive. Many improvements can be made to make the IRDP more beneficial. But before anything else is done the staff should be motivated and actually made to realise that what they are doing is of crucial importance to society as a whole and that their duty does not end with the identification and rendering of assistance to the poor, but the true responsibility lies in lifting them above the poverty line. On detailed discussions one had with the officials concerned with the IRDP, invariably every functionary is under the impression their only responsibility is to render assistance. Very little concern was shown on the need to lift them above the poverty line. They were happy and contended with simply following the directions laid down, if it actually benefited the poor, it was purely accidental and not contemplated. For them evidently, it was simply a case of assistance being and end in itself and not a means to achieving the end of the eradication of poverty.

Therefore, in the ultimate analysis, a committed set of officials who are fully aware of their duty should be in charge of IRDP, if eradication of poverty is not to remain a dream. The survey also highlights the opinion of the non-participants.

Reasons for Non-participation in IRDP as Reported by the Non-beneficiaries

(On the basis of an interview with 20 non-beneficiary households)

Reasons	No. of Households	Percentage of Total
1. Absence of detailed information	—	—
2. Not interested/indifferent	2	10
3. Delay in getting the assistance	—	—
4. Cumbersome procedure	2	10
5. Assistance not sufficient	2	10
6. Interest rate very high	—	—
7. Block officials not helpful	1	5
8. Applied but not received	1	5
9. Others:		
(i) Not willing to mortgage land	4	20
(ii) No persons to look after the scheme	—	—
(iii) No land to be given as security	3	15
(iv) Desiring to apply at a later date	—	—
(v) Fear that repayment may not be easy	5	25
(vi) Not specified	—	—
(vii) Reported	—	—
Total	20	100

At Kappady village, Kasargode, Tenzing reports that in 1986-87 nine persons had been assisted and in 1987-88, 35 persons. Loans ranged from Rs. 200 to Rs. 7482 given for various schemes. In this village preference was more for petty trade, handloom, boat and net. Only four ST and six SC people have been given loans. The guideline of 30 per cent SC/ST is not adhered to. In Koipady village there are 557 SC and 109 ST families. Yet only 10 persons have been assisted. On asset verification of Kunhikrishnan, who was given a loan of Rs. 7482 for a boat and net, said that the boat has been damaged while fishing and he has sold it. Lakshmi who was given a loan of Rs.967 for goats said that all the goats had died. Akkamma and Damodaran have improved their income through the IRDP loan. Repayment position is satisfactory.

In the same village under RLEGP scheme houses are sanctioned and road construction taken up. In many places the houses are incomplete.

Under the RFLP (Rural Functional Literacy Programme) in Koipady village 270 people were made literate. The balwadi at Kumbla is not functioning satisfactorily. He concludes that IRDP is good but NREP/RLEGP needs improvement.

G.K. Vardhana Rao in Pathanamthitta, 1990 reports that the development pattern has to be different. For the villagers the gulf returned people are the reference points. There has been a good support and participation for the housing schemes and also in women's programme. Under the IRDP nearly 50 per cent of the funds have gone to the dairy units. The SC/ST people have been benefited by the IRDP schemes.

Under JRY scheme construction of roads, school buildings, and bridges was taken up and completed. Pumpsets and wells are successful schemes for small farmers and marginal farmers. Under the NREP/JRY programmes the wages prescribed are not realistic. A closer interaction of the village officer and village extension officer will make the schemes more fruitful.

In 1985 Ajay Kumar from Pathanamthitta district of Iravon made a case study of 4 persons.

Chellappan Achari	— Blacksmithy
Sivaraman	— Welding set
Narayanan	— Dairy Unit
Soman Nair	— Cool Bar Shop

There was not much delay and assets have been given. Only in the case of dairy unit a bribe had to be paid to get the certificate from the veterinary officer. The IRDP assistance helped all the people. It is reported that assets in the dairy sector are misutilised.

There is lack of follow-up by the extension staff due to the various meetings and their sole concentration on achieving the targets. The beneficiaries loan off-take is very less and creates only marginal assets.

Alkesh Kumar Sharma observes in Ezhukone village, Quilon district, in 1990 that the loan recovery is 40 per cent due to alienation of assets and non-timely assistance of the second loan of funds.

The poor people do not benefit much due to ignorance about procedures, quantum of assistance, delay in second dosage of assistance etc. The unit cost fixed by NABARD norms lead to poor quality of assets. Appropriate training to the beneficiaries is a prerequisite for success.

The Janata Dal government's announcement of writing off loans upto Rs. 10,000 had affected loan oriented schemes and their recovery. Loaning to a group ensures higher rates of loan repayment.

Under TRYSEM production-cum-training centres can function as earn-while-you-learn centres and on-the-job training could be given. JRY schemes give freedom to the people for implementing their felt needs. Thus construction of borewells, retaining walls, water tank, waiting sheds and latrines has been taken up.

Jayathilak reports that poverty is acute in Chembu village in Kottayam district. There is widespread misutilisation. The group economic activity for women failed as they are fully employed but the men are not fully employed. The schemes should have been for men. IRDP loans to women are repaid promptly. Cow loans have failed, while goats have been a success. TRYSEM was also not need-based but target-based. Training for tertiary sector, short gestation period, low cost and less investments should be emphasised. The poverty that exists is 'alcohol induced poverty'.

B. Srinivas reports from Akatheathara village, Palghat district, in 1991 that the DWCRA cloth weaving unit started and then closed down as out of 15 members only seven repaid their loans. In DWCRA unit at Papopadi seven people were given loan for milch cattle and eight members for rice business. Only one had repaid. The Andimadan unit for pottery given to 10 women are functioning well. It is a mixed response. IRDP loans in some places reflects that they could give loan to only 46 persons (SC

22; ST 1 and others 23). The community assets are mentioned and the work and amount but to how many people employment has been provided, in which season or is it benefiting the local unemployed or migrant labour is not at all reflected. The encouraging factor is that houses, sanitary latrines, drainage, foot bridge, roads are the kinds of work taken up.

Tara reports in 1984 in Vellanad village of Trivandrum district the trend of IRDP assistance is 49.5 per cent in primary sector, 28 per cent in secondary sector and 21 per cent in tertiary sector. The quantum of assistance is also a critical input and maximum assistance was for less than Rs. 2500. Only 3.24 per cent beneficiaries got assistance above Rs. 8000. There is potential in the tertiary sector whereas officials concentrate on the primary and secondary sector. The popular schemes are dairying, goat rearing, cycle hiring, and tailoring.

About 20 per cent of the beneficiaries acknowledge that they have been benefited as their incomes have increased, 50 per cent voiced that they have benefited nominally and 30 per cent did not get any benefit out of IRDP. The average assistance works out to be Rs. 2767 which is comparatively less. The fact that out of 35 households, 27 (70%) are still holding the assets is commendable. The beneficiaries have said that delay at the banks, and at the block level, even extended upto 1 year. Some of them spoke about corruption.

The IRDP scheme had helped considerable number of people to generate income especially among the poorest of the poor, though undeserving and well-off persons have also benefited. As IRDP is the only poor-oriented scheme, all-out efforts should be made at all levels to improve the performance at the grassroots level. The following suggestions emanate from the socio-economic reports:

- Willing beneficiaries should only be selected.
- The beneficiaries present status and potential should be identified and accordingly many schemes be suggested so that the one she is confident of can be selected.
- Assets to be given preferably in the name of women, who are really responsible and their repayment is better.

— Effective training and exposure to be given in those places where similar schemes/trades are implemented.
— The quantum of assistance should be higher.
— Marketing arrangements in all sector and specially in dairy sector should be developed.
— Dairy sector projects should be given in those cases where there is a milk route operating or where there is possibility of extending milk routes in collaboration with government cooperatives or private sector schemes.
— Provide adequate veterinary care. If government veterinary facilities are not available then private veterinarians can be appointed on contract basis.
— To bring down the cost of production, fodder availability is a must and should be promoted and integrated with other schemes or departments.
— Successful IRDP beneficiaries should be selected and their performance highlighted. This could be a visiting centre for new beneficiaries.
— The official-beneficiary interaction should be encouraged.
— Effective monitoring necessary.
— Involvement of voluntary organisation right from selection.
— Awareness creation about the IRDP scheme should be done.
— Second dose of assistance at appropriate time should be given.
— Variety of programmes and successful programmes should be introduced.
— Short gestation projects should be preferred and official machinery to help them in marketing of produce also should be linked up.

Performance

What is the effect of IRDP in alleviating rural poverty? There is no doubt that IRDP is not the panacea for all ills of poverty. By evaluating its performance over a decade, it becomes clear that IRDP is a mixed bag of both success and failures.

On the achievements of physical target, it is a grand success and it has achieved more than its targets in all respects, like, number of beneficiaries assisted, number of women and SC, ST beneficiaries assisted, per capita subsidy disbursed etc. But if one looks minutely at the effects of this assistance it becomes clear that the picture is not that rosy. The number of really eligible beneficiaries assisted is a big question. But in Kerala with very high levels of awareness and the functioning of local bodies this problem can be eliminated. There is a scope for complete justice in selecting the beneficiaries with these changes:

— The number of assisted beneficiaries who crossed the poverty line is very difficult to judge, but number of beneficiaries whose income increased is considerable. The retention of assets even after two to three years gives the idea that the asset is beneficial. The pre-assistance income of the beneficiary heavily influences the stability of the assets and the income from it. As the amount of assistance is inadequate in most cases it is unable to bring them above the poverty line.

— The diversification of activities is appreciable. More funds going to secondary and tertiary activities is a welcome sign. But too much concentration on petty trade is not healthy.

— The recovery of loans is more than 50 per cent which is as good as the recovery rates in other loan activities.

— Thus it is a mixed bag and its efficiency has to be improved and can be improved by bringing in some more intellectual inputs which can introduce some other innovative activities. The implementing agencies have to look for new activities like electronics, rabbit farming, bee keeping etc. according to the capability of the beneficiary and the marketable potential of the area.

Some Thoughts

The general tendency of the critics is to advocate, not going for milch animals under this scheme. But this can be the most successful scheme as it does not have inter-beneficiary competition within a locality, unlike trade activity. In the case of trade, too many petty shops in a locality will give rise to too much competition and hence low levels of business, whereas if there are too many milch animals it is advantageous from the market point of view as there is scope for milk procurement by MILMA. The only problem is providing inputs. Some avenues have to be found to provide for fodder and feed. The feed part can be taken care of by giving extra assistance. Regarding fodder, I do not think the existing land is over-exploited. Research efforts can evolve shade loving and non-competitive grasses which can be grown under coconut.

The preference for petty shops is not healthy as there will be limited demand in the locality and hence the number assisted under this activity should be carefully chosen. Another general attitude would be to clamour for the same activity which is giving good income in the initial period when there would not be any competition. When more and more, people are assisted under the same activity the competition increases and the viability of the individual activity will be put to strain.

The concept of kitchen gardening or nutritional gardening has not been seriously attempted. There is vacant space in the compounds of most houses including the poor. The targeted group can be assisted to popularise kitchen gardening which would have a lot of impact on the nutritional status of the household.

Some Case Studies of IRDP

Case No. 1

Beneficiary's Past History: The beneficiary was working as daily wage worker in some hotel in Wadakkanchery, Palghat district. He used to earn about Rs. 25 per day. The monthly income used to be around Rs. 500 which of course was variable. Annual income would be Rs. 6000. This has to be considered as above poverty line case.

He has two kids, wife and mother. He is living with his sister and brother-in-law under the same roof, has a single ration card. The family as a unit is getting a subsidy of Rs. 3,000. But both the families are doing business separately and their income would be separately accounted and enjoyed. He shifted the tea shop and eating place from a remote village area to a place near the town.

Present position: He has some fixed assets like bunk, stove, vessels etc. and is selling tea and other minor eatables. He feels that after taking a loan his condition has improved. He gets a daily average income of Rs. 75 of which his net income would be Rs. 15 to 20 per day. That means he gets about Rs. 450 to Rs. 600 per month.

Problems

He complains that he does not have much working capital to expand his business. Since the household as a unit has reached the limit of subsidy obtainable, there is no scope for further assistance. He took loan from local money lenders at a very high interest rate. He has taken a loan of Rs. 300 two times which is to be repaid in 10 weeks @ Rs. 80 per week. That means on Rs. 600 he is paying Rs. 200 as interest in 10 weeks. This comes to about 8 per cent per month. He is repaying it very regularly and more regularly than the bank loan. He is planning to go for another loan soon.

But I could not see any reason for going for private borrowing. The whole amount must be going for some other purpose. The reason I elicited from his wife was his alcoholism and he spends daily minimum of about Rs. 5. This habit is depreciating his business earnings.

If this continues, he cannot become self-viable in his business. Another problem I understood was, they could not save on daily basis. They suggested that they should have facility of putting Rs. 10 or Rs. 15 aside daily, so that they can repay the amount easily.

Some Thoughts

Consideration of two families as a household though they are independent entities and limiting the subsidy, is not correct. It should be seen whether they are joint family in true sense. Simply living under one roof does not mean that they are one household. They can have two independent economic family units.

There should be a provision of giving some more expansion capital even when repayment is continuing.

A Local Entrepreneur in Udayamperoor village, District Ernakulam

This is a proprietary concern, manufacturing iron gate, grills etc. for houses. The proprietor is not technically qualified, but well experienced in the field. He was working in another workshop for the past ten years and has now started this workshop. He has three people under him. The major portion of the work comes from the village itself. The work he gets depends on the available housing loan by the government This unit is financed by State Bank of Travancore, Nadakkavu. The loan availed is Rs. 35,000 and it was taken in 1990 under Self-Employment Scheme. The monthly repayment instalment is Rs. 150 which he is not able to repay on time. The electricity bill comes to Rs. 150 per month, whether consumed or not. With the present conditions he is not able to pull on.

Case Study from Pananchery village, district Thrissur

Thankappan, aged 43, is a resident of Poovanchira, a remote corner of Pananchery village. He is by caste a Malayan, an Aadivasi of the Vellani hills extending just behind his homestead. One has to walk half-a-kilometre from the jeep track to reach his home. All these years he was living in a mud hovel on the land assigned to him by the government. Last year, he was one of the lucky nine to whom the Forest Department gifted a *pucca* house. His family consists of his wife Madhavi, son Jayan aged 20 and daughter Usha aged 17s. The responsibility of looking after his sister Narayani who has been recently widowed with two young children, is also on Thankappan. Thankappan has studied upto Class IV and knows to read and write Malayalam. The only 'skill' he knows is collecting forest produce like honey, wax and medicinal herbs. This, he does regularly every year during the 'season', i.e.

December to March. He sells it in the local market at Pattikkad. However, this is no assured income as there is heavy competition for collecting the produce and also the finding of wax and honey is a matter of chance. Alternatively, he does some daily wage labour if and when available. Thankappan's son Jayan failed in Class X and never bothered to study again. These days he is on the lookout for some daily wage labour. Usha is sitting idle at home after her failure in Class X.

Thankappan is aware that the Government has some programmes to help the poor. He had heard of it from the Village Extension Officer. But so far he has not applied for a loan. He wants to start a small stone crushing unit. But he does not know the extent of finances required, nor does he know whether the venture is viable. The successive failures of two petty shops started under IRDP assistance is making him doubtful as to whether he should apply for a loan. The VEO who comes to his area once in a week, has also cautioned him that he would be taking the loan at his own risk. Thankappan would like his son Jayan to earn a decent living. However, he does not have the knowledge or experience to counsel his son. On those days when work is not available, Thankappan sits idle puffing away his beedi. Even the only meal of gruel is a luxury. He very much wishes that his living conditions improve. But does not know how to. Can he be helped?

Based on the survey reports the following suggestions are made:

- A variety of employment generation programmes should be implemented.
- The felt needs of the people should be taken up on a priority basis.
- Appropriate schemes for different areas like foot bridges, suspension bridges, foot paths to interior inaccessible areas to be done with stone paving etc. so that it becomes all-weather road.
- Asset creation is given importance but not employment generation.
- Local unemployed unskilled labour should be given preference.

— Appropriate local technology in soil conservation, water harvesting, building construction should be adopted.
— In housing, standard design should be avoided. Peoples' preference could be provided.
— Employment generation programmes should not coincide with any agricultural season operation.
— The maintenance of the assets should be given to a group of people who are beneficiaries/users by forming a committee or any suitable agency.
— The wage rates should be realistic as it leads to other falsification of records and other complications.
— Any payment in kind if at all given must be given immediately according to the requirements.

Conclusion

IRDP

About 75 per cent of the probationers through their study support the fact that IRDP has been beneficial to the people and specially to the poor and SC/ST people. The success of the IRDP beneficiaries would have been more had the quantum of assistance been more, and the officials a little more innovative. Repayment is more than 50 per cent and this is a good sign. Assets are also with the beneficiaries. About 25 per cent of the probationers have concluded that there is misutilisation, proper beneficiaries have not been selected, proper monitoring is also not done, as a result there are failures.

Community Asset Creation Programmes

All the probationers have confirmed that assets like anganwadi building, drinking water wells, homes, footpaths, bridges, community halls, school buildings etc. created under the NREP, RLEGP, and IAY programmes are useful.

To conclude one can say that through government interventions there is good impact both at individual and community level. Peoples' participation in these developmental activities shows the awareness of the people. Certainly there is scope for further improvement.

10. A VILLAGE LIFE

The concept of a village in Kerala differs from the rest of the country. Villages in Kerala traditionally have houses distributed all over. Villages are comparatively modern. The houses in the villages are very modern in terms of design. Thatched houses with mud walls, tiled houses and concrete houses with modern design and architecture is very common. Almost every household has a coconut tree, banana or a kitchen garden. Houses are independent. The basic facilities like tap water, sanitary facilities etc. are generally available. A large number of houses are electrified.

There is no sign of untouchability anywhere in the state barring the boundary of Palghat district with Tamil Nadu. Houses belonging to SCs are dispersed among the caste Hindus and others. The housing colonies are those which are constructed under various government schemes. Social disabilities which were present in the past are no more due to awareness generated by voluntary agencies like Shastra Sahitya Parishad etc.

Both men and women of all communities go out to work according to their needs. Throughout Kerala the wage rate is Rs. 60 for men and Rs. 50 for women for manual labour.

Basic drinking water facilities are available, villages are electrified, and transport facilities either through kuccha or pucca roads are available. Even in the absence of public transport, local jeeps are available. Cycles and bikes are also common. Protected water supply through pipes is predominant because of the various rural water supply schemes. Panchayats and the district administration give top priority to this problem. By and large there is no waste land in the village. Panchayat hall is available for social functions.

Intercropping is very common in agriculture. Fertilisers and pesticides are widely used. There is a trend of shifting from paddy to other crops like rubber and coconut. Cross-bred cattle constitute 80 per cent of the cattle population. There is not much preference for buffaloes.

Each village is equipped with a PDS shop (Public Distribution System) supplying the statutory ration and Maveli stores or private provision stores are available. Each PDS shop serves an average of 300 families.

RATION QUOTA

RICE —

Children	:	110 gms. per day (1 unit)- 770 gms/week.
Adult	:	110 gms. per day (2 unit) - 1540 gms/week.

WHEAT —

Children	:	120 gms. per day (1 unit) - 840 gms/week.
Adult	:	120 gms. per day (2 unit) - 1680 gms/week.
SUGAR —	:	450 gms. per head/month
KEROSENE —	:	2 litres per month per house for electrified houses.
	:	5 litres per month per house for non-electrified houses

Services like electrical, electronic repair facilities, phone facilities including STD, cars for hire services are available in all rural areas.

A health centre/sub-centre or even a well equipped private dispensary is very common. Sanitary facilities are individually owned and houses are very neat and clean. Invariably there will be cooperatives, for many different purposes. There will also be a veterinary sub-centre, anganwadi centre, panchayat office, schools etc. in every village.

As the people are politically active, there is intense political debates and discussions among the common people and walls reserved for political parties are very common. There are a large number of newpapers and periodicals.

People are by nature very clean, hygienic and they keep the village premises neat and clean. Places of worship of different religions, situated next to each other and each following their own religious rites is a common sight.

11. DEVELOPMENT EXPERIENCE OF KERALA — AN OVERVIEW

The development of a state is a part of the overall development of the country. In many ways, the former is conditioned by the latter. But, depending upon the local conditions - physical, agro-climatic, demographic, historic, cultural and political - there is also room for some flexibility and local variations. Kerala has followed a path of development different from the rest of the country. There has been a much greater emphasis on social services and social infrastructure and the adoption of welfare measures. As a result, the service sector has grown far ahead of the productive sectors. This pattern of development has had both positive and negative aspects.

The positive aspects may be summarized as :

— The state has the highest general rate of literacy in the country 90 per cent. The effective rate of literacy (after leaving out those in the age group of 0 to 4 years) is well over 90 per cent. The all-India general rate of literacy is as low as 50 per cent.

— Female literacy is highest in Kerala and here the difference from other states are even sharper.

— School education is free and in the nearly 12,000 schools spread all over the state, 56 lakh children study. The enrolment of children in the age group of 5 to 14 is more than 90 per cent. The percentage of enrolment of girls is almost equal to that of boys except in a few pockets. Every year, over half a million students appear for the SSLC Examination.

— The emphasis on the spread of education to all sections of society has created a vast army of men and women with some basic level of education and training. The continuous supply of a large body of educated manpower ensured availability of personnel as more and more responsibilities were taken up by the Government in the field of development. The state did not have to look outside much for manpower requirements. In fact, Kerala has been an exporter of skilled manpower for a long time.

- The spread of education also created a populace aware of its rights and led to the general growth of an egalitarian approach amongst all sections of the society.
- Medical facilities are better compared to other states and there is at least one dispensary in every Panchayat. Except in the case of some special areas, the number of beds per lakh of population is highest in Kerala.
- Voluntary agencies have played a major role in establishing educational and medical institutions.
- The State has a very low death rate, namely six per thousand. This seems to be virtually the lowest that can be reached. In fact mortality rate is also the lowest in the country, namely 36 per thousand. Life expectancy is 70 years compared to the all-India average of 53 years.
- The birth rate has been falling during the last 10 years and is now about 24-25 per thousand as against 32-33 for all-India.
- The rate of growth of population was around 1.3 per cent in 1981-91 and is falling.
- Successive governments have laid emphasis on the development of physical infrastructure and the state has a wide network of roads. Other communication facilities like post offices and telephones are also well developed.
- Being a tropical evergreen area, there is some agricultural production everywhere, with the result that people live everywhere and the human settlement pattern is widely dispersed as individual homesteads. As a result, despite a very high density of population, there is no crowding.
- Water has been relatively plentiful (until recently) and water supply has been extended to more and more villages.
- Electricity has been taken at least to one part in every village of the state.
- Since industrial development has been limited, there is no pollution except in one or two isolated points. In general, the air is fresh and clean.
- Successive state governments have introduced a large

number of welfare measures, with the result that the state has now a large variety of welfare schemes in the form of pensions for the old, the widowed, the aged agricultural workers, unemployment allowances for the handicapped, etc.

— Generally, wages in the state are high due to a strong trade union movement backed by political power and this has meant that the organised sections are better off.
— Due to predominance of cash crops in the state's agricultural economy and the money income in the organised sector, the per capita consumption of non-food consumer items is very high. Thus per capita consumption of toiletries, medicines, building materials etc. are very high in the state relative to other parts of the country.
— The state has implemented land reforms in a much better manner compared to many other states.
— In recent years, the national programmes for rural poor and the implementation of schemes for Scheduled Castes have had a visible impact in some rural areas.

As a result of these positive aspects, one might say that the social consumption of people of all levels of income is high. As some observers have said, the physical quality of life of the people is highest in Kerala.

The negative aspects of the development that has taken place so far may be stated to be:

— There is extreme fragmentation of holdings — nearly 90 per cent of the holdings being less than half a hectare in size. As a single occupation, agriculture does not seem to generate adequate income for a family. Members of the family have to take up other occupations. Agriculture has ceased to be the sole or even principal source of income.
— Due to intense pressure on land, some sections of the people have encroached upon forests in the hills over

very large areas. Denudation of forests has been very fast until very recently. This has adversely affected the ecology in many parts of the state and the retention of water in the soil, so important for the evergreen vegetation and cash crops and for year-round flow of water for drinking purposes.

— Economic growth has been slow, lower than for the country as a whole; in particular, there has been very little growth of industry.

— As a result of very low growth rate in agriculture and industry, employment creation has been low and the state has the largest number of unemployed in the country relative to the population. Over 45 lakh persons are unemployed or severely underemployed. Of these, half are matriculates. Educated unemployment is particularly severe malady in the state, as such persons want only white-collar jobs.

— Government and public employment has become an end in itself and many of the public agencies have become overstaffed. Coupled with the ideology that promotion opportunity for an entrant in an organisation should be opened from the bottom level to the topmost level and should be based almost entirely on seniority, the fall in the quality of the educated has led to deterioration of professional competence in a number of development departments. The upgradation of professional competence in such organisations and the retraining and redeployment of personnel pose major challenges.

— The creation of a large number of departments under conditions of continuing political coalitions in the State led to excessive 'departmentalism'. The horizontal coordination which is essential for ensuring timely implementation of the components of a development programme and for reaching the benefits to the people is found to be very difficult to achieve, especially in the absence of decentralised people's bodies. It is hoped that the present Panchayat Bodies will compensate.

— Private incomes of large sections of the people have been

low. Generally speaking, private consumption in the State has been low, especially in food items. The per capita calorie intake is amongst the lowest in the country. The nutritional status of the population as a whole is therefore quite low. People live long, but seem do so at lower levels of physical strength and stamina.

— There is a natural tendency for prices to be higher in the state, because it is a food deficit area. This tendency has been aggravated by the cycle of higher wages and higher prices and by the flow of funds from the migrant labour of the state which moved to the Middle East in the wake of the oil boom there. As a result, prices are much higher in the state than in most other parts of the country.

— Though wages have been going up, there are indications that productivity in agriculture and industry and in services has been going down. There seems to be the absence of a work-ethic needed for increasing productivity.

— The advantage of a large national common market like that of India is that, if any part is competitive in its production, it can produce and sell in a readily available large market. But since productivity has not kept pace with the growth in wages in the state, Kerala has become a high-wage, high-cost, non-competitive economy. Investors do not find it attractive to invest and produce goods here. Kerala has, therefore, not been able to attract investors from the rest of the country and investors from within the state itself have been going outside the state for starting industries.

— Because of its heavy commitment to social services and welfare measures, the government finds it difficult to maintain them well. The momentum of expansion is still there though not really necessary. As a result, quality has been steadily going down in the maintenance of the social services.

— For want of resources, the maintenance of physical infrastructure, like roads, has also been suffering and their condition is deteriorating steadily.

— The heavy commitments on existing services and the

momentum of expansion in them makes the availability of resources for investment very tight. The per capita investment in productive sectors is, therefore, quite low. The per capita plan outlay in successive plans is also lower than the all-India average.

— The poorer sections of society who are not in the organised sector and who have not been benefited by the Gulf boom have suffered more in recent years. Their absolute and relative deprivation seems to have increased. They constitute about 30 per cent of the population — mainly the agricultural labourers, fishermen and those engaged in the traditional industries like handloom, coir, cashew etc.

— Every group in society has been demanding and getting subsidies and concessions, even if the groups happened to be affluent or relatively better off. Thus, the disparity of income distribution between the better-off sections and the organised sector, on the one hand, and those sections of the population engaged in traditional industries and in the unorganised sector, on the other, is increasing. Unless corrective measures are taken, social tensions are likely to increase in such a situation.

— The expectations of all sections of the people have been far in excess of the readiness to work for their fulfilment. In the field of development, a large number of schemes, institutions, programmes and projects have been sanctioned over the years. Since the resources available for development have been meagre, due to the large committed and consumption expenditure of Government, the available resources have been spread thinly over a large number of schemes and programmes. Timely completion, early enjoyment of benefits, economic utilisation of resources, quality and above all, accountability have turned out to be major casualties in this situation.

No strategy of development is for ever. The stage has come, in fact, had come some years ago, when a major mid-course correction in the strategy of development of the state has become essential. But it is precisely this that is extremely difficult to bring about. The economy of the state is in a kind of *Elipathayam* (Rat Trap), as portrayed in the famous award-winning film. The challenges facing the state is how to get out of it.

One of the objects of development in a traditional horizontally stratified society is to homogenize it. In our transitional stage, two negative developments seem to have emerged. One is the vertical fragmentation of society along political and communal lines, leading to dominance of group interests in the operational policies of political parties. The other is the way in which the growing numbers of the middle class, a product of development, conduct themselves. The middle level farmers, the small the medium industrialists, traders, professionals and employees of the Government and organised sectors (including the 'workers'), seem to form a loose and informal, but effective and highly vocal coalition of interests. Their main concern seems to be to take the maximum out of the common kitty. They operate through the first-mentioned set of political groups. The consequence is that at a time when the people and the economy are in need of a 'transforming' leadership that can motivate, take bold decisions in long-term public interest and in the interests of furthering homogenization, they seem to have only 'nominee' leadership of groups or a coalition of groups.

The middle groups have always responded to crisis and to the call for sacrifice and for working for higher values. Leadership should rise to the level necessary to do this. If this happens, the future path of development of the state is assured. If it does not happen, the state may linger for long in the transitional stage, with all its attendant consequences.

The achievements by the state and the people in the field of education, health, housing, awareness, cleanliness, sanitation and infrastructure in rural areas it is really monumental and quoted by one and all as a model in the social sector.

It is an unique model which has witnessed a coalition government all through. The future could be brighter if productivity is enhanced and the resources are judiciously used with appropriate technology. Non-polluting industries like tourism and electronics is the future of Kerala. People are the assets and participative whether in election, development, debate in all schemes of the government and in all walks of life.

The villages of Kerala will always remain a model of development for other places.

LIST OF SOCIO-ECONOMIC REPORTS

S.No.	Officer Trainee	Year	District & Village
TRIVANDRUM			
1.	N. Sathiyavathy	1982	Socio-Economic Study of Village Kottukal.
2.	Tara Kodiyan	1984	Socio-Economic Study of Village Vellanad.
QUILON			
1.	G. Rajasekharan	1983	Socio-Economic Study of Village Mulavana.
2.	P.A. Sharafudheen	1984	Socio-Economic Study of Village Sathamcotta.
3.	M. Ravi Kanth	1986	Socio-Economic Study of Village Chavara.
4.	Kiran Soni	1986	Socio-Economic Study of Village Clappana
5.	Visvas Mehta	1986	Socio-Economic Study of Village Paravoor
6.	T.R. Meena	1988	Socio-Economic Study of Village Sakthikulangra
7.	S.G.K. Kishore	1989	Socio-Economic Study of Village Ariankavu
8.	Alkesh Kumar Sharma	1990	Socio-Economic Study of Village Ezhukone
9.	K. Elangovan	1992	Socio-Economic Study of Village Thirkkovilvattom
ALLEPPY			
1.	J. Sudhakaran	1982	Socio-Economic Study of Village Arattupuzha
2.	Ramesh Negi	1984	Socio-Economic Study of Village Purakkad

S.No.	Officer Trainee	Year	District & Village
3.	Subbiah	1985	Socio-Economic Study of Village Ambalapuzha
PATHANAMTHITTA			
1.	Ajay Kumar	1986	Socio-Economic Study of Village Travon
2.	G.K. Vardhana Rao	1992	Socio-Economic Study of Village Naranganam
KOTTAYAM			
1.	Elias G.	1982	Socio-Economic Study of Village Bharanangaram
2.	Rajeev Sadanandan	1985	Socio-Economic Study of Village Trikodithanam
3.	U.K.S. Chauhan	1986	Socio-Economic Study of Village Panachikkad
4.	Pradeep Kumar	1987	Socio-Economic Study of Village Onamthuruthu
5.	Ashish Kumar Singh	1988	Socio-Economic Study of Village Kumarakom
6.	E.K. Majhi	1989	Socio-Ecnomic Study of Village Puthupally
7.	A. Jayathilak	1991	Socio-Economic Study of Village Chempu
8.	Sanjeev Kaushik	1993	Socio-Economic Study of Village Thalyazham
ERNAKULAM			
1.	Sheela Thomas	1985	Socio-Economic Study of Village Thrikkakara (South)
2.	Raj Kumar Sharma	1987	Socio-Economic Study of Village Muvathpuzha
3.	Gyanesh Kumar	1988	Socio-Economic Study of Village Mulavucad
4.	R.K. Singh	1989	Socio-Economic Study of Village Valakom

S.No.	Officer Trainee	Year	District & Village
5.	Ishita Roy	1991	Socio-Economic Study of Village Udayamperoor

IDUKKI

S.No.	Officer Trainee	Year	District & Village
1.	Paul Antony	1983	Socio-Economic Study of Village Kattappana

TRICHUR

S.No.	Officer Trainee	Year	District & Village
1.	V. J. Kurian	1983	Socio-Economic Study of Village Kattakampal
2.	Subrata Biswas	1985	Socio-Economic Study of Village Anjur
3.	W.R. Reddy	1986	Socio-Economic Study of Village Manlur
4.	Manoj Joshi	1989	Socio-Economic Study of Village Cheruthuru
5.	Venu.V.	1990	Socio-Economic Study on Tribal Settlement
6.	V. Ramakrishnan	1992	Socio-Economic Study of Village Panachary

PALGHAT

S.No.	Officer Trainee	Year	District & Village
1.	P. Michael	1982	Socio-Economic Study of Village Malampuzha-1
2.	P. Marapandiyan	1984	Socio-Economic Study of Village Puduseery (East)
3.	Kshatrapati Shivaji	1986	Socio-Economic Study of Village Muthalamada-I
4.	Satyajeet Rajan	1987	Socio-Economic Study of Village Puduseery
5.	Srinivas	1991	Socio-Economic Study of Village Akathethara

S.No.	Officer Trainee	Year	District & Village
KOZHIKODE			
1.	A.K. Dubey	1982	Socio-Economic Study of Village Elathur
2.	Thomas Mathew	1983	Socio-Economic Study of Village Villiappally
3.	Tom Jos	1984	Socio-Economic Study of Village Rapoth
4.	Prakash Kumar	1985	Socio-Economic Study of Village Puduppady
5.	James Varghese	1986	Socio-Economic Study of Village Kuttiadi
6.	Sanjeev Dubey	1987	Socio-Economic Study of Village Cnathamangalam
7.	T.K. Jose	1988	Socio-Economic Study of Village Iringal
8.	Raju Narayana Swamy	1991	Socio-Economic Study of Village Eramala
MALAPPURAM			
1.	T.K. Manoj Kumar	1987	Socio-Economic Study of Village Areacode
KASARGOD			
1.	P.G. Tenzing	1986	Socio-Economic Study of Village Koipady

BIBLIOGRPAHY

Agricultural Development Policy, 1992, Government of Kerala.

Annual Report 1992-93, Spices Board.

Coir Board Thirty Eight Annual Report 1991-92 by Coir Board.

Economic and Statistical News Letter 1993 by Department of Economic and Statistics.

Economic Review,1994, State Planning Board.

Eighth Five Year Plan 1990-91, Govt. of Kerala.

FARM Guide, 1994, FARM Information Bureau, Govt. of Kerala.

Government of Kerala, Agricultural Development Policy, Govt. of Kerala.
Kerala Budget in Brief, Govt. of Kerala.

Kerala Fisheries - An Overview, 1992, Department of Fisheries, Govt. of Kerala.

Kerala's Economy: Performance, Problems and Prospects, edited by Prakash.

Kerala's Water Resources, DWRDM, Calicut.

Land Use & Water Management Practices in Kerala (A Status Paper) Govt. of Kerala.

Plan Outlays & Expenditure Kerala (1951-52 to 1989-90), State Planning Board, 1992.

Policy on Science and Technology, Govt. of Kerala.

Scheduled Tribes Development Schemes, Department of SC/ST Development, Govt. of Kerala.

Science, Technology and Environment, State Planning Board.

Selected Indicators of Development Kerala and India 1962 to 1986.
Spices Statistics 1991 - Trade Information Service, Spices Board.
Statistics for Planning, 1993, Govt.of Kerala.

The Economies of the States of the Indian Union, Edited by Malcolm Adiseshiah, Lanzer International.

4

KARNATAKA

SUDHIR KRISHNA

1. INTRODUCTION

Brief Political History

The state of Karnataka was formed on November 1, 1956, by merging the states of Mysore and Coorg, and parts of the erstwhile states of Madras, Bombay and Hyderabad. This was part of the reorganisation of the states on linguistic basis. After reorganisation, the state had 19 districts, which have now become 20, with the bifurcation of Bangalore district into Urban and Rural districts. The 20 districts are organised into four divisions: Belgaum, Gulbarga, Mysore and Bangalore.

The Belgaum division (also called the Bombay-Karnataka) consists of the four districts, namely: North Kanara (or Uttara Kannada), Belgaum, Bijapur and Dharwar. The Gulbarga Division (also called the Hyderabad-Karnataka) consists of three districts of the former Hyderabad state, namely: Gulbarga, Bidar and Raichur, and the district of Bellary (which came to Karnataka from the then Madras State). The Mysore division includes the district of Coorg, which was a separate state, Dakshina Kannada (which was until then a part of the Madras State) and four other districts of the former state of Mysore, namely: Mysore, Chickmagalur, Mandya and Hassan. The remaining six districts of the state (Bangalore Urban and Rural, Chitradurga, Tumkur, Kolar and Shimoga) came from the old Mysore state and now fall in the Bangalore Division. Thus, each of the four divisions has some distinct historical flavour also.

Current Status of Karnataka

Karnataka now ranks 8th in India in terms of area as well population. It is a relatively more 'urban' state, with 30.9 per cent of its population in urban areas, as compared to 25.7 per cent for India (1991 census). The density of population is 234 persons per sq. km., which is slightly less than the national average of 257. Nearly 36 per cent of its rural population lived below the poverty line (1987-88) while the figure for the rest of the country was 33.4 per cent.

While Karnataka's share of the country's population is 5.3 per cent (1991 census), and 5.8 per cent in terms of total geographical area, the state has 7 per cent of the total cultivable area and 7.7 per cent of the net sown area of the country. As for the forests, Karnataka owns 4.5 per cent of the total forest area of the country. The gross irrigated area of the state was 2.58 million ha. (1989-90), which was 4.3 per cent of the national figure.

Development Strategy Pursued by the State

Like other states, Karnataka too has been pursuing the twin goals of all-round development of the state on the one hand and, on the other, equity in the process of planning and implementing development programmes. It is generally recognised as a very progressive state. This was true even when it was the princely state of Mysore.

The development strategy pursued so far by the State has given mixed results. To quote from the Draft Eighth Five-year Plan (1992-97) Document of the State Planning Department: "After the State achieved a long term growth rate higher than that for all-India during the two and half decades preceding the 1990s, the rate of growth has been lower than the all-

India average. The growth rate in agriculture has exhibited decelerating trends in recent years; particularly the foodgrain production has stagnated for over a decade."

However, the state focused on social and economic reforms more as a socialistic measure than commercial. For instance, land reforms were implemented vigorously in the 1970s and 1980s. This measure gave the rural masses a great moral and social boost, though its impact on the overall direct economic growth of the State was not significant. Rural housing has been yet another popular programme in the State, particularly since the 1970s.

Administrative Measures

The administrative set-up of the state has had a tremendous bearing on the development of the people. This set-up included not only the government functionaries and establishments, but also the schemes designed by the state for betterment of the economic condition of the people. Thus, one has to reckon with the way the development schemes and programmes are designed and implemented. Further, the arrangement of programme monitoring and evaluation would need to be looked into.

Karnataka has a long tradition of Panchayati Raj Institutions (PRIs). Till 1987, the PRIs in the state were at two tiers, namely the Village Panchayats (for each village or for a group of villages) and the Taluka Development Boards, for each of the 175 talukas of the state. Side by side, the National Extension Service (NES) Programme also continued, though in a modest way. In the year 1987, new Panchayati Raj systems were introduced, bringing in elected local governments at the Mandal level (the Mandal Panchayats) and the District level (Zilla Parishads). The new Act bestowed large powers on these bodies, particularly on the Zilla Parishads, for planning and implementing the various rural development programmes. In 1993, a fresh Panchayati Raj Act came in to force, to bring the composition and the administrative set-up of these rural local bodies in line with the recent Constitutional Amendments. All these changes in the administrative set-up did influence the rural development efforts.

Social Structures

Indian society, particularly in rural areas, is still a close knit one, notwithstanding liberalisation and the concomitant metamorphosis of various social values. Class differentials are closely intertwined with economic stratification of the rural population in rural Karnataka, akin to what it is prevalent in many other parts of the country. Yet, the operation of the land reforms legislations, particularly in the 1970s and the 1980s coupled with the implementation of special measures for the Scheduled Castes (SCs), the Scheduled Tribes (STs) and Other Backward Classes (OBCs), much before the implementation of the Mandal Commission Report, has had a tremendous equalisation effect on the social values and structures. But two questions remain:

(a) Was the social equalisation adequate? and
(b) Did economic equalisation too come, along with the social equalisation?

Nature and Scope of Study

This study would, in its broad vision, attempt to bring out the trends and current status in the socio-economic scenario of rural Karnataka during the past one and a half decade. The specific indicators of this assessment would be as follows:—

(a) Land holding patterns;
(b) Housing scenario;
(c) Implementation of minimum wage laws;
(d) Social discrimination against the scheduled castes; and
(e) Impact of rural development programmes.

The study would give greater emphasis on the impact of government interventions, than on other influencing factors, on the aforesaid indicators of the social and economic life of the rural people.

Inter-regional imbalances among the different parts of Karnataka would be an important fall-out of the study.

The study would draw primarily from the 46 village survey

reports prepared by the IAS probationers, which they did as a part of their field training during 1980-81 to 1993-94. The division and district-wise break-up of these surveys is as follows :

Table 4.1 : Division and district-wise break-up of the study reports

Belgaum Division	12
Uttar Kannada District	3
Belgaum District	3
Bijapur District	3
Dharwar District	3
Gulbarga Division	9
Gulbarga District	3
Bidar District	1
Raichur District	2
Bellary District	3
Mysore Division	17
Coorg (or Kodagu) District	0
Dakshina Kannada District	5
Mysore District	7
Mandya District	2
Chickmagalur District	2
Hassan District	1
Bangalore Division	8
Bangalore Urban District	0
Bangalore Rural District	1
Chitradurga District	1
Tumkur District	3
Kolar District	1
Shimoga District	2

Thus these studies cover almost all the districts of the state. The excluded districts are two, namely Coorg and Bangalore Urban. Though 46 is not a large sample to represent the whole state, yet it is certainly an indicator of the situation prevailing in the state. It would be our attempt to supplement the information available in these reports with that from other sources, to draw more logical conclusions.

Therefore, in addition to the above mentioned efforts of the probationers, this study would also refer to some other available literature, such as the Plan Documents, publications of the

Government's Bureau of Economics and Statistics, research studies of universities etc. Some of these documents would be made use of directly in this report, while some others would be cited as materials for further studies.

Some Limiting Factors

These 46 surveys cover almost a 15-year time span. Hence it would be not be very appropriate to compare them. Secondly, not all probationers have given equal attention to each issue. Some have given greater attention to housing while some others to land-holding pattern. Thus to compare these reports would need some caution.

2. LAND HOLDING PATTERNS IN RURAL KARNATAKA

Restrictions on holdings of agricultural lands has been a very important component of the Karnataka Land Reforms Act, 1961, particularly after it was amended with effect from 1-3-1974. The studies by the probationers has covered a very crucial period, namely, from 1980 to 1993. This was the period which saw the largest part of implementation of Land Reforms Law in the State. In this chapter, the following three major issues would be analysed :

(a) The pattern of land holding in different regions/districts of the State;
(b) The pattern of land holding *vis-a-vis* the Scheduled Castes; and
(c) The nature and extent of benami land holdings and concealed tenancy.

We would also use some of the macro-level data published by the state government and compare that with the picture emanating from the reports of the probationers.

Pattern of Land-holding Size

The natural tendency of land holdings in the country is to get fragmented and reduced in size because of the property laws which allow equal share among all male children. (A recent amendment in Karnataka in 1994 has allowed equal share for daughters as well). Thus one should expect decline in average size of operational holdings across the board. Government statistics give the same picture, namely, the average operational holdings in the state which was 3.20 hectares in 1970-71, fell steadily to 2.13 hectares in 1990-91, as the Table 4.2 indicates.

Table 4.2 : Average Size of operational holdings in Karnataka — By districts

(Area in Hectares)

Sl. No.	Name of District	1970-71	1976-77	1980-81	1985-86	1990-91
1.	Bangalore (Rural)	1.35	1.86	1.74	1.82	1.61
2.	Bangalore					1.51
3.	Belgaum	3.26	3.03	2.88	2.60	2.38
4.	Bellary	4.32	2.37	3.14	2.94	2.70
5.	Bidar	5.46	4.61	3.90	3.38	2.80
6.	Bijapur	5.88	5.27	4.82	4.25	3.75
7.	Chikmagalur	2.71	2.55	2.47	2.21	1.97
8.	Chitradurga	3.98	3.64	3.42	2.89	2.56
9.	D. Kannada	1.59	1.32	1.50	1.28	1.17
10.	Dharwad	4.20	3.95	3.60	3.14	2.90
11.	Gulbarga	5.94	5.43	4.79	3.87	3.28
12.	Hassan	2.16	1.99	1.78	1.54	1.32
13.	Kodagu	3.70	3.68	4.05	3.25	3.10
14.	Kolar	1.88	1.81	1.72	1.60	1.46
15.	Mandya	1.37	1.23	1.08	0.96	0.83
16.	Mysore	1.89	1.81	1.60	1.48	1.39
17.	Raichur	4.89	4.65	4.11	3.46	2.97
18.	Shimoga	2.22	2.21	2.12	1.89	1.75
19.	Tumkur	2.15	2.15	1.87	1.82	1.65
20.	U. Kannada	1.39	1.31	1.24	1.16	1.04
	State	3.20	2.98	2.73	2.41	2.13

Source : District Socio-economic Indicators; published by the Director of Economics & Statistics, Karnataka, Bangalore, 1993.

The study reports offer interesting information regarding the ratio of small holders (i.e., holding upto 5 acres) as a percentage of total number of land holders. In some districts, this ratio was reaching the figure of 100 per cent, whereas in some others, it was much less. The following picture emerges:

Table 4.3 : Classification of the Districts (as per the studied villages) according to the ratio of small holders (i.e., upto 5 acres) to number of holders.

Percentage of small holders to total pattadars	Districts that fall in that category
10 to 20	Bellary
20 to 40	Dharwar, Bijapur and Gulbarga
40 to 60	Chikmagalur, Hassan, Belgaum, Bijapur, Chitradurga and Raichur
60 to 80	Mysore, Dakshina Kannada, Uttara Kannada, Shimoga and Bellary
Above 80	Dakshina Kannada, Mandya, Uttara Kannada, Tumkur &
Bangalore	(Rural)

The two studied villages of Bellary District offer extreme situations: While Sirwar Village had as high as 65.3 per cent of holders falling in the category of small holders, Sreedharagadda village had only 16.8 per cent of holders coming in this category. Both villages were quite similar in terms of irrigation facilities.

Let us now analyse the data on land holding patterns, given in Tables 4.2 and 4.3. As for Dharwar, Bijapur and Gulbarga, the situation of having hardly one-third of the land holders as small farmers gives an impression of throwing out the small holders from the orbit of land holdings. It is also true, however, that Gulbarga and Bijapur districts are largely dry and land holdings in purely average terms in these two districts is the highest in the State (above 3 hectares per capita on crude average method), as seen in Table 4.2.

On the other hand, the coastal districts of Uttar Kannada and Dakshina Kannada have the smallest average operational holdings in the state, being 1.04 and 1.17 hectares, respectively, as against the state average of 2.13 hectares (1990-91). Thus it is not surprising to find that more than 80 per cent of the operational holdings in these two districts are less than 5 acres. The same situation prevailing in Mandya district can, however, be explained away as due to high degree of irrigation with Government sources, which would lead to happy survival of the farmer even with small holding. As for Bangalore (Rural) and Tumkur districts, they were very close to hubs of commercial activities, which would account for high degree of marginalisation of operational holdings. The remaining districts fall in intermediate places.

It would be useful to compare this information with the previous table giving district-wise average size of operational holdings. It should, however, be kept in mind that these data do not differentiate between irrigated holdings and unirrigated ones.

One can draw the following conclusions from the probationers' reports and the data of the State Directorate of Economics and Statistics :

(i) Land holdings are relatively larger in dry land districts, such as Bijapur and Gulbarga;

(ii) In Coastal Districts of Uttar Kannada and Dakshina Kannada as also in the areas close to major industrial/ commercial activities in Tumkur and Bangalore Rural Districts, smaller holding dominate the land holding pattern;

(iii) In highly irrigated district of Mandya too, smaller holdings are prominent; and

(iv) Other districts present an intermediate picture.

Skewness in Holding

The question now arises as to whether the smaller holdings are dominating only in number or also in substance. Some typical reports from the probationers give an idea about this issue and are presented in Table 4.4.

Table 4.4 : Ratio of small holdings and area held under them, as a percentage of total land holdings, in some typical villages.

Village	District	Year	Percentage of small holdings (<5 acres) to total	Total extent held by small holders to the total of holdings (%)
Harohally	Mysore	1992-93	70	88
M.H.Hally	Mysore	1987-88	92	70
Nekkilady	D.Kannada	1988-89	88	43
Bukinakere	Mandya	1992-93	94	73
Hattikere	U.Kannada	1992-93	73	19
Amatur	Belgaum	1989-90	61	30
Byadanur	Tumkur	1989-90	51	20
Kesaramadu	Tumkur	1987-88	78	55
Sreedhargadda	Bellary	1989-90	17	3

The above Table 4.4 indicates that very high degree of marginalisation of small holders was seen in the studied villages in Bellary, Tumkur, Belgaum, Uttara Kannada and Dakshina Kannada Districts.

If we see Karnataka as a whole, the land holding picture that is projected in the Statistical Outline of Karnataka, published by the State Directorate of Economics and Statistics (1989-90) (pp. 25-26) is as follows :

Table 4.5 : Distribution of operational land holdings in Karnataka

	1970-71		1985-86	
Holdings (Size)	Number	Area ('000 ha)	Number	Area ('000ha)
Marginal (Below 1 ha)	1081	549	1792	866
Small (1 to 2 ha)	840	1221	1293	1889
Medium & Large (above 2 ha)	1680	9598	1834	9124
All	3551	11368	4309	11879
Marginal & small (below 2 ha) as percentage of all	54	16	72	23

Source: Directorate of Economics & Statistics, Karnataka, Bangalore, 1989-90.

Thus in Karnataka, the number of small (and marginal) holdings went up by 18 per cent (from 54 to 72) during 1970-71 to 1985-86. But the area held by these holdings went up by only 7 per cent, from 16 to 23. This would indicate that the sub-marginalisation of small holdings has continued.

Pattern of Landholdings vis-a-vis the Scheduled Castes

The Scheduled Castes and Scheduled Tribes constitute nearly 15 and 5 per cent, respectively, of the State's population. Their average operational holding size *vis-a vis* the state average, as reported by the State Directorate of Economics and Statistics, is given in Table 4.6.

Table 4.6 : Average size of operational holdings of SCs and STs in Karnataka (Area in ha)

	1970-71	1980-81	1990-91
State	3.20	2.73	2.13
SCs	NA	1.93	1.53
STs	NA	2.55	2.17

Source : Directorate of Economics and Statistics, Karnataka, 1992-93.

Thus the average operational holding size has declined for SCs, STs as well as for State as a whole, though for SCs the average holding size is consistently less than the State average for all castes put together.

Table 4.6 also gives an impression that the marginalisation of holdings of STs, though it has reduced over 1980-81 to 1990-91, has been less than what it was for the State as a whole. Perhaps the special protective measures and laws designed to prevent alienation of lands of the SCs and STs has been of some help.

The study reports of the probationers present a more stark picture, in respect of SCs at least. For instance, in M.H.Hally (Mysore District), K. Shivaramu had noted that the SCs being 2.4 per cent of the total number of Khatedars, held just 0.11 per cent of the land (1987-88, p.7).

In Kutethur village of Dakshina Kannada District, the average family holding was 4.91 acres of dry land (equivalent), whereas for the SCs this was just 0.68 acre. Moreover, the land held by SCs was almost totally dry land, as the following Table 4.7 would indicate (Kapil Mohan: 1991-92, pp. 15-16):

Table 4.7 : Land holdings of SCs & STs *vis-a-vis* others in Kutethur Village of Dakshina Kannada District (1991-92) Land Holdings (in acres)

Social Group	No. of Families	% to total	Dry	Wet	Garden	Equivalent Dry	% To Total
SC	23	5.7	17.73	0.32	0.87	19.67	1.00
ST	13	3.2	0.57	0.00	0.00	0.57	0.03
Others	365	91.1	695.24	564.14	89.65	1950.55	98.97
Total	401	100.0	713.54	564.46	85.52	1970.79	100.00

Kapil Mohan observes, and it is fairly clear from his data cited in Table 7 above, that the interface of the SCs (and STs) with agricultural lands can thus hardly be given in terms of ownership. They are largely agricultural labourers.

The picture that is emerging from some other study reports that have given clear statistical data, is consolidated in the following Table 4.8.

Table 4.8 : Average holding size of SCs *vis-a-vis* all pattadars in some villages.

Village	District	Year	Average Holding Size (in acres)		
			SCs	STs	All
M.H.Hally	Mysore	1987-88	0.87	NA	1.89
Kutethur	D.Kannada	1991-92	0.86	0.04	4.91
Vandse	D.Kannada	1990-91	0.40	0.90	4.20
Salekina - Koppa	Dharwar	1977-78	0.66	NA	4.90
Bellambari	Kolar	1990-91	0.50	NA	4.35

The marginalisation of SCs in land holding system is described carefully in some of the study reports. In Chittakula village of

Uttara Kannada district, there were 11 SC families (out of total of 1987), but no SC family owned any land (Rajeev Chawla, 1988-89, pp. 5 & 12). In Narendra village of Dharwar district too, Nagambika reported that though there were 42 SC families in the village, none of them owned any land (1990-91, Ch. 4). Similarly, in Agumbe village of Shimoga District, though the SCs made up 15 out of the total 30 households, yet no SC family held any land (Anshu Bharadwaj : 1993-94, pp. 3 & 9).

It is also mentioned in many studies that wherever the SCs held lands, if at all, it was normally the unirrigated dry land even though other social groups held wet and garden lands. A typical case is narrated by S.D. Meena from Amatur village in Belgaum district (1989-90): "The large holdings are in the areas irrigated by borewells, dug wells and Jalikoppa Lift Irrigation on Malaprabha Reservoir. Such holdings are generally held by Caste Hindus and a few Muslims. Nearly all the SC families and most of the Backward Class families do not have any wet lands. Their holdings are limited to dry lands, which are at higher levels, where the Jalikoppa Lift Irrigation cannot supply water."

This marginalisation of SCs is noticed even in case of D.K. district where tenancy reforms were implemented with great intensity as observed in two study reports, namely from Jawaid in Vandse village and from Kapil in Kutethur village.

Benami Land Holdings and Concealed Tenancy

The Karnataka Land Reforms Act, 1961 prescribed a ceiling on land holdings and prohibited creation or continuance of tenancy and lease with effect from 1-3-1974, exemption being granted in the case of land holders who were either soldiers or seamen, (sec. 5). All land which was tenanted as on that date, vested with the State Government (sec. 44). Occupancy rights over such lands were conferred, after due enquiry by the Land Tribunal, on the tiller (sec. 45), Any land leased or tenanted after 1-3-1974 was to be forfeited to the Government (sec. 58). With effect from the scheduled date (i.e. 1-3-1974), no person who had an annual family income of Rs. 12,000 or more from non-agricultural sources, could acquire any agricultural land (sec. 79A). Further, no person other than one cultivating the land personally, was entitled to hold such lands after that date (sec. 79B). Transfer of agricultural lands to non-agriculturists was also banned (sec. 80).

These and some other stringent provisions of land reforms law relating to acquisition, holding and operation of the land holdings had a profound impact on the farming community. For instance, as per sections 84 and 85 of the KLRF Act, no land holder can keep his lands uncultivated for more than two consecutive years and if he does so, the Government can take over his land temporarily and give it to some one else for cultivation. This provision was meant to put psychological pressure on the landlords not to lease their lands uncultivated.

The study reports indicate, however, that there are certain categories of holders who are unable to cultivate the lands personally and tend to lease it out unofficially. Such situations occur normally due to:

(a) Old age of the lessor,
(b) absence of any male member in the lessor's family,
(c) lack of bullocks with the lessor family, and
(d) non-residence in the village.
(Shivaramu, M.H.Hally, Mysore district, 1987-88, p.5)

But the land reform laws do not provide any relief to such categories of land-holders. The law ordains that such landlords could at best engage casual labourers to help them out. The message has gone very well with the land holders that if they either hire tenants or lease out their lands, they could very well lose their lands (Jayanthi, Varuna village, Mysore district, 1989-90, p. 15). This situation is seen clearly from several study reports, from the districts of Mysore, D.K., Hassan, U.K., Tumkur etc.

Whereas the bigger farmers would rather keep their lands fallow than give it for cultivation to others for fear of losing it under the land reform laws, the marginal farmers' plight is different. Such marginal farmers who did not have the capacity to cultivate their lands, leased it out informally (e.g. Nilaya, Bukinakere village, Mandya district, 1992-93), and themselves worked as coolies (para 5.5).

There is yet another facet to the situation wherein the land holders are reluctant to lease out their lands. As we have seen before, 72 per cent of land holdings in the state are small or marginal though they contribute only 23 per cent of the total operational area. Still, the numerous small and marginal farmers would anyday prefer to work on their own land unless driven by abject poverty to lease out their holdings. This social value system has further prevented leasing out lands. Moreover, in rural areas, alternative means of employment are almost non-existent (Anshuli, in Jamboti village, Belgaum district, 1990-91, pp. 9-11).

The cases of benami leasing out of land was recorded by about eight out of 46 study-reports. In each case, the number of such instances was usually less than 5 per cent of total number of holdings. In most such cases, the landlords were prevented from tilling their land due to some disability or due to non-residence in the village.

There was not much of organised system of leasing in or leasing out of lands recorded by these studies.

Conclusion

(a) Small holdings dominate the rural land holding scenario. As many as 72 per cent of the holders are small or marginal (i.e. holding upto 2 ha.). The rural development programmes should take note of this situation for macro planning.

(b) Though 72 per cent of land holders are in the category of small and marginal holders, their holdings put together constitutes less than one-fourth of the total agricultural land holdings. This proportion has gone up, against such holders, over the past few decades (Ref. Tables 4.2 and 4.5). This trend needs to be taken note of while deciding the socio-economic policies.

(c) The average size of land holdings for the SCs is very much less than that for the State as a whole (1.53 ha. as against 2.13 ha.). However, this figure for the STs is 2.17 ha., which is marginally higher than the State average (All figures for 1990-91, *vide* Table 4.6).

(d) The various laws enacted to prevent alienation of lands of the SCs and the STs seem to have been effective in preventing the decline in the land holdings of the SCs and STs.

(e) However, in several villages, the SCs and STs do not hold any significant lands and are generally surviving as agricultural labourers (Ref. Tables 4.7 and 4.8).

(f) The lands held by the SCs and STs are usually dry and unirrigated type. Conversely, the participation of these communities in the holding of agricultural lands in the command areas of the government owned irrigation projects has been relatively minimal.

(g) Though the land reforms laws insist that the land owners cultivate their lands personally or else lose it, yet, in reality, these provisions are not being enforced. A significant number (say, about 10 per cent) of the land holders do not cultivate their lands personally due to reasons of old age, non-residence, absence of a male member in the family etc.

(h) Due to stringent application of the tenancy related provisions of the land reforms laws, a good number of the landlords have stopped giving their lands for cultivation to others on lease. Rather, they take recourse to wage labour and change the wage labourers frequently. In some extreme situations, such landlords would keep their lands fallow. At times, they engage in benami tenancy, i.e. a *de facto* tenancy but *de jure* self-cultivation. This arrangement gives a mixed bag of help and problems to the land lords, but is positively detrimental to the labourer class.

3. HOUSING SCENARIO OF RURAL KARNATAKA : SOME ISSUES

In this part, the dwelling patterns in the surveyed villages would be examined. Specifically, four questions would examined, namely :

1. Was any spatial segregation noticed in the dwelling pattern?
2. What was the typology of house construction?
3. What is the extent of houselessness prevailing in the villages?
4. To what extent is the sanitation/toilet facility available in

villages?

In all the four enquiries, effort would be made to find out the caste/community-wise variations also, wherever possible, giving particular attention to the SCs and STs.

It should be pointed out that not all the reports have given attention to all these four questions. Even while addressing an issue, some have given only qualitative description, without supporting data. Hence, the database gets somewhat constrained.

Another difficulty encountered in analysing these study reports is that there is no uniform terminology and specifications used by individual probationer. For instance, the definition of a kutcha house, or a terraced house etc. This vagueness in definition would make some of the observations open to error.

However, these limitations have not seriously impaired the analysis and the conclusions drawn could be termed as reasonably accurate.

Spatial Segregation of the Caste Groups

Spatial segregation of dwellings based on caste and community was keenly observed by many of the studies. Here they are examined in terms of the four revenue divisions.

Mysore Division

Traditionally, in a village setting in Karnataka, the SCs are physically segregated and live on the outskirts of the village. The study reports of Mysore Division generally confirm this. Even those SCs who have converted to Christianity, were found to be so segregated (Perumal in Deveerammanahally village, Mysore taluk 1983-84, p.1), while major communities such as Lingayats were found to be living in the main village.

However, Jayanti, in Varuna village of Mysore taluk (1989-90, para 1.2), found no such spatial segregation of caste groups.

In Maravanthe (Yogendra, 1986-87, p.1) and in Nekkilady (Ajay Seth, 1988-89, pp.1-2), both in the Dakshin Kannada district, houses were found to be scattered and in the agricultural lands itself, thanks to the land reforms. This has made the question of segregation in housing irrelevant.

In M.H. Hally village of Mysore taluk (and district), K. Shivaramu observed (1987-88, p. 1) that: "Generally, Harijans live in separate colonies. But recently, the other Hindus also live side by side with the Harijans."

In Harohalli village in Mysore District (Vandana: 1992-93, p.10), a clear division of dwellings was noted, with the SCs residing on the left side of the main road (Mysore-HD Kote Road), and similar groupings noticed for other communities/castes.

In Sakrepatna village of Chikmagalur district, Vandita (1987-88, pp. 2-3) notes existence of separate colonies of agricultural labourers and Lambanis.

In Kutethur village of the same district, Kapil positively found such spatial segregation (1991-92, para 2.3.3). He has found partial explanation in tradition and also in the fact that *the Rural Housing Programmes for the STs and SCs had provided sites and houses to them in a cluster and such clusters had to be away from the existing village. (Emphasis added).*

In Kandali village of Hassan district, Sandeep Dave observed that out of 150 houses, nine belonging to the SCs were in a separate colony within the village precincts (1988-89, p.2). He has further noted that in the Government (Janatha) Housing area, beneficiaries belonging to all communities lived together. This observation confirms the theory that the *Government, through its housing programmes, can catalyse the abetment or diminution of the social segregation on caste/community lines at least in the context of habitat. (Emphasis added).*

Belgaum Division

S.D. Meena had found in Amatur village of Belgaum District (1989-90) that though none of the villagers were ready to accept that untouchability was practised there, but all 24 Harijan families lived in a separate corner of the village, slightly away from the main cluster of houses. This sub-cluster of Harijan houses had a separate hand pump which was the only source of water for them.

In Jamboti village of Belgaum district, Anshuli (1990-91, pp.

1-2) had found that, "Traditionally, different castes have their own areas. For example, there is a Harijan Keri, a Desai Galli and a Brahmin Galli. Muslims are also concentrated in one place. However, in recent constructions, some amount of intermingling is seen. In the newly built Janatha Housing Colony, families of all religions and castes are living side by side. Each colony has its own well."

Segregation on caste and community lines was noted in Narendra village of Dharwar district also, by Nagambika Devi (pp. 4-5). This village is just about 8 kms. from the district headquarters and is hardly 2 kms. away from the Pune-Bangalore National Highway. She has recorded that : "The dwellings of various communities like SCs, STs, Muslims, etc. are concentrated in separate colonies or 'cheries' of the village. But the taboo of untouchability is not seen. The coming up of Janatha Colony in the village has further helped the eradication of untouchability because the caste Hindus, SCs, STs and others live harmoniously as next door neighbours." In the same district, Subhash Chandra had also made reference to separate colony or 'thanda' for the lambanis in Timmapur village (1987-88, pp. 1-2).

In a much earlier study (1977-78), M.R. Sreenivasa Murthy had reported in Salakinakoppa village of Dharwar district that, "As is usual in villages, each street in this village has houses belonging to a particular caste group. Thus, the Kelagina Oni has houses belonging to the Patil (Kshatriya) community and it is also called the Gowdar Oni. The Naduvina Oni has mainly Lingayat households and the Melina Oni has the houses of people belonging to the Valmiki community. The houses of the Harijans are all concentrated along the Samaj Karya Street (p. 3)."

In village Malapur of Bijapur district, Basavaraju (1989-90, p. 3) had noted that the members of the SCs lived separately from the caste Hindus. However, he had also found examples of progress towards being together: "The houses of SCs are adjoining to the houses of caste Hindus. There is no harassment from the caste Hindus."

In Anjutagi village of Bijapur district, Kumar Naik (1991-92, para F, p. 2) had reported that, "The houses of the SC families are concentrated in part of the Gairana land, but there is no tendency to harass on sheer caste criterion."

We had seen earlier the reports from the coastal district of Dakshin Kannada in Mysore Division that the houses were usually scattered in the small agricultural fields, and this had eliminated the possibility, if any, of social segregation of houses on caste or communal lines. Similar report is made from the other coastal district of Uttar Kannada, which falls in the Belgaum Division. In this district, Ramana Reddy has reported from Basolli village (1989-90, p.2) that, "Each house is situated within the cultivator's land and this is one reason for the scattered pattern of the village. There is no defined pattern of dwelling based on caste."

In another village, Chittakula, in the same district, Chawla (1988-89, p.4) found that, "The members of the SCs live separately in a colony which is at the end of the caste Hindu dwellings.They all live in absolute peace and utmost understanding."

Bangalore Division

Bangalore Division consists of the districts of Bangalore (Urban), Bangalore Rural, Shimoga, Tumkur, Kolar and Chitradurga.

In Agumbe village of Shimoga district, Anshu noticed (1993-94, p.4) that the colony for SCs was outside the village. They had a separate borewell and interaction between them and the higher castes was minimal.

Shalini, in Bellambari village of Kolar district, recorded (1990-91, p.2) that, "People from various communities are staying side by side. Even the members belonging to the SCs/STs have their house sites adjacent to the biggest landlords of the village."

In Chitradurga district, Kharola noted in Madekeripura that while the Lambani Colony was about 300 metres away from the village, the A.K. Colony was in the centre of the village (1986-87, p.14). He also reports that there were about 10 Muslim households in the village, but their houses were scattered all over the village and not located in a single place.

In Mathur village of Shimoga district, Kamble (1987-88, p.1) noted thus: "Though the entire village is in one place, the people stay according in community-wise colonies. There is no dearth of sites for dwelling. Though the SCs/STs stay in the same village, but in different colonies, there are no traces of harassment to them."

In Kesarmadu village of Tumkur District, which is just 9 kms. from Tumkur town, Rajneesh Goel records: "The houses have been organised into a number of localities. While the SCs stay in a separate colony, persons of other castes and communities are having their houses in the same localities" (1987-88, p.4).

Solur village in Bangalore Rural District also had segregation of SCs and STs, as found by Gauri in 1988-89. This village is situated on the Bangalore-Mangalore National Highway. She writes (pp. 2-3) that, "The SCs/STs live in two areas, at both ends of the village. At the far end, the Harijans intermingled with the poorer Christians."

Gulbarga Division

Gulbarga Division consists of the district of Bidar, Gulbarga, Raichur and Bellary.

A very telling citation from H. Baskar, who reported for Begur village in Raichur district (1984-85, pp. 2-3):

> "There are 67 families, of whom 23 belong to the Kurubas (shepherds by tradition) forming the biggest caste group in the village. The SCs, represented only by Madigas come second with 16 families. The 10 Kaberu (fishermen) families occupy the third position followed by the Lingayats represented by eight families and Nayakas with five families. The other residents include Agasaru (dhobies), Jangams and Panchala Vishwakarmas. Though the Kaberus, Kurubas, Lingayats and Nayaks co-exist, a certain degree of localisation of castes in pockets can be distinguished. As is common in most Indian villages, the SCs are concentrated in the Harijanwada and live separately from the caste Hindus."
>
> "The SCs live in *kuccha* houses consisting of mud walls and thatched roofs; stone is rarely used. Most of their houses are in a dilapidated state, cramped and lack ventilation. The Harijanawada is unhygienic with puddles of stagnant water

> and decaying debris strewn all over. Houses belonging to the Lingayats are the best with stone walls, mortar and stone mixed roofs, wooden doors and windows and many of them even have decorated pillars. Dwellings belonging to the other castes are intermediate in nature, ranging from pucca to semi-pucca. As every rule has an exception, one does come across a Lingayat family living in a *kuccha* house or a SC residing in a semi-pucca one."

But for this excellent impressionistic description, Baskar has not given any statistical information.

In another village, Sreedharagadda of Bellary district, Raj Kumar Khatri (1989-90, p. 2) has given a good, though brief, description, which goes as follows:

> "There are 850 dwellings in total. In the main village site, majority of the houses belong to the Hindus (Lingayats). On the southern side of the village site, there are two Harijan Cheris (one old and the other new). On the eastern boundary of the village and across the *kuccha* road, which passes through the village, the people belonging to the Scheduled Castes and other backward classes live. In the main village site, there is not a single house belonging to the members of the Scheduled Castes or Backward Classes."

In Sirwar village of Bellary district, M. Laxminarayana noted (1988-89) that the SCs lived at the entrance of the village in a separate pocket (p. 7). He continues to find that the Government had built 91 Janatha houses of which 40 were given to the SCs and rest to others. This is another example of removal of caste based compartmentalisation of society through government intervention.

V. Umesh has reported in Halbarga village of Bidar district (1982-83) that different communities and castes lived in different areas: "The SCs like Harijans, Christian converts, Kurubas, Wodders and Chamars are segregated and reside in separate areas of the village, while Lingayats and Marathas live in the main village. In other words, it can be said that there is colonisation of the village community."

A distinctly different picture comes across in Miryan village of Gulbarga district in the report of Vidyavathi, (1992-93, p.10, para 16). She records that : "Quite surprisingly, the SC colony is located right in the centre of the village. I have visited this colony quite a few times and it has been an enlightening experience."

In Kurugodu village of Bellary District, Parmesh Pandey observed (1986-87, p. 2) that : "By and large, the SC population of the village was living separately from the caste Hindus. But some SC families also live in mixed localities in the lands that they had purchased from the landlords."

Conclusions and Recommendations

Spatial segregation, particularly of the Scheduled Castes, is fairly common though its degree is less in the coastal districts. The picture that emerges from these 46 reports can be summarised in Table 4.9.

Table 4.9 : Caste-based segregation of dwellings in study villages.

Division	Segregation found	Segregation positively	Picture not found absent	Total analysed
Mysore	6	2	9	17
Belgaum	8	1	3	12
Bangalore	4	2	2	8
Gulbarga	5	1	3	9
Total	23	6	17	46

Such segregation is largely traditional. This tradition continues and is followed by all castes and communities. Yet some unmistakable peculiarities are listed below :

1. The Lambanis live far away, from about 200 metres to a kilometre from the main village. There abode is popularly called the 'thanda'.
2. The SCs live on the outskirts of the village, with few

exceptions.

3. The caste Hindus also have community/caste-wise habitats, though their caste-based segregation is relatively less rigid.
4. Usually, members of the SCs live in a pocket on the outskirts of the village. However, this is not always true. At times, their 'cheri' is well within the village 'gramthana'.
5. Some of the rural housing schemes sponsored by the government seem to be aiding and abetting such segregation, as they come for different caste groups, particularly for SCs and STs and provide for group habitat for them, thus perpetuating their isolation.
6. On the other hand, land reforms measures, particularly in the districts of Dakshin Kannada and Uttar Kannada, have provided small pieces of agricultural lands to a large number of marginal farmers and agricultural labourers, who have preferred to have their houses on such lands. That has automatically solved the problem of spatial segregation.

One would recommend to the policy makers to have a mixed housing for all castes and communities developed under rural housing programmes. Such housing colonies should have all utilities on sharing basis, including the drinking water source, public toilet, reading room, park, and community hall.

Typology of House Construction

The houses of rich and poor, all are usually independent single units. Most of the houses have tiled roofing. Thatched roofing has been replaced by tiles or zinc-sheet or even asbestos roofing, thanks to the various housing programmes launched by the government, particularly since the 1970s. However, none of the reports have alluded to the zinc or asbestos roofing.

Many of the reports have given statistical data regarding house construction typology. These are presented in Table 4.10 below:

Table 4.10 : Roof types of the rural houses in the studied villages

Village Name	Total No. of houses	Thatched/ Kuccha	Tiled asbestos	Zinc/ terraced	RCC/stone
Mysore Division					
DM Hally	292	35	257	—	
Vandse	378	188	190 (Break up not indicated)		
Varuna	239	10	228	—	1
Maravanthe	620	263	336	—	21
Nekkilady(details not given) nearly 70%					
Naravi	644	41	603	—	—
KK Hally	1085	263	816	—	6
Timmapur	147	80	59 (Total does not tally)		
Bukinakere	All, except one, of the surveyed houses had tiled roof				
Sakrepatna	N.A.	10%	90%		
Belgaum Division					
Amatur	292	120	172	—	—
Hebsur	803	78	725	—	—
Jamboti	368	12	356	—	—
Malapur	213	12	—	—	201
Basolli	62	47	15	—	—
Chittakula	1867	628	1229	—	10
Banglore Division					
Bellambari	75	14	41	—	20
Madekeripura	610 80	80	—	75	
Byadanur	70	12	52	—	6
Amruthur	975	76% of sampled dwellings are pucca units			
Gulbarga Division					
Sreedhara-gadda	850	832	18	—	—
Halbarga	321	218	—	—	103

Thus about 60 to 90 per cent of all dwelling units are tile roofed or have similar other roofing of higher level. This is a significant achievement attributable to state intervention for welfare of the people. Tile roof has by now become a symbol of economic well-being of the households. However, several instances of existence of thatched roofing was noticed by the study reports. From a closer scrutiny of these reports, some more insight is visible into the typology of roofing. This is being presented in groupings of Revenue Divisions hereafter.

Mysore Division

Yogendra Tripathi observed that even in a forward district like Dakshin Kannada (1986-87 : Maravanthe Village), most (21 out of 23) of the houses belonging to the SCs and STs had thatched roofs. In the same district, Jawaid noticed in Vandse village (1990-91) that of the 15 houses belonging to the SCs/STs, 10 were *kuccha* and five *pucca*. In K.K. Halli of Mandya District, Baderiya (1990-91, p.2) had enumerated that of the 447 houses belonging to the SCs, 135 were thatched while 310 were tile-roofed and two had modern terrace.

Belgaum Division

While noting that only 725 of the total of 803 families had proper houses (rest had huts) in Hebsur village of Dharwar district, B.H. Anil Kumar found no difference in the standard of roofing in respect of caste Hindus as well as the SCs and STs (1988-89, p. 2).

In the same district, in Narendra village, Nagambika (1990-91, p. 5) has noted that, "The dwellings in the village are terraced. The houses have along with them, hutments for the women to reside during their menstrual and delivery period."

In Timmapur village of the same district, Subhash Chandra (1987-88) has described the house construction as follows: "The village has no *pucca* houses, the traditional style of construction in the region being that of roofing by tiles by those who can afford it or by simple thatching using hay. While the caste village has 73 thatched and 11 tiled houses, the SC portion has seven thatched and 48 tiled houses."

Sreenivasa Murthy found in Salakinakoppa village in Dharwar district more than 15 years ago, i.e. in 1977-78 (pp.3-4): "Out of the total 92 houses in the village, five are *pucca* houses with cement roof and brick walls. All of them belong to the *Kshatriya* community. There are 35 houses with tiled roofs and brick walls and they belong to an assortment of communities from Harijan households to Lingayat families. All the harijan households have semi-pucca houses with good tiled roofs and brick walls."

The study by B. Basavaraju (1989-90) in Malapur village of Bijapur district has found a vast majority of houses (201 out of 213) to be terraced. His definition of a terraced house is, however, not clear. Perhaps he meant it to be stone-roofed. He has, however, not found that the situation is no different for SCs in this respect as compared to the rest of the population in the village (p. 4).

In the village Agumbe of Shimoga, which is famous for its heavy rainfall, Anshu noted (1993-94, p. 4) that, "Almost all the houses are tiled and made up of bricks. It is inevitable, because a *kuccha* house cannot withstand the heavy rains that come pounding down each year. All the dwellings in the SC colony are tiled. In fact, they are all new houses, built under the Ambedkar Scheme." In another context, the same report of Anshu (p.6) states that, "A typical feature of villages in this area is that dwellings are scattered. The farmers prefer to build houses within the farms or close to them." Among the reasons cited by Anshu for this preference are better protection of lands, trees and crops from wild animals and high price of lands in the main habitat areas.

In Kolar district, Shalini found in Bellambri village (1990-91, pp. 2-3) that construction specifications of the houses depended on the economic status of the families. While the people from the SC communities had 14 thatched houses, six tiled houses and four terraced houses; the other families taken together had got 35 tiled houses and 16 terraced houses.

In Madekeripura village of Chitradurga district, Kharola found most of the dwellings of the SCs to be thatched huts (1986-87, p. 14). In Byadanur village of Tumkur district, A.K. Jha (1989-90, p. 16) found no correlation between tiled roofing and socio-economic status. Among SC/ST dwellings, 14 out of 20 were tiled, among Muslims, 8 out of 10 and among others, 30 out of 40 were tiled. In Kesaramadu village of this district, which is just 9 kms from the district headquarters, Rajneesh (1987-88, p. 4) noted that: most of the houses were *kuccha*, using locally available materials and had thatched roofs. However, some of the affluent did have houses of bricks and tiled roofs. There was no double-storeyed house in the village.

Gulbarga Division

In Chandrabanda village of Raichur district, A.K. Tiwari (1991-92) noted that most houses were made up of big stone blocks and were flat roofed, while the poorer families' houses were made up of mud and thatched roof. Unfortunately, Atul has not given a clear statistical support to his observation.

We get an excellent data table in the report of R.K. Khatri in Sreedharagadda village (1989-90), listing out the typology of house construction community-wise:

Table 4.11 : Types of dwellings in Sreedharagadda village, Bellary district (1989-90)

Caste	No. of houses	Type			Facilities	
		Pucca	Kuccha	Huts	Bathroom	Toilet
Sch. Castes	175	—	32	143	—	—
Muslims	90	2	30	58	2	—
Lingayats	310	15	215	80	15	6
Kuruba (BC)	31	—	10	21	—	—
Medars	36	1	6	29	7	—
Gollaru	20	—	9	11	—	—
Valmikis	130	—	90	40	10	—
Agasaru (Washermen)	30	—	10	20	2	—
Barbers	4	—	4	—	1	—
Goldsmiths	5	—	4	1	2	1
Edigas (Arrack vendors)	12	—	4	8	2	—
Barikeru	5	—	—	5	—	—
Kumbar-(Potters)	2	—	1	1	—	—
TOTAL	850	18	415	417	41	7

Thus Sreedharagadda gives a picture of high relative deprivation in case of the SCs, of whom about 82 per cent lived in huts, whereas for rest of the population, this percentage was only 41. Even among the non-SC households, some had higher deprivation than the others. For instance, among the Agasarus (washermen) and Medars (bamboo weavers), it was 67 per cent and among Muslims 65 per cent.

Conclusions

It seems to be the experience of many probationers that the percentage of inferior type of house construction was more among the SCs and STs as compared to the others. The probationers have not thrown light on the reasons for this situation and hence I am using the indirect hints that I get from their reports and cross-verify it with my own experience to explain it. One reason is that the economic situation of SCs and STs has come in the way of improving their houses and they have to depend on the government. But the system of having funds earmarked for the SC and ST families by way of SCP and TSP has tended usually to limit the flow of government programmes such as housing to them. Perhaps such programmes should not have SCP and TSP component. All the funds under rural housing should be pooled and extended to the beneficiaries under the Antyodaya concept. Automatically, the SCs and other deprived sections would get due attention.

Secondly, it is also a question of awareness among the beneficiary groups, besides their capacity to organise procurement of better quality building materials. This is another issue needing the attention of policy-makers. When the government has been providing subsidised ration through Fair Price Shops, there could be a system of making available housing materials also to the rural poor at subsidised prices, using the FPS or a similar mechanism.

Houselessness

In this part, we attempt to identify the nature and extent of scarcity of houses and of house-sites that prevails in the surveyed areas. Here too, the analysis has been made for the different divisions.

Mysore Division

Most studies have found varying degree of houselessness prevailing in the rural areas. Maravanthe (D.K. District) had only 30 huts (a hut indicates lack of a proper house), as against 620 proper houses (Yogendra: 1986-87). In Vandse village of the same district, housing shortage is mentioned by Jawaid (1990-91, para 2.3.4.3), though the exact details are not given.

In Varuna village of Mysore taluka (Vandana: 1992-93), 92 persons needed new houses as against 239 houses that existed. In Deveerammanahalli (Mysore District, Perumal: 1983-84) the number of persons needing houses was 15 as against 292 houses that already existed. In M.H. Hally of Mysore District, K. Shivaramu (1987-88, p. 1) noted that the Hindus and the Harijans residing in the village did not have adequate house-sites.

In Sakrepatna village of Chickmagalur District, Vandita recorded (1987-88, p.1) that the dwellings were more or less sufficient.

In K.K.Halli of Mandya District, Baderiya (1990-91, pp. 3,4) did not enumerate specific instances of houselessness, but has noted nevertheless that the houses were overcrowded with inhabitants.

Belgaum Division

Here too, while none have described anyone living on the streets, yet many of the studies have noted that there was a pressure for independent dwelling units owing to increasing population and division of families (e.g. S.D. Meena: 1989-90, in Amatur village of Belgaum district, p.2; Anshuli Arya: 1990-91, in Jamboti village of Belgaum district, p. 2; Nagambika: 1990-91 in Narendra village of Dharwar District, p. 5).

However, Basavaraju, in Malapur village of Bijapur district did not find any shortage of house-sites either for the SCs or for others (1989-90, p. 3). Similar is the finding of Ramana Reddy in respect of Basolli village of Uttara Kannada district (1989-90, p. 2).

In the village Chittakula of Uttara Kannada district, Chawla reported that out of 1,867 households, 1,663 had sufficient dwelling facilities, whereas the remaining 204 did not (1988-89, Annexure I). In another village, Hattikere, of this district, Atheeq did not find any noticeable shortage of dwelling houses (1992-93, para VI).

Bangalore Division

In Bellambari village of Kolar District, Shalini (1990-91, pp. 2-3) found all the villagers, caste Hindus as well as Harijans, having sufficient area for their house sites.

Jha reported, in Byadanur village of Tumkur district (1989-90, p. 3), that out of a total village population of 4100, 150 persons were houseless and they were finding it quite difficult to secure house-sites. In the same district, in Kesarmadu village, 9 kms. from Tumkur city, Rajneesh (1987-88, p. 4) found that just two years ago, 47 house-less people were granted sites by the authorities and, as a result, there was no problem of house-sites in the village.

In Amruthur village of Tumkur district, Manjula found (1988, p. 13) that 71 per cent of surveyed households had own houses. Further analysis of houselessness by Manjula indicated that 33 per cent of Muslim households were houseless, whereas this percentage was 9 for SC/ST households and 22 for all others.

Gulbarga Division

In Sirwar village of Bellary district, Laxminarayana reported that out of total 544 households, the number of houseless was 148, of whom 26 were SCs and rest OBCs (1988-89, p. 8).

Khatri studied the Census data and also made physical verifications for the unit strength of the dwellings. As per Census data, there should be 7 persons per dwelling (population 5906 and number of houses 850). On physical verification too, he found the occupancy for each unit to be 6 to 8 persons. As a general rule, he found the living space for the individuals highly insufficient (1989-90).

In Halbarga village of Bidar district, Umesh enumerated 15 houseless persons, out of a total number of 321 dwellings. Out of these 15, ten were SCs (1982-83).

In another major village, Kamalapur, of Gulbarga district, Rakesh found from the Census data that as against 1553 households, only 1170 houses existed, which clearly indicated an acute shortage of housing (1990-91).

Conclusion and Recommendations

The various study reports indicate housing shortage to the tune of about 20 to 30 per cent in most rural areas and the immediate need to give it serious attention.

One also gets a fairly clear impression that housing shortage is a more acute problem in larger villages, as compared to the smaller ones.

It is not possible to make a comment that the SCs need house-sites more badly than non-SCs. Indeed, there are instances of a particular caste requiring house-sites more acutely. However, this situation varies from village to village.

None of the study reports have examined the financial structures of the rural housing programmes. For instance, all such schemes envisage beneficiary's contribution, which is often missing. Thus the effectiveness of the housing programmes can be further enhanced by creating awareness and involvement among the beneficiary households.

Housing has been given another special thrust by the State Government in recent years, i.e. since 1992-93. Housing Schemes such Ashraya and Ambedkar aim at providing about a lakh of houses per year to the urban and rural poor. The procedure for acquisition of lands under these schemes is highly simplified and decentralised. One can hope that the shortage of housing would come down drastically by the end of the century in the state.

Again, since 1994-95, the three-tier Panchayati Raj system has been introduced in the state. Involving these bodies can help in proper and expeditious identification of the needy and in better implementation of the housing programmes.

Sanitation and Toilet Facilities

In this part, we ascertain the nature and extent of availability of sanitary and toilet facilities available in the rural dwellings.

Mysore Division

All the studies have noted absence of latrines in the villages. In Nekkilady (Dakshin Kannada district), 10 per cent of the surveyed houses had toilet facilities (Ajay Seth: 1988-89, p. 26). However, that situation seems to be an exception, as we will see.

Baderiya has noted in K.K. Halli (Mandya District, 1990-91) that absence of toilet facilities caused great inconvenience and embarrassment to the womenfolk.

Jayanti has mentioned that in Varuna village (Mysore District, 1989-90), only 20 of the 239 houses had a bathroom, and that 50 houses had recently acquired individual latrines under a Pilot Project, with Rs. 500 contributed by each beneficiary.

Gaurav, in Pura village of Chikmagalur District (1991-92, p.17) had noted total absence of toilet facilities.

In Harohalli of Mysore District, Vandana found no latrines (1992-93, p. 73), though as per Panchayat records 24 latrines had been provided. In M.H. Hally village of the same district, K. Shivaramu (1987-88, p.10) has recorded that sanitation arrangements in the Harijan Colony were not satisfactory.

In Bukinakere village of Mandya District, Nilaya (1992-93) recorded that 95 per cent houses did not have a latrine, though he does not give exact figures.

Belgaum Division

The situation in this division is no better. Anshuli in Jamboti Village of Belgaum district (1990-91, p. 2) has reported that no house in the village had a latrine or a separate bathroom. However, a proposal for construction of community latrines had been sanctioned by the Zilla Parishad and construction was to start the next year.

Anil Kumar had found in Hebasur village of Dharwar district (1989-90, p. 2) that all the houses in the village had bathrooms as an integral part of the house, but only few had latrines because of the age old practice of going out in the open for defecation. Even then, Anil's finding of a bathroom in every dwelling unit is rather matchless: no other study report has found so many bathrooms.

In the same district, Nagambika has recorded for Narendra village, which is quite close (8 kms) to Dharwar City, that, "Because of open drainage and lack of latrines, typhoid is prevalent. The sanitary condition in Harijan cheri is similar to that of the other places" (1990-91).

In Timmapur village of Dharwar district, Subhash (1987-88)

had reported that, "There are no public latrines and the ones that were constructed by the Land Army on an individual site lies unused. Consequently, roads and lanes in the village are like open lavatories. The sanitary conditions in the SC area are particularly bad.

In Bijapur district, Basavaraju noted (Malapur village, 1989-90, p. 23) that, "There is no drainage facility in the village. People use open area for toilet purposes..."

Ramana Reddy reported in Basolli village of Uttara Kannada district (1989-90, p. 2) that none of the houses had proper bathrooms and they did not have latrines either.

In another village, Chittakula, of Uttara Kannada district, Chawla (1988-89, p. 37) reported gross inadequacy of latrines, though he has not indicated the exact position as it existed.

Bangalore Division

In case of Bellambari village of Kolar District, Shalini (1990-91, p. 3) had noted that most of the houses did not have attached bathroom and latrine facilities and that there was no planned system of drainage and for disposal of sewerage.

In Solur village of Bangalore Rural District, Gauri found that though the total population was 2800, yet the facilities like latrines and bathrooms were woefully inadequate, except for a small Christian Missionary Project area called Jerusanagar (1988-89, p.3).

In Amruthur village of Tumkur District, Manjula (1988-89) noted that 77 per cent of the sampled households had no household latrines, whereas 100 per cent of SC/ST households lacked this facility (p.14).

Gulbarga Division

Gulbarga division seems to be no better in respect of toilet facilities for the people in the rural areas. In fact, the few reports that were available, showed a rather worse situation.

Rakesh Singh has recorded in Kamalapur that this major village had a poor drainage system. There were very few latrines and people went out for defecation, while children used the roadsides for the purpose (1990-91, p. 16, para IV).

Vidyavathi too has alluded to poor drainage system in Miriyan village of Gulbarga district (1992-93, para 11).

In Bagur village of Raichur district, Basker (1984-85) writes about the condition of sanitation thus: "Though the village lacks drainage facilities, yet the bylanes are clean and well maintained. Unhygienic conditions prevailed in the harijanwada."

A similar observation is made by A.K. Tiwari in Chandrabanda village of Raichur district (1991-92). He records the "total absence of ventilation and sanitation inside the house. The fields around the house are used for the calls of nature (p.17). The village awfully lacks sanitation facilities. The existing drains are not well made and pigs roam about in the village. The scenario is turned worse by the road-side relieving habits of the people. Recently, one public toilet for women has been constructed, but it has no clear-cut drainage facility, nor is the running water facility available nearby" (p. 10).

In Halabarga village of Bidar district, Umesh had noted that out of a total of 321 houses, only three had bathroom and lavatory facilities (1982-83, p. 2).

A very detailed account of toilet facilities in a large village is given by Raj Kumar Khatri in Sreedharagadda village of Bellary district (1989-90). Out of the total 850 houses in the village, bathrooms existed in 41 and toilet in only 7. Of the 41 bathrooms, the largest number (15) was found in the houses of Lingayats, followed by those of the Valmikis (10) and Medars, or Bamboo-weavers (7). In respect of the toilets in the dwelling units, of the seven toilets, six were in the houses of the Lingayats and one in that of a goldsmith (p. 2). None of the 175 houses of the SCs had either a bathroom or a toilet.

An instance of government intervention in this respect is found in the report of Laxminarayana in Sirwar village of Bellary district (1988-89, p. 8). He notes that, "People go to the fields or road-sides to answer nature's call. Recently, the Zilla Panchayat had constructed a common latrine for women, but its maintenance is pathetic, especially for want of water.

Conclusion

Several conclusions can be drawn. One is that there is a great need to launch a rural sanitation programme including individual as well community latrines. Women are the biggest sufferer in the existing situation.

The second is to improve the delivery system for construction and maintenance of such schemes. The PRIs on the one hand and the beneficiaries on the other, need to be brought in as co-partners in planning, implementing and monitoring such programmes.

Lastly, awareness among the population is to be generated about sanitation programmes, so that they also create demand for such programmes and participate in its management/maintenance. A rural sanitation programme, that is thrust upon the people, may not click, as most of the study reports have indicated.

4. IMPLEMENTATION OF MINIMUM WAGES ACT FOR AGRICULTURAL LABOURERS

The provision of Minimum Wages Act in respect of agricultural labourers has been examined by the probationers. Their reports are being analysed here to examine the following questions:

(a) What was the prevalent wage rate *vis-a-vis* the prescribed minimum wages?
(b) Was there a gender bias in the wage structure?
(c) What were the constraints, if any, in implementing the minimum wage laws?

Many probationers have not given the number of workers interviewed by them before reporting the prevalent wages. In such cases, one gets a feeling that the report was based on rather inadequate impressions. Yet, the overall picture emerging from a set of such reports is expected to provide a reasonably accurate picture.

Some of the key issues emanating from the study reports are shown in Table 4.12. Thereafter, a more detailed analysis from each report is presented.

Wages Paid *vis-a-vis* the Statutory Minimum Wages

During the study period, i.e. 1983-84 to 1993-94, the statutory minimum wages rose from Rs. 5 to Rs. 12 per day. During this period, the Government also launched the National Rural Employment Programme (NREP) and the Rural Landless Labourers Employment Guarantee Programme (RLEGP). In the early 1990s, these two programmes were merged to start the Jawahar Rozgar Yojana (JRY). These employment programmes were aimed at providing gainful employment to the rural poor during the lean agricultural seasons for upto 100 days in a year, thereby creating durable assets useful to the local people. The study reports have shown perceptible gap between the legally prescribed minimum wages and the wages actually prevalent rural areas. Of the 46 study reports, 31 have given statistical information in this regard, which is enlisted in the table below :

The above information, which has come from 31 of the 46 study reports, can be consolidated in Table 4.13, as follows :

Table 4.13 : Consolidated picture of the wage situation

	Total	Mysore	Belgaum	Bangalore	Gulbarga
No. of villages reported	31	11	7	4	9
No. of villages where actual wages paid were found to be less than the statutory M.W.	16	3	4	3	6
No. of villages where more than the statutory minimum wages were paid	15	8	3	1	3

Let us now analyse the situation by Revenue Divisions and districts.

Mysore Division

In Mysore Division, three of the studied villages of the coastal district of the Dakshina Kannada — one in the coffee-rich district

Table 4.12 : Minimum wages : Certain key issues as noted in the studied villages

Village	District	Year of study	Prescribed Min wages (per day) for dry land agri. labourers (Rs.)	Wages in vogue as per study Reports (Rs.)	Gender bias noticed	Awareness among the people
1	2	3	4	5	6	7
Mysore Division						
Mysore District :						
1. Deveeram manahally	Mysore	1983-84	5	M:8,F:6 (1981 data)	Yes	N.A.
2. Varuna	-do-	1989-90	12	M:12to15 F:10to12	Yes	Fair
3. Harohalli	-do-	1992-93	12	M:10 F:10	No	N.A.
4. M.H.Hally	-do-	1987-88	10	M:10,F:6	Yes	N.A.
5. Jothigowdanpura	-do-	1986-87	10	8 to 25	Yes	N.A.
6. Nekkilady	D.K.	1988-89	12	M:15,F:12 (+Meal)	Yes	N.A.
7. Kutethur	-do-	1991-92	12	25 to 30 (+Meals)	N.A.	N.A.
8. Vandse	-do-	1990-91	12	M:26-28 F:13-15	Yes	N.A

(Contd.)

Table 4.12 : (Contd.)

1	2	3	4	5	6	7
9. K K Halli	Mandya	1990-91	12	M:15;F:10 (+Tea&Meal)	Yes	N.A.
10. Bukinakere	-do-	1992-93	12	M:20 to 25 F:10 to 15	Yes	N.A.
11. Pura	Chikmagalur	1991-92	12	M:15;F:12	Yes	N.A.
Belgaum Division						
1. Chittakula	Uttar Kannada	1988-89	12	18 to 20	No	No
2. Basolli	-do-	1989-90	12	M:12-15 F:10-12	Yes	Yes
3. Hebsur	Dharwar	1988-89	12	M:18,F:4to8	Yes	No
4. Narendra	-do-	1990-91	12	M:10-15 F:8-10	Yes	Yes
5. Jamboti	Belgaum	1990-91	12	M:10-12 F:8-9	Yes	N.A.
6. Amatur	-do	1989-90	12	M:15-20 F:12-15	Yes	N.A.
7. Katgeri	Bijapur	1990-91	12	8 to 12	N.A.	No
Bangalore Division						
1. Amruthur	Tumkur	1988-89	12	M:10-20 F:8-10	Yes	N.A

(Contd.)

Table 4.12 : *(Contd.)*

1	2	3	4	5	6	7
2. Byadanur	Tumkur	1989-90	12	In-season 8 to 10 off season 8 to 15	N.A.	N.A.
3. Bellambari	Kola	1990-91	12	9 to 10	N.A.	N.A.
4. Agumbe	Shimoga	1993-94	12	M:35,F:25	Yes	N.A.
Gulbarga Division						
1. Sirwar	Bellary	1988-89	12	Season 8 to 10 Off Season 6 to 8	N.A.	No
2. Sreedharagadda	-do	1989-90	12	8 to 14	N.A.	N.A.
3. Kurugodu	-do	1986-87	10	M:8to10 F:6to8	Yes	N.A.
4. Bagur	Raichur	1984-85	10	M:5to6 F:3to4	Yes	N.A.
5. Chandrabanda	-do	1991-92	12	12 to 15	N.A.	No
6. Kamalapur	Gulbarga	1990-91	12	M:20,F:15	Yes	N.A.
7. Miryan	-do-	1992-93	12	M:20,F:15	Yes	N.A.
8. Malkhed	-do-	1986-87	10	7 to 8	N.A.	N.A.
9. Halbarga	Bidar	1982-83	5	M:12,F:8	Yes	N.A.

of Chickmagalur and two in the highly irrigated district of Mandya — and two of the five studied villages of Hassan district, reported more than the statutory minimum wages being paid to the rural agricultural labourers. The possible causative factors for this positive situation could be as follows.

The Dakshina Kannada economy itself is such that wage rates in all sectors are high. Beedi rolling, for instance, which gives good income to workers while sitting at home, dissuades the rural poor from working for any poor wage in agricultural activities. It is estimated that every third household in rural areas is engaged in beedi rolling, in the coastal belt.

As regards Chickmagalur, though the studied village, Pura, itself was not growing coffee, yet the report indicates that the high wage rates available in the coffee-economy in the same district as well as in the neighbouring districts of Hassan and Kodagu influenced the wage rates in Pura also. There is, however, a strong seasonality in the labour wage economy. In his study report, Gaurav Gupta (1991-92, pp. 12-13) states that the wage rates were Rs. 15 for male workers and Rs.12 for female. He further states that, "The seasonal factors tremendously influence the wage rate. In the coffee picking season, i.e. from December to January, there is a significant rise in the demand for labour in the (neighbouring) Malnad terrain of the district. At the same time comes the harvesting season for the 'Hingaru' (i.e. the second or Rabi) crop in the village. As a consequence of both these factors, the wage rates in the village shoot up seasonally to Rs. 20 for male workers and Rs.18 for the female. Unemployment is also seasonal. From February to April, many are unemployed. In other months too, there may be days in which no work is available to agricultural workers. The total number of days of employment available to a worker would be close to 100 days in year."

In Dakshin Kannada district, though the wage rates are high, being double or even more than the statutory minimum, yet, there is a strong seasonal effect. A special feature of this district is the culture of paying wages in form of grains and the additional facilities offered to workers such as meals and coffee. Though these facilities are offered in some other districts too, but not as an additional wage, usually. Some instances are stated below, taken from the three reports of this district :

(a) In Nekkilady, Ajay Seth (1988-89) has reported (pp. 14-15) that, "A male agricultural labourer gets Rs.15 plus a meal per day, whereas a woman gets only Rs.12 plus a meal. Agricultural operations within the village offer employment for nearly 100 days in a year for all the agricultural labourers.The labourers who go to Uppinangadi village (2 kms. from Nekkilady, on the National Highway) to work as coolies, get Rs. 15 to 20 per day, and they manage to get employment for at least 200 days in a year."

(b) In the same district, Jawaid Akhtar (1990-91) has reported in Vandse village that: "Wage rates of for male workers vary from Rs. 26 to 28 per day. In case of females, the wage rates are between Rs 13 and Rs. 15 per day, but they are generally paid in kind at the rate of 7 seers of paddy per day, which comes to about twelve rupees. Lean periods are the months of January, March and April."

(c) In a later year (1991-92), Kapil Mohan found in Kutethur village of this district (p.28) a specific work-wage norm which is reproduced in Table 4.14.

Table 4.14 : The prevailing agricultural wage rates and terms in Kutethur village of Dakshin Kannada District (1991-92)

Sl No.	Type of Work	Daily wages Cash/Kind	Additional facilities to the worker	Work hours
1.	Ploughing, tilling, carrying seedlings	Rs.25/30 or 5 seers of rice	1 meal 2 coffee	7.00 to 5.30 (1 hour break)
2.	Transplanting, harvesting and threshing	3 seers of rice	1 meal 2 coffee	8.00 to 5.30 (2 hour break)

In Kutethur, thus, we find a wage environment very favourable for the working class. Kapil has, however, not discussed other issues such as gender bias or awareness about the Minimum Wages Act etc.

Sivasailam's study in Jothigowdanapura Village of Mysore District (1986-87, p.5) has noted a link between the land reforms and agricultural labour economic practices. According to him, the traditional practice of payment of wages in kind was being replaced by payments in cash, due to interpretations of certain provisions relating to tenancy under the Land Reforms Act, 1961. Owing to the same reasons, he notes, agricultural employment was essentially on a seasonal basis, and continuous and permanent employment was discouraged. Sivasailam has also noted the high degree of seasonal fluctuation in wage rates: In the off-season, the wage rates for a male agricultural labourer could be as low as Rs. 8, while in the peak season, the same could be as high as Rs. 25.

In Mysore district, we thus notice a situation of somewhat lower than legal minimum wages prevailing, coupled with gender-based wage differentials. But the bigger problem seems to be the lack of employment opportunities available during the lean agricultural seasons. In respect of Mandya district, we have to note that in addition to NREP etc., the canal construction work was also in progress in one of the studied village, viz. Bukinakere. This factor had an effect on the wage structure as the contractors in the civil constructions offer wages linked to output, whereas the statutory minimum wages are not linked to output. In agricultural operations, there is no declared link between output and wages, but the employer does determine the wage to be paid depending on the capacity of the labourer to show output (Nilaya, Bukinakere village, 1992-93, pp. 33-35).

Belgaum Division

Only few of the study reports from Belgaum division have discussed this aspect. The coastal district of Uttar Kannada showed prevalence of higher than statutory minimum wages in both the studied villages, for which reasons are quite akin to those discussed above for Dakshin Kannada district in Mysore Division. Proximity to urban centre in the case of one of these two villages led to the work force periodically migrating for better wages [Rajiv Chawla, Chittakula village, 1988-89 p. 45 (1)].

Bangalore Division

A situation similar to the one described above for Chittakula village of Mysore Division is noted in the Kesarmadu village of Tumkur district in Bangalore division by Rajneesh Goel (1987-88, p. 7).

In Tumkur district, in the study of Amruthur village by V. Manjula (1988-89), we find an interesting analysis of the Census data (Table 5 of her report), which is listed in Table 4.15 below:

Table 4.15 : Land as a source of livelihood in Amruthur village, Tumkur district (1988-89)

Census Year	Total main workers	Culti-vators	Agrl. Labourers	(2)+(3)	(4) as a pro-portion of (1)
(1)	(2)	(3)	(4)	(5)	
1971	1260	592	187	779	61%
1981	1531	474	432	906	59%

Thus, while the number of cultivators had gone down by 20 per cent during the decade 1971-81, the number of agricultural labourers had gone up by almost 150 per cent.

In the highly rainfed Agumbe village of Shimoga district, where paddy is the most prevalent crop, Anshu had found very high wage rates prevailing in agriculture causing difficulties in getting workers for other employment programmes such as the JRY. "The offered wage in JRY is Rs. 16 per day while if they work as agricultural labourers, they get upto Rs. 30, plus afternoon meals. So there are no takers for JRY."

Gulbarga Division

In Gulbarga division, out of nine villages studied, six showed that the wages being paid were below the statutory minimum. In this division, Bellary is a very dry district with neither any significant irrigation project (except for the Tungabhadra project in the northern parts), nor does the district receive much rainfall. However, Laxminaryana reports that in Sirur village of Bellary Taluka, labourers did not prefer to go out of village in search of employment, even for the NREP or RLEGP works (1988-89, p. 10). Similar observation is made by Parmesh in Kurugodu village of this taluk (1986-87, p. 4). In the same taluk of Bellary, Khatri studied Sreedhargadda village, just 7 kms. from Bellary City, and found that in the lean season, the rural labourers cut the bushes (called 'Jali') to sell in the city as firewood (1989-90).

Deodurg and Raichur are among those talukas of Raichur district which are, in good parts, irrigated by the Tungabhadra Project. However, the villages studied in these talukas, were almost totally dry.

In case of Bagur village of Raichur district, Basker explains the existing position as follows (pp. 15-16): "Agricultural wages are mostly given in the form of cash but rarely in kind. The rates vary according to season and are also based on sex. During the summer season and when the crops are standing the rate is much lesser than that given during harvesting and ploughing. For weeding jobs, the labourers are paid less. Children also work as labourers and are paid between Rs. 2 and 3. It is only during the peak season that work is available in plenty, otherwise under-employment prevails and during the summer season, the labourers go without work."

Basker has presented the wage rate situation in the form of as following Table 4.16 (Table XIII of his report):

Table 16 : Daily wage rates and seasonal fluctuations, Bagur village (Raichur district, 1984-85)

	Male	Female
I. Season :		
June-August Oct-Dec Mar-Apr	Rs. 6	Rs. 4
II. Off-Season :		
Mid Aug-Mid Oct Mid Dec-Mid Feb Mid Apr-Mid Jun	Rs. 5	Rs. 3
III. Children	Rs. 2 – 3	

As for the caste and gender composition of the workers, Basker mentions that both men and women of the lower and intermediate castes worked in fields, whereas Lingayat women stayed indoors.

In Chandrabanda village of Raichur District, Atul K. Tiwari

found the prevailing agricultural wage rate to be between Rs. 12 to 15 and that no case of bonded labour was found or reported. He further reports that people were not aware of the technicalities of the Minimum Wages Act and cases under the Act were very rarely booked.

Of the three reports from Gulbarga district, two give an impression that the wages prevalent were higher than the statutory minimum wages. However, a closer scrutiny will reveal that it was only for key agricultural operations that such higher wages were provided. The normal agricultural wages were well below the prescribed minimum wages. Secondly, the gender differential appears to be so common that it seems to have been accepted even by the probationers.

In a relatively older report from Bidar District (Halbarga Village), V. Umesh (1982-83) has quoted (p. 11) from a DRDS survey of 1981, when the statutory minimum wages were Rs. 5 per day, that there were 75 families of agricultural labourers. Majority of these labourers were daily wages workers, though some were on monthly wages and few on annual payments. The prevailing wage rates were as follows :

Daily Wages : Men: Rs. 5; Women : Rs. 3
Monthly Wages : Men: Rs. 150; Women : Rs. 90
Annual Wages : Rs. 1800 to 2000 (Men only)
Very few were being paid in kind.

The net picture in Gulbarga Division is thus of a very low wage rate, violation of Minimum Wages Act and Equal Wages Act, and very high degree of seasonality in the availability of private agricultural employment. Awareness among the workers and the public also appeared to be very low in these districts.

Gender Bias in Wages

Equal wages for equal work and no differentiation between men and women in regard to payment of wages is a legal as well as Constitutional mandate. But in a significantly high majority of cases studied, the gender based wage differentiation was noticed, as could be seen from the following consolidated Table 4.17.

Table 4.17 : Gender bias in usual agricultural wages in rural Karnataka

No. of villages studied	46
No. of villages in which gender bias was noticed	21
No. of villages in which no gender bias was noticed	02
No. of villages in which the issue of gender bias was not analysed	3

Absence of gender based wage-differentiation was noticed in only two of the 46 villages studied. These villages were Harohalli of Mysore District (Vandana, 1992-93) and Chittakula of U.K. district (Rajiv: 1988-89). No specific reasons can be assigned for these two cases, nor, have the study reports given any reason.

In general, however, gender differentiation seems to be widespread, so much so that most of the probationers appear to have accepted it as a fact of life and have not analysed it in detail. Some probationers have, however, made interesting observations in this regard. For instance, Nilaya, who studied Bukinkere village of Mandya District (1992-93), states thus: "The concept of equal wages has not come to the village and it is violated without compunction (except in arecanut cutting and stone crushing). Even within a labourer's family, the male labourers were opposed to the idea of equal wages as they live in a notional world that they can work more and better than their wives/sisters/daughters."

Conclusions

(a) Of the 46 study reports examined, the fact as to whether the wages actually paid were more or less than the statutory minimum wages, was analysed in 31 reports only. Of those 31 reports, 16 found the actual wages being paid to be less than the statutory minimum, whereas 15 found it to be otherwise.

(b) There seems to be no conscious attempt by the employers to adhere to the statutory minimum wages, though it is quite apparent that in a hidden manner, the statutory minimum wages have been acting like unseen hands to strongly influence the wage structure that prevails.

(c) In overt manner, the wages rates are being determined by the market forces of supply and demand. Wherever, for instance, the alternative sources of high wage employment are available either in the same village or even in the vicinity, the prevailing agricultural wages go up. To cite instances, beedi rolling in Dakshina Kannada district, canal construction works, coffee cultivation etc.

(d) The wage rates also go up with the capacity of the employee to pay. For instance, in paddy or sugarcane growing areas, the employers have been found to be paying much above the statutory minimum wages.

(e) The wage rates prevailing for the agricultural labourers in the open market are highly seasonal in nature. Most studies have reported that employment was available to agricultural labourers in field for just about 100 to 150 days. In fact, the wage rates quoted by all the studies refer to this period only. What happens to the rural labourer outside this period? Some studies have reported that the rural work force migrates to cities. But in many instances workers are unable to migrate and remain in the village doing odd jobs, surviving on sporadic income. It is here that the role of employment schemes such as the EAS, JRY, NREP on the one hand and of self-employment schemes such as IRDP and TRYSEM on the other, come into play.

(f) Very few of the study reports have confirmed that the employment programmes, such as JRY, were being tuned carefully so as to match the lean period of agricultural operations. In fact, most studies have revealed that there is an unhealthy competition between the agricultural employment and the employment programmes, as both run concurrently. It is noticed that April to June being lean agricultural season, they also mark the beginning of new financial year, when the project reports are being studied and funds and approvals are not finalised. By the time these are done, it is July when the agricultural sowing operation begin. This situation has adversely affected the employment programmes also, as they suffer from lack of availability of workers. The need is, therefore, to finetune the employment programmes so that they are run during the agricultural lean season.

(g) Gender bias is very much prevalent in market wages, though it is legally banned. Women continue to get lesser wages than men. The popular justification for this situation is that the work output of women is less than that of men.

(h) Workers are not aware about wage related laws, especially regarding minimum wages and equal wages. Such awareness needs to be created not only among the workers but also among the employer (agricultural land holders) as well as among the government staff.

(i) Violation of the Minimum Wages and the Equal Wages laws is not being taken to the designated courts of law. This has led to loss of credibility of these legislations. A drive needs to be undertaken to enforce these legislations. Government and non-government functionaries both should be involved in these efforts.

(j) Caste-based wage differentiation was not found in the study reports, at least wherever it has been analysed, though indirectly.

5. SOCIAL DISCRIMINATION AGAINST THE SCHEDULED CASTES

The Constitution prohibits social, economic and religious discrimination on the grounds of caste. Several laws such as the Prevention of Untouchability Act, Protection of Civil Rights Act, and the Scheduled Castes and Scheduled Tribes (Prevention of Atrocities) Act have been enacted to effectively prevent any discrimination and oppression to the Scheduled Castes.

The study reports have given fair degree of attention to the practices in vogue in this regard in the surveyed villages. What is interesting is to find that some regions of the state, particularly the districts of Mysore Division exhibit high prevalence of caste-based discrimination against the Scheduled Castes. Such discrimination was found to be the least in the district of Belgaum

Division. In other two divisions, it did exist, but only slightly. A more detailed division-wise analysis follows:

Mysore Division

From Mysore District, we have three reports which have given fairly clear attention to this issue. Of them, two have found no overt practice of untouchability in the sense that the SCs were allowed open access to temples, hotels and other public places (D.M. Halli and Varuna villages). The third report (Harohalli, by Vandana 1992-93), however, gives a strikingly different picture. In this village, the report notes that SCs were not allowed to enter the kitchen of the household of other castes. More significantly, the SCs were not allowed to enter the tea shops and *dhabas*. Separate cups and plates were kept for the SCs: "They use them, wash them and are expected to drink tea, etc. outside the *dhaba*. Nobody eats or drinks from the hands of the SCs. The older generation of SCs seem to have accepted this plight, but the younger generation is seething with anger and disgust" (pp. 82-84).

In Dakshin Kannada district, where the literacy rate is the highest, we have some interesting reports. From Kutethur (25 kms. from the sea coast), Kapil reports (1991-92, p. 43) that, "Rigid caste structure still prevails and SCs are not allowed to offer © at the Devasthanas or the Bhootasthanas, claiming the exemption as family deities. The SCs have to make do with their own Bhoothas." A similar report comes from Maravanthe, a coastal village in this district (Yogendra: 1986-87, p. 27). He reports, "In the open, no one discovers such differentiation, but at the private level it does exist. The SCs cannot take water from the caste well." Similar situation is reported from Vandse village in this district by Jawaid (1990-91, p. 34).

In Mandya District, the report of Nilaya for Bukinakere village is quite significant. This survey revealed that except for a few, majority of the households did not allow SCs to enter their houses, at least not in the kitchen. They would not drink tea or water from the hands of the SCs, much less dine with them. Even the backward classes, such as the dhobis, would not wash the clothes of the SCs and the barbers would not cut their hair. For these services, the SCs would have to go to the nearby town. The local Venkataraman temple was officially open to SCs, but they did not use it. The SCs had their own Maramma Temple.

In Pura village in Chikmagalur District, Gaurav (1991-92, p. 22) found untouchability absent. The SCs were free to enter temples, hotels and other public places. However, in the neighbouring Hassan District, Sandeep found (Kandali village, 1988-89, p. 18) that there was a half-baked untouchability still prevalent. The local archak would perform *pooja* for the SCs also, but only from outside the house of the latter. The SCs were formally allowed entry into local temple, but they did not enter for fear of God. People did not take food from the SCs, but attended their functions.

Belgaum Division

In the coastal district of Uttar Kannada, Rajiv noted in Chittakula village (1988-89, p. 45) that the SCs were still treated as untouchables, though allowed entry into temples. Similar is the report from Basolli village in this district by Ramana Reddy (1989-90, p. 18) and in respect of Hebsur village of Dharwar district (Anil Kumar, 1988-89, p. 23), Timmapur village of Dharward district (Subhash, 1987-88, p. 80) and Narendra village of Dharwar district (Nagambika, 1990-91, p. 24).

In the Belgaum district, Anshuli reported from Jamboti village (1990-91, p. 26) that though untouchability was generally not prevalent and there was no bar on the SCs entering temples etc., yet, at the time of festivals, it was apparent: people belonging to the SCs sat together, away from the caste Hindus. Similar report has been made by S.D. Meena from Amatur village of this district (1989-90, p. 20).

In Anjutgi village of Bijapur district, Kumar Naik reported that though the SC families were concentrated in a specific area, there was no tendency to harass them on caste considerations. The SCs would go to tea stalls and use the same utensils as the others and take part in festivities together with other castes. However, the SCs did not visit the houses of caste Hindus during festivals.

Bangalore Division

Amathur village of Tumkur District, studied by Manjula in 1988-89 had a major communal clash just a year ago on the issue of entry of SCs into the village temple. At the time of her study, however, Manjula found tempers to have cooled down. But untouchability still existed, notionally at least. For instance, though the SCs were allowed entry into the village temple, they were wary of doing so. In the village proper, the village hotels provided services to the SCs in the same containers, but not so in the hamlet. The village barber and dhobi offered services to the SCs too.

In Byadanur village of Tumkur district, Jha has reported (1989-90, p. 11) that though untouchability was totally absent, the upper caste people did not dine with the SCs. But all shared the water sources, schools, etc.

In Solur village of Bangalore Rural district, Gauri Jha reported (1988-89) no case of social or economic discriminations against the SCs.

In Chitradurga district, Kharola found in Madekeripura (1986-87, p. 13) that untouchability was still practised in the village. Their housing was a separate block, their temples were separate. Though they could visit the village temples, they could not enter the 'garbha gruha'. But as far as social mixing was concerned, all persons mixed freely, especially the younger generation.

From Shimoga district, we have the report of Kamble in Mathur village (1987-88, pp. 11) which states that there were no instances of harassment of SCs. In Agumbe village also of this district, Anshu found no caste based tension (1993-94) and the SCs seemed to have accepted a submissive role.

Gulbarga Division

From Bellary District, the report of Laxminarayana in Sirwar village (1988-89, p. 12) found that untouchability was non-existent. The SCs indeed lived in a separate colony, but were not subject to any social discrimination. In the same district, in Sreedharagadda village, Khatri too found that the members of the SCs were allowed entry into temples, hotels and other public places, they were permitted to take water from public sources, worship the same tree as members of upper castes, send their children to same school, etc. However, Khatri noted some psychological discrimination to be still persisting (1989-90, p. 59).

In Raichur district (Chandrabhanda village), Atul found that the tea shops had separate utensils for the SCs and that their wells were different, even though they took part in all festivities (1991-92 p. 17). In another village, Bagur, in this district, Basker (1984-85, p. 26) noted that though untouchability was not practised overtly, yet the Madigas (SCs) were not allowed to enter the houses of the higher castes. By an established practice, Madigas drew water from an open well and other caste people from two borewells.

Coming to Gulbarga district, in Kamlapur, Rakesh (1990-91, p. 20) reported that untouchability was still seen. People interacted with the SCs but did not eat or drink in their houses. However, SCs were allowed to enter the temples and other public places on equal footing. There was no discrimination among the SCs themselves. However, in Miriyan village in this district, Vidyavathi (1992-93) found no situation of caste-based discrimination but only some underlying tension.

In Bidar district, Umesh reported in Halbarga village (1982-83, p. 36) that members of SCs were not treated as untouchables. They were allowed entry into temples, hotels and other public places. However, among the SCs themselves there was some discrimination. But he has not reported any situation of overt tension on caste considerations.

Conclusions

(a) The Constitutional provisions prohibiting social discrimination on grounds of caste, does not appear to have been imbibed fully by society, at least in so far as the SCs are concerned.
(b) The social discrimination against the SCs is declining in the rural parts, though with varying pace among different districts and regions.
(c) The remnant social discrimination is most visible in tea-

shops and temples.

(d) The popular notion that the educationally and economically progressive coastal districts of Dakshin Kannada and Uttar Kannada have got rid of untouchability altogether, is not true. The problem exists in these two districts more or less in the same degree as it is in the other districts of the state.

(e) The older generation among the SCs have by and large reconciled to the situation of the social discrimination. But the younger lot resents it consciously.

(f) In some cases, this social discrimination is quite subtle and requires careful probing to discover its dimensions.

(g) All in all, the social discrimination against the SCs is on the wane. It is quite apparent that if the legal, administrative and economic measures are continued, coupled with social efforts, the remaining edifice of social discrimination would wither away soon.

6. IMPACT OF RURAL DEVELOPMENT PROGRAMMES

We have already examined the status of certain specific development measures, such as rural housing, sanitation, minimum wage laws, land reforms laws etc. In this chapter, we shall analyse the impact of certain other important rural development programmes, such as the IRDP, NREP/JRY etc. Most of the study reports have not captured any solid statistical information to enable one to make a proper analysis of the impact of such programmes on the targeted beneficiaries. These reports have, however, made several empirical comments, which are significant.

The most important of such programmes is the IRDP, and it has accordingly been given maximum coverage by the study reports. This is followed by NREP (and later, JRY), housing schemes etc.

Integrated Rural Development Programme (IRDP)

The IRDP was launched in 1980 to provide direct assets to the rural poor families to improve their economic lot. The general impression prevailing in the country is that this scheme has been, by and large, a flop. However, the study reports give a mixed picture.

In Varuna village, Mysore district, all the 11 families were given assets such as pair of bullocks, goats, cows and petty business items. While all the 11 had benefited generally two had done extremely well. These two belonged to SCs and had been given a pair of bullocks each. Within a year, they repaid the loan of Rs. 1200 each (Jayanthi 1989-90, p 43).

In the same district, in Harohalli village, Vandana observed (1992-93, p.105) that under the IRDP, wherever the beneficiaries had actually bought the animals, they had gained a lot especially in case of sheep and goat, which multiplied very fast and fetched a good price in the market.

K. Shivaramu made 16 specific case studies of IRDP beneficiaries. In all cases, he found loans being repaid though with varying degrees of punctuality. In several cases, he found the animal to have died mid-project. Apparently, the cattle insurance scheme was not made use of. None of the beneficiaries seem to have been given any form of training in management of these projects, which could surely have accentuated the sad plight of some of them. On the whole the beneficiaries have generally secured positive economic benefits from the projects. These benefits are, however, not adequate to sustain the family. At best, the IRDP supplements the family income.

The question of sustainability of IRDP assets was proved by Ajay Seth in Nekkilady village of Dakshin Kannada district in 1988-89 (p. 23). He examined 15 beneficiaries of the years 1981 to 1986. Only one beneficiary (poultry unit) was sustaining his project since 1982. All others had sold off their units within a year or two, and repaid part of the loan amount from that sale realisation. Declining productivity was cited as the main reason for abandoning the project.

In Kutethur village, Dakshin Kannada district, Kapil made a study of 70 IRDP units (1991-92, Ch.19). The loans given were for irrigation wells and pumpsets (19), milch animal (12), petty business (37) and 'others' (4). Kapil has observed several deficiencies, of which the important ones are :

(a) More than 60 per cent of the beneficiaries had annual family income above the limit of Rs. 3,600.

(b) Recovery was just 6 per cent under ISB and 20 per cent overall.

(c) There were no personal visits to the beneficiaries by either the bank or government officials.

(d) Selection of beneficiaries through Gram Sabhas under the supervision of Mandal Panchayats had led to really poor families being selected.

(e) Banks were ill-motivated to participate proactively in this programme.

Kapil has also cited that three (of the total nine) ST families in the village had got IRDP loans four times each, in seven-year period, because of the imperfect procedure of selection of beneficiaries.

Mid-project collapse of the assets was noticed by Rajdeep also in Naravi village of Dakshin Kannada district (1989-90, p. 16), particularly in case of cross-bred cattle units, as these exotic imported animals could not bear the heat and humidity of the region. Another significant observation in this report is that most of the beneficiaries were from road-side households, who were comparatively richer.

Rajdeep and several other surveyors have noted that most beneficiaries were remiss in loan repayment and were in fond hopes of loan waiver schemes.

Though the IRDP guidelines provide for supplementary dose of assistance to the beneficiaries in majority of cases, it was not provided which thus failed to lift the beneficiaries above the poverty line (Jawaid, in Vandase village of D.K. district, 1990-91, para 19.2.4).

Recovery of IRDP loans has been found to be almost nil (5 per cent) by Nilaya in Bukinakere village of Mandya district (1992-93, p. 46). In fact, Nilaya found that recovery was less than 35 per cent in cases of loans sanctioned under all government sponsored schemes such as IRDP, DRI, SEEUY, whereas it was almost 100 per cent in case of schemes where banks extended loans directly. The reasons cited by Nilaya are that direct lending was given for more viable activities and the quantum of loan was also adequate.

In several cases, the beneficiaries feel that the IRDP loans are actually, not to be repaid at all (Gaurav, in Pura village, Chickmagalur district, 1991-92, p.19).

Lack of appropriate skills among the beneficiary families in managing the IRDP assets is cited as the chief reason for lack of success of the IRDP micro-enterprises by Atheeq, reporting from Hathikere in Uttara Kannada district (1992-93, Ch.VII). This would call for a systematic training programme for IRDP beneficiaries, howsoever, formidable it may appear it terms of number and variety.

In contrast, Ramana Reddy in Basolli village of the same district found that out of 13 IRDP beneficiaries, all except four were utilising the scheme. Subhash, in Timmapur village of Dharwar district (1987-88, pp. 18-19), found that in about 70 per cent cases, the assets were maintained, while in the remaining cases, they were either partially sold out or had died. Subhash cites two reasons for the death of animals: one is the poor quality of the animal and second, the poor skills of the beneficiaries in managing such assets. Added reasons are lack of supporting infrastructure facilities such as drinking water, fodder, veterinary care, etc.

Subhash has also found that loan repayment was better in cases of ISB sector. But he makes a strong argument to diversify the kind of projects to be taken up under the IRDP (pp. 19-20). He has also recommended regular training of extension staff.

Poor maintenance of the project leads to poor returns, as observed by Nagambika in case of milch animals which yielded less than 2 litres a day (Narendra village Dharwar District, 1990-91, p. 26).

That the IRDP has certainly benefited the rural poor, is reported by Anshuli in Jamboti village of Belgaum district (1990-91, p. 28). She found that this programme had succeeded especially in cases of ISB sector such as basket and net weaving, she-buffaloes and I.P. sets.

In Kesaramadu village of Tumkur district, Rajneesh (1987-88) found most assets to be in good condition and yielding as much as Rs. 2000 per annum. Similar positive results are reported by Anil Jha from Byadanur village in this district (1989-90).

In Sirwar village of Bellary Taluk (Lakshminarayana, 1988-89) and in Kurugodu village of the same taluk, (Parmesh, 1986-87), the IRDP assets were found to be largely intact and paying. So was the case in Sreedhargadda village of the same taluk (Khatri, 1989-90) and in Kamalapur village in Gulbarga taluk (Rakesh, 1990-91, p. 22).

In Raichur district, which has the lowest literacy rate in the state, Atul reported zero repayment of loans and prevalence of corruption in the BDO office (1991-92, Chandrabanda village, p. 13).

Role of PRIs and Gram Sabhas in IRDP

Some of the study reports have commented on the role of the PRIs, in IRDP. Sivasailam studied this aspect in Jothigowdanapura village of Mysore district in the very first year (1987) of the new PRI set up. He noted a sincere yearning on the part of the Panchayat members to make a success of the programmes such as the IRDP and NREP.

Kapil in Kutethur village of Dakshin Kannada district (1991-92, Ch. 19), too has observed that more eligible (poor) families got selected for IRDP after the selection was done through Gram Sabhas under the supervision of the Gram Panchayats. Similar observation is made by Jawaid in Vandase village of this district (1990-91, para 19.2.4).

That the deficiencies in the process of selection of beneficiaries is reduced if the selection is made through Gram Sabhas, is noted also by Anil Kumar in Hebsur village of Dharwar district (1988-89, p. 25) also. He, however, sees a lot of nepotism in this process.

Conclusions

The reports make a number of observations. To summarise, the IRDP is a useful programme to help the rural poor. It has succeeded in some places and failed in some other. Sectorally speaking, in some villages sectors such as ISB or milch cattle, have succeeded, while the same is not the case in some other villages.

The net impression that we get from these reports is that to make IRDP more effective and efficient, the following set of recommendations need to be kept in view :

(a) Involvement of the beneficiaries in purchase of assets leads to better quality of asset being procured.

(b) Involvement of Gram Panchayats and Gram Sabhas in the selection of beneficiaries improves the quality of the selection process. However, Panchayat members need to be given orientation training in this respect.

(c) Fodder availability needs attention, particularly for marginal farmers and landless labourers who have been given milch cattle or other animal husbandry items under IRDP.

(d) Marketing arrangements such as milk routes under the Operation Flood have a direct positive bearing on the success of the micro enterprises that are sanctioned under the IRDP.

(e) While the success of dairy projects depended heavily on the availability of milk routes, the projects of sheep and goat units had no such dependence. These animals multiply very fast and fetch good price also. However, lack of availability of grazing lands is a concern.

(f) The insurance schemes for the various IRDP micro-projects need to be made more popular among the beneficiaries, considering the high rate of mortality of these assets and high degree of economic vulnerability of the beneficiary families.

(g) The beneficiaries need to be given training in management of assets, insurance procedures, loan repayment etc.

(h) Support infrastructure, such as veterinary care, needs to be made available more easily.

(i) The post-sanction interface between the beneficiary and sponsoring agencies needs to be made sustainable. Organisation of IRDP beneficiaries would be a good step in this respect.

(j) More varieties should be introduced in the types of micro-enterprises being assisted under the IRDP. The ISB sector needs to be given greater prominence in this regard.

(k) The strategy should be to make use of the available infrastructure, raw materials and markets, so as to make the gestation period small and to improve the viability of the project.

Other Employment Programmes

The earlier study reports have focused on the National Rural Employment Programme (NREP) as the key government sponsored rural employment programme. The later reports have examined the Jawahar Rozgar Yojana (JRY). However, all the reports, without exception, have examined only the assets created out of the NREP/JRY. The employment guarantee aspect of these programmes have not been touched at all.

Therefore, we can safely conclude that NREP and JRY are universally viewed predominantly as asset creation programme. Their role for ensuring employment to the rural poor, especially during the lean agricultural season is somewhat incidental in nature.

Most reports have noted that the assets created were: village roads, drainage, school building, anganwadi building, repairs to drinking water well etc., which have all helped the village. Several reports, cutting across the regions, have talked of better wages available outside the NREP/JRY fold and hence the import of workers for these programmes from outside. Many reports have noticed that these programmes are run when agricultural operations are also at their peak, which leads to shortage of local labour.

Therefore, it is necessary to schedule the rural employment programmes in such a way that they are run in full swing during non-agricultural seasons and are kept rather dormant during peak agricultural season.

The study reports have not alluded at all to the system of registration of job seekers, which is very much prescribed in the JRY manual. This aspect needs to be brought home among implementing agencies by giving them proper guidance and orientation training.

The following recommendations come out of the study reports in respect of the other employment programmes :

(i) The procedure of registration of job-seekers under the JRY should be popularised among both, the people and the programme implementation machinery.

(i) The JRY should invariably be implemented in such a way that its competition with the normal agricultural operation is minimised.

(ii) Involvement of village people should be given a continued thrust, for the purposes of programme planning, implementation as well as supervision.

8. DETAILS OF THE FORTY-SIX STUDY REPORTS

Village Name	District	Year	Officer Trainee
MYSORE DIVISION			
1. Deveerammanahally	Mysore	1983	I.R. Perumal
2 Varuna	-do-	1989	M.V. Jayanthi (Ms.)
3. Harohalli	-do-	1992	Vandana Gurnani (Ms.)
4. Brahmagiri	-do-	1988	G. Kalpana (Ms.)
5. Antharsanthe	-do-	1993	Uma Mahadevan (Ms.)
6. M.H. Hally	-do-	1987	K. Shivaramu
7. Jothigowdanapura	-do-	1986	N. Sivasailam
8. Nekkilady	Dakshina Kannada	1988	Ajay Seth
9. Kutethur	-do-	1991	Kapil Mohan
10. Maravanthe	-do-	1986	Yogendra Tripathy
11. Naravi	-do-	1989	Rajdeep Saxena
12. Vandse	-do-	1990	Jawaid Akthar
13. K.K. Halli	Mandya	1990	G.R. Baderia
14. Bukinakere	-do-	1992	Nilaya Mitash
15. Pura	Chikmagalur	1991	Gaurav Gupta
16. Sakrepatna	-do-	1987	Vandita Sharma (Ms.)
17. Kandali	Hassan	1988	Sandeep Dave
BELGAUM DIVISION			
18. Hattikere	Uttara Kannada	1992	L.K. Atheeq
19. Chittakula	-do-	1988	Rajiv Chawla
20. Basolli	-do-	1989	E.V. Ramana Reddy
21. Hebsur	Dharwar	1988	B.H. Anil Kumar
22. Salakinakoppa	-do-	1977	M.R. Sreenivasa Murthy
23. Thimmapur	-do-	1987	Subhash Chandra
24. Narendra	-do-	1990	N.Nagambika Devi (Ms.)
25. Jamboti	Belgaum	1990	Anshuli Arya (Ms.)
26. Amatur	-do-	1989	S.D. Meena
27. Katgeri	Bijapur	1990	Raj Kamal
28. Malapur	-do-	1989-90	B. Basavaraju
29. Anjutgi	Bijapur	1991	G. Kumar Naik

(Contd.)

Village Name	District	Year	Officer Trainee
BANGALORE DIVISION			
30. Amruthur	Tumkur	1988	V. Manjula (Ms.)
31. Byadanur	-do-	1989	A.K. Jha
32. Kesarmadu	-do-	1987	Rajneesh Goel
33. Solur	Bangalore Rural	1988	Gauri Jha (Ms.)
34. Madekeripura	Chitradurga	1986	P.S. Kharola
35. Bellambari	Kolar	1990	Shalini (Ms.)
36. Agumbe	Shimoga	1993	Anshu Bharadwaj
37. Mathur	-do-	1987	M.R. Kamble
GULBARGA DIVISION			
38. Sirwar	Bellary	1988	M. Laxminarayana
39. Sreedharagadda	-do-	1989	R.K. Khatri
40. Kurugodu	-do-	1986	Parmesh Pandey
41. Begur	Raichur	1984	H. Basker
42. Chandrabanda	-do-	1991	Atul K. Tiwari
43. Kamalapur	Gulbarga	1990	Rakesh Singh
44. Miryan	-do-	1992	V. Vidyavathi (Ms.)
45. Malkhed	-do-	1986	E. Venkataiah
46. Halbarga	Bidar	1982	V. Umesh

BIBLIOGRAPHY

Bhat, L.S. (1988), *Strategy for Integrated Area Development: Case Study of North Kanara District.* New Delhi: Concept Publishing Company.

Cariappa, M.P. and Cariappa, P. (1981), *The Coorgs and their origins,* Mysore: Geetha Book House.

Giriappa, S. (1987), *Bidi-rolling in rural development,* Delhi: Daya Publishing House.

Ismail, K. (1984), *Karnataka temples : Their role in Socio-economic life,* Delhi: Sundeep Prakashan.

Karnataka's Agriculture in the March 1913-1988, Bangalore, Department of Agriculture, Karnataka.

Janata experiment in Karnataka: five eventful years (1988), Bangalore, Government of Karnataka.

Madaiah, M. & Ramapriya, R. (1989), *Karnataka Economy: Growth, Issues and Lines of Development,* Bombay: Himalaya Publishing House.

Mane (1987), A new initiative in public housing for Karnataka's middle income and weaker sections, New Delhi : A HUDCO-Sandeep prints.

Menefee, Selden (1984), The Pais of Manipal, Manipal: The Academy of General Education.

Mukhopadhyay, Arun K. (1982), *Farmer's Services Societies: A Study in Karnataka.* Hyderabad: National Institute of Rural Development.

Muniramappa, C.M. (1982), Co-operative Marketing in Karnataka. Mysore: The Director, Prasaranga, Manasagangotri.

Naik, Murahari D. (1989), *Agrarian Unrest in Karnataka,* New Delhi: Reliance Publishing House.

Narayan, B.K. & Reddy M.V. (1987), Land Development and Water Management; Ghataprabha and Malaprabha Command Areas, Bangalore: Institute for Society and Economic Change.

Narayan, B.K. & Reddy, M.V. (1986), Not a Story but a Fact: Maharashtra-Karnataka Border Issue, Bombay: Directorate of General Information and Public Reliance.

Pani, Narendar (1983), *Reforms to Pre-empt Change: Land Legislation in Karnataka,* New Delhi: Concept Publishing Company.

Parthasarathy, Jakka (1984), *Rural Population in Indian Urban Setting,* Delhi: B.R. Publishing Corporation.

Prasad, H.Y. Sharada (1981), Exploring Karnataka, Bangalore: Department of Information and Publicity.

Rajapurohit, B.B. (1982), Acoustic characteristics of Kannada, Mysore: Central Institute of Indian Languages.

Ramu, G.N. (1989), *Women, Work and Marriage in Urban India: A Study of Dual and Single-Earner Couples,* New Delhi: Sage Publications.

Rao, L.S. Seshagiri (1983), *A History of Kannada Literature.* Bangalore:

Vishwa Kannada Sammelan.

Rao, N.J. Usha (1981), *Deprived Castes in India : A Profile of Karnataka*, Allahabad: Chugh Publications.

Shetty, B. Vasantha (1984), *Studies in Karnataka History*, New Delhi: Sterling Publishers (P) Ltd.

Singh, N.P. (1988), *Flora of Eastern Karnataka*, New Delhi: Mittal Publications.

Sivakumar, Chitra (1982), *Education, Social Inequality and Social Change in Karnataka*, Delhi: Hindustan Publishing Corporation.

Thimmaiah, G. and Aziz, Abdul, *The Political Economy of Land Reforms*, New Delhi: Ashish Publishing House.

Vivekananda, M. (1986), Rural Landless Employment Guarantee *Programme in Karnataka*: An Evaluation. Bangalore: Institute for Social and Economic Change.

Hill, Polly (1982), *Dry grain farming families*, Cambridge: Cambridge University Press.

Hill, Polly (1989), Karnataka, Significant Six Years: pledges redeemed, Bangalore: Directorate of Information and Publicity.

Khan, Mumtaz Ali (1980), *Scheduled Castes and their status in India*, New Delhi: Publishing Corporation of India.

Khan, Mumtaz Ali (1985), Characteristics of migrants into Karnataka, Bangalore: Planning Department.

Ahmed, Syed Thanvir (1994), Karnataka State: finances and economic reforms, *Southern Economist*, Vol. 33, No. (15&16), December 1&15.

Akki, Basavaraj N. (1993), Origin of municipal administration in princely state of Mysore, *Local Government Journal*, Vol. 64, No. 4, Oct.-Dec.

Ambrose, Pinto S.J. (1994), Atrocities on dalits in Gulbarga, *Economic and Political Weekly*, Vol. XXIX, No. 16&17, April 16.

Azer, Rahman (1994), Karnataka tourism, *March of Karnataka*, Vol. 32, No. 11, November.

Babu, M. Devendra (1991), Profiles of Industrial Backwardness, *Southern Economist*, Vol. 30, No. 13, November 1.

Baglodi S.S. (1991), Many abandoned Gold Mines all over Karnataka, *March of Karnataka*, Vol. 29, No.6, June.

Bhanu, T. (1995), Karnataka's dismal power scenario, *Financial Express*, New Delhi, April 18.

Bhanu, T. (1995), No longer pollution-free, *Financial Express*, New Delhi, July 7.

Bhargava, B.S. (1995), Political empowerment of women, *Political Economy Journal of India*, Vol. 3, No. 3&4, July-Dec.

Bhargava B.S. (1994), Working of Gram Sabhas in Karnataka, *Journal of Rural Development*, Vol. 13, No. 2, April-June.

Bhargava B.S. (1992), Panchayati raj in Karnataka, *Kurukshetra*, Vol. 40, No.4, January.

Bhat, M.G. (1993), Private property rights and forest preservation in

Karnataka Western Ghats, India. *American Journal of Agricultural Economics*, Vol. 75, No.2, May.

Bhat, M.G. and Huffaker, R.G. (1991), Property Rights and Forest Preservation, *American Journal of Agricultural Economics*, Vol.73, No.2, May.

Chachadi, N.G. (1994), Two decades of development in Karnataka, *Southern Economist*, Vol.33, No. 15&16, Dec 1&15.

Chakravartty, N. Mikhil (1992), Storm over Cauvery, *Mainstream*, Vol. XXX, No. 11, Jan. 4.

Chandrasekhar, B.K. (1991), Profile and particpation of women zilla parishad and mandal panchayat members, *Journal of Rural Development*, Vol. 10, No. 5, Sept.

Chaturvedi, Yogananda Sastry (1991), Nutritional Ecosystems: A Study in Two States, *Journal of Rural Development*, Vol. 10, No. 4, July.

Cowda, G. Nanjunda (1994), Karnataka economy - a comparative analysis, *Southern Economist*, Vol. 33, No. 15&16, Dec., 1&15.

Date, B.M. (1994), Recommendations of State Finance Commission - Karnataka, *Quarterly Local Government Journal*, Vol. 65, No. 3-4, July-Dec.

Deshpande, S.V. (1994), Administering land reforms in Karnataka, *Economic and Political Weekly*, Vol. XXIX, No. 33, August 13.

Deshpande, S.V. (1994), Impact of Karnataka 1974 land reforms act on the beneficiaries, *Southern Economist*, Vol. 32, No. 18, Jan. 15.

Dikshit, G.S. (1994), Irrigation tanks of Karnataka. *March of Karnataka*, Vol. 32, No. 11, November.

Engineer, Asghar Ali (1994), Bangalore violence, *Economic and Political Weekly*, Vol. XXIX, No. 44, Oct.

E.R. Gopinath (1991), Cauvery defies solution, *LINK*, Vol. 33, No. 53. Aug. 11.

Erappa S. (1995), IRDP : Experiences of SC/STs in Karnataka, *Southern Economist*, February 15.

Erappa, S. (1992), IRDP as catalyst for upliftment of Scs and STs, *Kurukshetra*, Vol. 40, No. 10, July.

Gadhari, J.P. (1991), Danger signals in Karnataka, *Link*, Vol. 33, No. 47, June 30.

Gadkari J.P. (1991), LTTE haunts Karnataka, *Link*, Vol. 34, No. 4, September 8.

Ganesh, Kumar N. (1994), Impact of cooperative credit on income and employment patterns in Dakshina Kannada district of Karnataka, *Indian Cooperative Review*, Vol. 31, No. 3, January.

Gayithri, K. (1993), Credit delivery in rural Karnataka. *Journal of Rural Development*, Vol. 12, No. 3, May.

Ghorpade, M.Y. (1993), Karnataka Panchayati Raj Act, 1993, *Southern Economist*, Vol. 32, No. 3, Jun. 1.

Ghorpade, M.Y. (1992), Karnataka Budget 1992-93, *Southern Economist*, Vol. 30, No. 22, Mar 15.

Girijesh, G.K. (1994), Social forestry progress in Karnataka, *Southern Economist*, Vol. 33, No. 15&16, Dec 1&15.

Gopalan, M. Santhana (1994), Banking scenario in Karnataka, *Southern Economist*, Vol. 33, No. 15&16, Dec. 1&15.

Gowda, Channe, (1991), Problems and Prospects of Sericulture in Karnataka, *Southern Economist*, Vol. 30, No. 13, Nov 1.

Gowda, D.T. Nanje, (1994), Karnataka's small and marginal holders' farming needs to be strengthened, *Southern Economist*, Vol. 33, No. 15&16, Dec. 1&15.

Gupta, A.R. Chandrahasa (1992), Karnataka Marches Ahead, *March of Karnataka*, Vol. 30, No. 8, Aug.

Hegde Pandurang (1995), Alien science spells doom for country's forests, New Delhi, *Pioneer*, Mar 31.

Hittamani, S.V. (1991), The precious 'drop' that matters in drip irrigation, *March of Karnataka*, Vol. 29, No. 4, April.

Hora, Vinoo (1992), Universalising primary education, *Mainstream*, Vol. XXX, No. 39, July 18.

Inamdar, Y.L. (1994), Agricultural wages and employment, *Southern Economist*, Vol. 33, No. 15 & 16, Dec. 1 & 15.

Jena, A.C. (1991), Panchayati Raj development administration, *Journal of Rural Development*, Vol. 10, No. 5, Sept.

Kalkundrikar (1991), Banking industry in Belgaum district, *Mysore Economic Review*, Vol. 76, No. 9, Sept.

Kamath, Suryanath U. (1991), Irrigation works in Pre-British days in Karnataka, *March of Karnataka*, Vol. 29, No. 6, June.

Kanaginahal, M.B. (1991), Integrated rural development programme in Dharwad district, Karnataka, *Indian Cooperative Review*, Vol. 29, No. 2, Oct.

Karanth, G.K. (1992), Privatisation of common Property resources, *Economic and Political Weekly*, Vol. XXVII, No. 31&32, Aug. 1-18.

Karnad, Girish (1994), The Idgah controversy in Hubli, *Mainstream*, Vol. XXXII, No. 42, Sept. 3.

Kerutagi, M.G. (1994), Problems of sericulture enterprises in Bijapur Dist., Karnataka, *National Bank News Review*, Vol. 10, No. 3. July-Sept.

Khare, Harish (1994), BJP and Muslims after Karnataka, Hindu, Dec. 7.

Kittur, A.T. (1992), The Mandal Panchayat Taxation, *Mysore Economic Review*, Vol. 77, No. 8, Aug.

Kripa, A.P. (1995), Karnataka : Raitha Sangha's political dilemma, *Economic and Political Weekly*, Vol. XXX, No. 3, Jan. 21.

Krishnaswamy, K.S. (1993), Panchayati Raj : Karnataka's new step backwards, *Economic and Political Weekly*, Vol. XXVIII, No. 18, May 1.

Leelavathi, D.S. (1994), Role of industrial estates in developing small scale industries in Karnataka, *Southern Economist*, Vol. 33, No. 15&16, Dec. 1&15.

Lele, Sharachchandra (1993), Private property rights and forest preservation in Karnataka Western ghats, India, *American Journal of Agricultural Economics*, Vol. 75, No. 2, May.

Mahadev, M. (1991), Foodgrains production in Karnataka, *The Mysore Economic Review*, Vol. 76, No. 10, Oct.

Mahadeva, M. (1991), An evaluation of housing schemes in Karnataka, *Southern Economist*, Vol. 30, No. 13, Nov. 1.

Mandanna, P.K. (1994), Agricultural economy : a case study of Kodagu district in Karnataka, *Southern Economist* (Annual Issue), May 1.

Mansur, Hasan (1992), Communalisation of politics and the 10th Lok Sabha elections in Karnataka, *Islamic Perspective*, Vol. 8, No. 1, Jan-Jun.

Mathew, George (1994), Karnataka political tragedy, New Delhi, *Hindu*, May 17.

Mathew, George (1993), Karnataka puts the clock back, New Delhi, *Hindu*, April, 19.

Mathur, J.S. *et al.* (1992), Physical and operational performance of road transport, *Southern Economist*, Vol. 31, No. 8, Aug 15.

Mattigatti Rabeendra (1991), Operation Flood Programme and Resource Use Efficiency in Karnataka, *Margin*, Vol. 23 No. 4, July-Sept.

Mendonca, Allen J. (1993), Where self-help is the best help, *Indian Express*, New Delhi, Nov 17.

Meti, S.K. (1994), Consumer cooperatives in educational institutions, *Cooperative Perspective*, Vol. 29, No. 1, April-June.

Murthy, C.G. Venkatesha (1993), A comparative study of criminals and non criminals of Karnataka with regard to their personality factors, *Social Defence*, Vol. 3, No. 113, July.

Murthy, H.G. Shankra (1990), Performance of Markfed, Karnataka, *Indian Cooperative Review*, Vol. 28, No. 2, Oct.

Nadkarni, M.V. (1991), Developing Uncultivated Lands, *Indian Journal of Agricultural Economics*, Vol. 46, No. 4, Oct-Dec.

Nadkarni, M.V. (1992), Social forestry projects in Karnataka, *Economic and Political Weekly*, Vol. XXVII, No. 26, June 27.

Naik, Gopal and Kalro, Amar H. (1991), Government Silk Filature, Chikkahalli, *Vikalpa*, Vol. 16, No. 3, July-Sept.

Nair, Janaki (1993), Badanavala killings : Signs for the dalit movement of Karnataka, *Economic and Political Weekly*, Vol. XXVIII, No. 19, May 8.

Nair, Janaki (1994), Kannada and politics of state protection, *Economic and Political Weekly*, Vol. XXIX, No. 44, Oct. 29.

Nanjundappa, D.M. (1994), Karnataka has immense tourism potential Karnataka's growth, *Southern Economist*, Vol. 33, No. 15 & 16, Dec. 1 & 15.

Narayana, K.S. Mohan (1991), Rural Development in Karnatka, *Yojana*, Vol. 35, No. 17, Sept. 30.

Narayanaswamy (1994), Sir Mark Cubbon's monumental regime, *March of Karnataka*, Vol. 32, No. 12, Dec.

Natraj, V.K. (1995), Karnataka : elections and after, *Economic and Political Weekly,* Vol. XXX, No. 2, Jan. 14.

Natraj, V.K. (1995), Karnataka: Steady advance to backwardness, *Economic and Political Weekly*, Vol. XXIX, No. 28, July 9.

Pasha, Syed Ajmal (1992), CPRs and rural poor, *Economic and Political Weekly*, Vol. XXVII, No. 46, Nov. 14.

Patil, A.P. Biradar (1991), Belgaum District, *Southern Economist*, Vol. 30, No. 13, Nov. 1.

Patil, R.L. (1993), Growth of population of Karnataka state, *Southern Economist*, Vol. 32, No. 8, Aug. 15.

Patil, R.L.M. (1992), Wanted political settlement, not court verdict, *Mainstream*, Vol. XXX, No. 28, May 2.

Pinto, Ambrose (1992), Caste conflict in Karnataka, *Economic and Political Weekly*, Vol. XXVII, No. 28, July 11.

Pinto, Ambrose (1995), Karnataka : Badanvalu-emerging dalit paradigm, *Economic and Political Weekly*, Vol. XXX, No. 15, April 15.

Pinto, Ambrose (1995), Karnataka : hoisting national flag at idgah maidan, *Economic and Political Weekly*, Vol. XXX, No. 5, Feb. 4.

Pinto, Ambrose (1994), Karnataka : politics of capitation colleges, *Economic and Political Weekly*, Vol. XXIX, No. 1&2, Jan. 1-8.

Pinto, Ambrose (1994), Karnataka : politics of reservation, *Economic and Political Weekly*, Vol. XXIX, No. 35, Aug. 27.

Pinto, Ambrose (1994), Karnataka Assembly elections, *Economic and Political Weekly*, Vol. XXIX, No. 53, Dec. 31.

Prahladachar, M. (1994), Insights for policy from Karnataka's experience, *Financial Express*, New Delhi, Jun 18.

R., Sri Ram (1992), Energy conservation in Irrigation pumpsets, *Urja*, Vol. 31, No. 4, April.

Rajarama, K.E.T., (1993), Pre-puberty marriages in Belgaum district of Karnataka, *Social Change*, Vol. 23, No. 1, March.

Ramachandra, T.V. (1991), Analysis of Energy Utilisation in the small scale industries in Karnataka, *Energy Management*, Vol. 15, No. 1, Jan.-March.

Ramiah, P. (1994), Action plan for the Krishna, *Hindu*, New Delhi, Aug. 30.

Ramiah, P. (1994), Karnataka's quota policy, *Hindu*, New Delhi, June 20.

Ramiah, P. (1994), Liquor lobby bottled? *Hindu*, New Delhi, July 5.

Ramiah, P. (1994), Reservation in Karnataka, *Hindu*, New Delhi, May 6.

Ramiah, P. (1994), Trial of strength? *Hindu*, New Delhi, May 1.

Ramoo, S.K. (1993), Doing and undoing in Karnataka, *Hindu*, New Delhi, March 5.

Ranganathan, V. (1991), Electricity Tariffs in Karnataka, *Economic and Political Weekly*, Vol. XXVI, No. 21, May 25.

Rangaswamy, N. (1993), Financing social services in Karnataka state, *Southern Economist*, Vol. 32, No. 14, Nov. 15.

Rannorey, D.K. Sainath Kumar (1994), Social forestry progress in Karnataka, *Kurukshetra*, Vol. 42, No. 6, March.

Rao, L.S. Seshagiri (1992), Kanada - Official Language, *March of Karnataka*, Vol. 30, No. 4, April.

Rao, Sri (1991), Educational reforms in Karnataka, *Mysore Economic Review*, Vol. 76, No. 12, December.

Rao, Sri (1991), Educational reforms in Karnataka, *Mysore Economic Review*, Vol. 76, No. 11, November.

Rayappa, P. Hanumantha (1993), Issues in tribal development, *Journal of Rural Development*, Vol. 12, No. 2, March.

Reddy, B. Muralidhar (1993), Whose game is it? *Hindu*, New Delhi, October 3.

Reddy, B. Sudhakara (1995), Transportation, energy and environment, *Economic and Political Weekly*, Vol. XXX, No. 3, Jan. 21.

Sethuram, E.R. (1993), Karnataka tackling problem of street children, *March of Karnataka*, Vol. 31, No. 7, July.

Shashikala, S. (1993), A study of silk marketing with reference to Silk Exchange in Karnataka, *Journal of Rural Development*, Vol. 12, No. 6, November.

Shastri, Sandeep (1994), Elections to the Lok Sabha from Karnataka, *Journal of Parliamentary Information*, Vol. 40, No. 3, September.

Shastri, Sandeep (1994), Karnataka : crisis management, *Mainstream*, Vol. XXXII, No. 15, February 26.

Shastri, Sandeep (1994), Karnataka assembly elections 1994, Southern *Economist*, Vol. 33, No. 14, November 15.

Shastri, Sandeep (1994), Looking back on Karnataka poll, *Mainstream*, Vol. XXXIII, No. 17, March 18.

Shastri, Sandeep (1991), The Dynamics of Electoral Politics, *Indian Journal of Social Sciences*, Vol. 4, No. 3, July-Sept.

Shenoy, P.D. (1992), Corporate turn-around in 400 days, *Journal of Institute of Public Enterprise*, Vol. 15, No. 1, March.

Shenoy, P.D. (1995), How the KSRTC saw a turnaround in 400 days, *Indian Journal of Transport Management*, Vol. 19, No. 3, March.

Shenoy, T.V.R. (1994), Just roll out the red tape, *Economics Times*, September 22.

Sheshadri, T. (1991), District Industries Centres, *The Mysore Economic Review*, Vol. 76, No. 10, October.

Shet, M. Muktha (1995), Socio-economic conditions of fishermen in Dakshina Kannada, *Southern Economist*, Vol. 33, No. 22, March 15.

Shivappa, H. (1992), Marketing of Groundnut, *Southern Economist*, Vol. 31, No. 1, May 1.

Shivappa, H. (1991), Cultivation of Groundnut and other competing Crops, *Southern Economist*, Vol. 30, No. 7, Aug 1.

Shukla, Rajiv (1994), Karnataka : rights of admission reserved, *Hindustan Times*, New Delhi, Nov 15.

Siddappa, B. (1993), Some suggestions to improve PDS in Karnataka, *Southern Economist*, Vol. 32, No. 7, August 1.

Singh, Katar (1991), Dryland Watershed Development and Management, *Indian Journal of Agricultural*, Vol. 46, No. 2, April-June.

Singh, Narendra (1992), Dalit and caste Hindu clashes in Karnataka, *Economic and Political Weekly*, Vol. XXVII, No. 3, Jan. 18.

Sitaraman, Sudha (1994), Karnataka - burdens of interpretation, *Economic and Political Weekly*, Vol. XXIX, No. 24, June 11.

Sriram, R. (1991), The Dichotomy of Environmental Concern, *Urja*, Vol. 30, No. 1, July.

Subrahmanya, K. (1991), Bangarappa collectivism, *Link*, Vol. 34, No. 11, October 27.

Subrahmanya, K. (1992), Cauvery dispute takes a dangerous drift, *Link*, Vol. 34, No. 21, Jan. 5.

Subrahmanya, K. (1991), Cauvery issue backfires on Bangarappa, *Link*, Vol. 34, No. 17, Dec. 8.

Syed, Thanvir Ahmed (1993), Karnataka's budget recognises need for fiscal reforms, *Southern Economist*, Vol. 31, No. 23&24, April 1-15.

Tandon, B.N. (1994), Community participation in the management of ICDS projects, *Southern Economist*, Vol. 32, No. 17, Jan. 1.

Thimmaiah, G. (1994), Karnataka's patchwork reservation policy, *Times of India*, Aug. 11.

Thippaiah, P. (1994), Estimation of informal sector in an industrially backward, *Southern Economist*, Vol. 33, No. 3&4, June 1 & 15.

Tilak, Jandhyala B.G. (1994), The pests are here to stay : capitation fee in disguise, *Economic and Political Weekly*, Vol. XXIX, No. 7, Feb. 12.

Upadhyay Madhu (1995), Job generation through rural industries, *March of Karnataka*, Vol. 33, No. 2, Feb.

Upendranadh, C. (1994), Industrial growth and structure, *Economic and Political Weekly*, Vol. XXIX, No. 48, Nov. 26.

Vaikunthe, L.D. (1991), Agricultural cooperative Credit, *Indian Cooperative Review*, Vol. 29, No. 1, July.

Veerashekerappa (1994), Determinants of institutional credit flow to agriculture, *Journal of Rural Development*, Vol. 13, No. 3, July-Sept.

Vishveshwar (1994), Precious forests of Karnataka, *March of Karnataka*, Vol. 32, No. 11, Nov.

Viswanath, A.R. (1992), Agricultural Credit & Overdues problem of PACS in Karnataka Mysore, *Economic Review*, Vol. 77, No. 1, Jan.

Ambedkar (Yadav), J.B. (1992), *Communication and rural development: a village of North Karnataka*, New Delhi: Mittal Publications.

Mutbiab, S. (1992), *Splendour of South India*, New Delhi: UBS Publishing Distributors Pvt. Ltd.

Mutbiab, S. (1989), State Manpower profile study: Seventh five year plan, Banglore: Manpower and Employment Division.

Mutbiab, S. (1993-94), Karnataka's economy in brief, Bangalore,

Directorate of Economics and Statistics, Karnataka.

Karnataka at a glance (1994), Bangalore, Directorate, Economics & Statistics, Karnataka.

Karnataka Panchayat Raj Act, 1993, Mysore, Department of Law & Parliamentary Affairs, Karnataka.

Moraes, Dom (1976), The open eyes : a journey through Karnataka, Bangalore, The Directorate of Information and Publicity, Karnataka.

Moraes, Dom (1992), Evaluation of the training imparted to women in electronics trade in industrial training institutes, Bangalore: Manpower and Employment Division, Planning Department, Karnataka.

Krishan, M.G.(1992), Panchayati raj in India : an analytical study of Karnataka, New Delhi: Mittal Publications.

Karnataka Mandal Panchayat members' social background (1990), New Delhi: Institute of Social Sciences.

A paper on women employment in Karnataka (1989), Bangalore, Planning Department, Karnataka.

Singh, Katar (1988), Managing dry land watershed development programmes : Lessons of Karnataka experience, Anand: Institute of Rural Management, Anand.

Rajan, M.A.S. (1979), Land reforms law in Karnataka: Description of context and relationships, Bangalore: Government Press.

Directorate of Census Operations, Karnataka (1981), Census handbook of Kolar district, Bangalore.

Directorate of Census Operations, Karnataka (1981), Census handbook of Tumkur district, Bangalore.

Directorate of Census Operations, Karnataka (1981), Census handbook of Mandya district, Bangalore.

Directorate of Census Operations, Karnataka (1981), Census handbook of South Karnataka district, Bangalore.

Directorate of Census Operations, Karnataka (1981), Census handbook of Bijapur district, Bangalore.

Kamath, Suryanath U. (1981), Gazetteer of India: Karnataka State Gazetteer, Bangalore rural district, Bangalore: Government of Karnataka.

Kamath, Suryanath U. (1981), Gazetteer of India: Karnataka State Gazetteer, Uttara Kannada district, Bangalore: Government of Karnataka.

Kamath, Suryanath U.(1981), Gazetteer of India: Karnataka State Gazetteer, Belgaum district, Bangalore: Government of Karnataka.

Kamath, Suryanath U. (1981), Gazetteer of India: Karnataka State Gazetteer, Mysore district, Bangalore: Government of Karnataka.

Kamath, Suryanath U. (1981), Gazetteer of India: Karnataka State Gazetteer, Bangalore district, Bangalore: Government of Karnataka.

Kamath, Suryanath U. (1991), Irrigation works in Pre-British days in Karnataka, *March of Karnataka*, Vol. 29 No. 6, June.

Controller and Auditor General of India, Report of the Comptroller and Auditor General of India for the year ended 31st March 1988 No.

5 (Civil), Bangalore: Government of Karnataka.

Agriculture population in Karnataka (1981), Bangalore, Department of Agriculture, Karnataka.

Energy conservation in selected power intensive industries in Karnataka: Report for discussion in the economic and Planning Council (July, 1988). Bangalore: Technical Consultancy Services Organisation of Karnataka, Planning Department, Karnataka.

Karnataka Preservation of Trees Act, 1976 and the Karnataka Preservation of Trees Rules, 1977 (as amended upto 25th May 1983) and notifications, Bangalore, Law and Parliamentary Affairs Department, Karnataka.

Inter State Economic Indicators (1981), Bangalore, Planning Department, Karnataka.

Draft Annual Plan 1991-92, Bangalore: Planning Department, Karnataka.

Economic Survey 1989-90, Bangalore, Planning Department, Karnataka

Planning guidelines for the watershed development programme (1987), Banagalore: State Watershed Development Cell, Karnataka.

Draft Eighth Five Year Plan 1992-97, Planning Department, Karnataka.

Draft Annual Plan 1992-93, Bangalore: Planning Department, Karnataka

Plan of Action: Anthyodaya in Mysore district for 1986-87 (1986), Mysore: District Rural Development Society, Karnataka.

Report on study on wastage and stagnation in medical education at diploma/degree/postgraduate level in Karnataka (1989), Bangalore: Planning Department, Karnataka.

Social background of Zila Parishad members in Karnataka (1989), New Delhi: Institute of Social Science.

Ramu, G.N., (1988), *Family structure and fertility : Emerging patterns in Indian city*, New Delhi: Sage Publications.

A report on the representation of Scheduled Castes and Scheduled Tribes in the state civil services: as on 31st March, 1991 (1992), Bangalore: Directorate, Economics & Statistics, Karnataka.

Karnataka's economy in brief 1991-92 (1992), Bangalore: Directorate, Economics & Statistics, Karnataka.

Report of the Comptroller and Auditor General of India for the year ended 31 March 1991 No. 3 (Civil) (1992), Bangalore : Govt. of Karnataka.

New Panchayti Raj in Karnataka : an evaluation(1992), New Delhi: Institute of Social Sciences.

Report on the second All India census of small scale industrial units (1992), New Delhi: Development Commissioner Small Scale Industries.

Brochure on co-operative movement in Karnataka : as on 30th June, 1987 (1989), Banglore: Research & Evalution cell, Department of Co-operation, Karnataka.

Narayan, B.K. (1978), land development and water management: Concurrent study-I, Bangalore: Institute for Social and Economic

Change.

Aziz, Abdul (1993), *Decentralized Planning : the Karnataka experiment*, New Delhi: Sage Publications.

Karnataka Land Reforms Act, 1961 (as amended) and Karnataka Land Reforms Rules (1982), Bangalore: Department of Law and Parliamentry Affairs, Karnataka.

Mathew, George (1986), *Panchayatraj in Karnataka today: its national dimensions*, New Delhi: Institute of Social Sciences and Concept Publishing Company.

Working together: State, People and Forests of Uttara Kannada (1993), New Delhi, Society for Promotion of Wastelands Development.

Narayan, R.K. (1977), The Emerald route, Bangalore: Director of Information and Publicity, Karnataka.

Narayan, R.K.(1989), Report of the Finance Commission for Zilla Parishads and Mandal Panchayats, Bangalore: Rural Development & Panchayatraj Deptt., Karnataka.

Statistical outline of Karnataka 1989-90 (1989), Bangalore: Directorate of Economics And Statistics, Karnataka.

Karnataka Zilla Parishads .Taluk Panchayat Samithis, Mandal Panchayats and Nyaya Panchayats Acts, 1983 (1987), Bangalore: Department of Law and Parliamentary Affairs, Karnataka.

Karnataka Village Panchayats and Local Boards Act, 1959, Bangalore: Government Press.

Karnataka Budget 1995-96 (1995), Bangalore: Government Press.

Index numbers of industrial production in Karnataka 1992-93 (1994), Bangalore: Directorate of Economics and Statistics, Karnataka.

Report on areas, production, productivity and prices of agriculture crops in Karnataka 1992-93(1994), Bangalore: Directorate of Economics and Statistics, Karnataka.

Report on timely reporting of estimates of area of principal crops in Karnataka 1993-94, (1995), Bangalore: Directorate of Economics and Statistics, Karnataka.

Industrial policy and incentives package (1993) Bangalore: Directorate of Industries & Commerce, Karnataka

Karnataka's State Domestic Product 1980-92(1993), Bangalore: Directorate of Economics and Statistics, Karnataka.

An economic-cum-purpose classification of the Karnataka government budget 1994-95(1995), Bangalore: Directorate of Economics and Statistics, Karnataka.

T.K. Meti (1976), '*The Economy of Karnataka-An Analysis of Development and Planning*', New Delhi, Oxford & IBH.

K. Puttaswamiah (1980), *'Economic Development of Karnataka', (2 Volumes)*, New Delhi, Oxford and IBH.

K. Puttaswamaiah (1972), 'Indicators of Develpment', Bangalore, Department of Planning.

D.M. Nanjundappa (1971), 'Surplus Rural Manpower and Economic Development in Mysore', Dharwad, Karnataka University.

Hemalatha Rao & Devendra Babu (1994), *'Scheduled Caste and Scheduled Tribes: Socio-Economic Programmes'*, Ashish Publishing House, New Delhi.

G. Thimmaiah (1993), *Power Politics and Social Justice', Backward Castes in Karnataka*, Sage Publications, New Delhi.

T. Govindaiah (1989), *'Irrigation Development in India'*, Allahabad, Chugh Publications.

Nanjundappa, D.M. (1991), Surplus rural manpower and economic development in Mysore. (An evaluation report on service man power programme, Bangalore, Karnataka University Press.

APPENDICES

Appendix-I
Village Schedule

1. **Name of Village:**

   Block:

   District:

   State:

2. ***Demography**

2.1. Total population of the village as per 2001 Census data #

2.2 Male [ ] Female [ ]

SC [ ] ST [ ] OBC [ ] Others [ ]

[# take the help of the school teacher, Patwari or ANM/ MPW or key informants]

(* implies all demographic figures should be as per 2001 Census data)

2.2 Rate of growth of population over different Censuses:

Year	Population	Rate of Growth
1981		
1991		
2001		

2.3 Languages spoken:

3. **Location of the Village**

3.1 No. of hamlets:

3.2 Distance of the village (in km) from

(a) District hd. Qrt. [ ]

(b) Block hd. qrt. [ ]

(c) Nearest Bus Stop

(d) Nearest Rly. Station

(d) Nearest town

(f) Nearest market

(g) Nearest branch of a bank

(h) Nearest post office

(i) Nearest PHC

(j) Nearest grain storage facility

3.3 **Basic Amenities in the Village (Y/N)**

(a) Electrification

(b) All weather approach road

(c) Bank

(d) Primary school

(e) Middle school

(f) High school

(g) Primary health sub-centre

(h) Veterinary dispensary

(i) PDS shop

(j) Hatt

(k) Adult literacy centre

(l) Community latrine

(m) Community based safe drinking water sources

(n) Public Telephone Service

(o) ICDS centre

(p) Panchayat Bhavan

(q) Street light

(r) PACS

(s) Other (Specify)

4. **Status of Primary School**[1]

4.1 **Enrolment and attendance**[2]

	No. of children enrolled in Govt. School (GS)			No. of children enrolled in Private School (PS)			Attendance on the day of Survey (GS)			Attendance on the day of Survey (PS)			No. of children who are not enrolled		
	Boys	Girls	Total	Boys	Girls	Total	Boys	Girls	Total	Boys	Girls	Total	Boys	Girls	Total
All Classes															
Class I															
Class V															

4.2 **Teachers in the Primary School:**

No. of Teachers in G.S.			No. of Teachers in P.S.			Are the teachers regularly coming to school	
Male	Female	Total	Male	Female	Total	Yes	No.

4.3 **Literacy:**

Literacy Rate (2001)	Male		Female	
Literacy as on survey date:	Male		Female	

1. As on the day of survey collect information from the Principal/Teachers.
2. You have to visit schools (government and private) to collect information about the attendance.

4.4 **Incentives in Primary School:**

Whether mid-day meals is in operation (1/2)[3]	If yes, whether it has helped in reducing drop-outs (1/2/3)[4]	Whether free text book/ uniforms are provided		Whether scholarship is given to SC/ST/ Girl Students	
		Govt. School (1/2)[5]	Pvt. School (1/2)[5]	Govt. School (1/2)[5]	Pvt. School (1/2)[5]
☐	☐	☐	☐	☐	☐

4.5 **Basic Amenities in Primary School:**

Whether drinking water is (1/2)[5]		Whether toilet available (1/2)[5]		Whether play ground is available (1/2)[5]		Whether Black Board is available (1/2)[5]		No. of teaching rooms for primary section (1/2/3/4)[6]		Whether school has its own building (1/2)[5]	
GS	PS	GS	PS	GS	PS	GS	PS	GS	PS	GS	PS
☐	☐	☐	☐	☐	☐	☐	☐	☐	☐	☐	☐

3. 1. Yes 2. No.
4. 1. Nil 2. Partially 3. Significantly
5. 1. Yes 2. No.
6. 1. Nil 2. 1-2 3. 2-4. > 4

5. **Health Status**[7]

No. of births in last one year		No.of deaths in last one Year		No. of infant deaths in last one year		Services provided by the PHC (1/2/3/4/5/6)[8]	Functioning of the PHC (1/2/3)[9]	Functioning of the Sub-PHC (1/2/3)[9]	Whether the ANM/MPW visit your village (1/2/3)[10]	In general, in the case case of illness, whose services people seek (1/2/3/4)[11]
M	F	M	F	M	F					

5.1 **Family Planning and Maternity Care**
Number of persons of the village in the reproductive* age group: Male [ ] **Female** [ ]

Total No. of married couple	Total No. of eligible couple for Family Planning	Total No. of males adopted family Planning methods	Total No. of females adopted family planning methods

7. Collect information from ANM/MPW/School Teacher/Mukhiya/TBA/PHC/PHC Doctors and Staff.
8. 1. Immunisation 2. Ante-natal care 3. Treatment of minor illness 4. Paediatric care 5. Availability of Contraceptives & IUD insertion 6. Others. There could be more than one response.
9. 1. Fully functional 2. Partially functional 3. Non-functional
10. 1. Very often 2. Sometimes 3. Never
11. 1. Govt. health functionaries 2. Local rural health practitioner (Quake) 3. Private qualified services 4. Others.

Rank the family planning methods according to Villagers preference (1 to 4 in ascending order): Vasectomy Tubectomy ☐ IUD ☐ Contraceptives ☐

Number of domestic deliveries ☐ Number of Institutional deliveries ☐

6. **Total area of the village at present*** (in acres): [ ]

7. **Land Details** (strictly in acres)

7.1 **Types of land**

a. Land for cultivation [ ]

b. Land under forest cover [ ]

c. Fallow land [ ]

d. Pasture and grazing land [ ]

e. Wasteland [ ]

f. Land for homestead [ ]

g. Net sown area [ ]

h. Community land [ ]

i. Miscellaneous [ ]

7.2 **Total land under irrigation** [ ]

(a) Types and number of Govt. irrigation projects:

(b) Capacity of providing irrigation:

(c) Present condition of the Govt. irrigation project (functional/ non-functional):

(d) To what extent farmers depend on them:

(e) Water rate under (i) Private irrigation project:

(ii) Govt. irrigation project:

7.3 **Nature and classification of soil:**

7.4 **Rainfall**

a. Average rainfall:

b. Rainfall last year:

7.5 **Land under**

a. Ownership cultivation [ ]

b. Tenancy [ ]

c. Others (specify) [ ]

---

* Record information from patwari.

7.6 **Distribution of landownership*** (householdwise)

a. Landless

b. < 1 acre

c. 1-3 acres

d. 3-5 acres

e. 5-10 acres

f. 10-20 acres

g. 20 acres

7.7 **Distribution of operational holdings**

a. <1 acre

b. 1-3 acres

c. 3-5 acres

d. > 5-10 acres

e. > 10-20 acres

f. > 20 acres

7.8. **Area under cultivation yielding**

a. One crop

b. Two crops

c. Multi crops

7.9 Any watershed development work in the village, either by the Govt. or the villagers themselves? [Y/N]

If yes, write a note on it in the Socio-economic report.

8. Write a note on the role of **Command Area Development Agency/Drought Area Development Programme** in the village in your Socio-Economic report (if applicable)

9. **Is the village drought prone or flood prone?**

If any of these two, write a note in your Socio-economic report on reasons and measures undertaken to overcome the problem?

---

* Record information from patwari.

10. **Common Property Resources**

    Note down the available Common Property Resources in the village and collect the necessary other data in order to write a note, usage rights enjoyed by sections of the people, average collection of itemised produce per week, shrinkage of CPR in past 30 years due to various reasons, etc. in your Socio-economic report.

    ____

    ____

    ____

    ____

11. Collect information on prevailing wage rate, seasonal Write a note* on local employment conditions including wage rates, extent of unemployment, etc. by peak and lean seasons.

    ____

    ____

    ____

    ____

12. **Agriculture and Allied Activities**

12.1 Crops grown by the villagers and seasonality of the cropping (for all crops)

	Crops	Months of Sowing	Months of Harvesting
i			
ii			
iii			
iv			
v			
vi			
vii			
viii			

12.2 Cropping pattern of major crops:

	Kharif crops	Area under Cultivation	Area under irrigation	Source of irrigation
a.				
b.				
c.				
d.				

	Rabi crops	Area under Cultivation	Area under irrigation	Source of irrigation
a.				
b.				
c.				
d.				

12.3 What are the non-farm activities currently undertaken by the villagers (specify activities[1] with number of units and scale of operation): ☐

12.4 Nearest grain market from where villagers usually sell and purchase grains:

12.5 Nearest place from where villagers purchase farm inputs (seeds, fertilisers, etc.):

Distance from the village (in km.) ☐

12.6 Estimate of surplus agro produce sold out by the villagers (items and quantity sold during last year):

12.7. Approximate number of milch and other cattle in the village.

12.8. Grazing facilities actually availble in the village:

1. It includes all types of activities like vending, petty trade, traditional trade and craft, cottage industry, food processing, poultry, fishery, sericulture, forestry, horticulture, etc.

13. Migration

13.1 Whether people in or outmigrate*? [ ]

[*In migrate = 1, Outmigrate = 2, Both = 3, None = 4]

13.2 No. of persons outmigrating: [ ]

13.3 Places of out migration:

13.4 Nature of work they generally outmigrate for:

14. Panchayat

14.1 Whether Panchayat exists? [Y/N] [ ]

14.2 If yes, last election held (year) [ ]

14.3 Mukhiya of the Panchayat M/F [ ]

Age [ ]

Caste [ ]

Land Ownership [ ]

14.4 Members of the panchayat:-

	Name	M/F	Age	Caste	Land Ownership
1.					
2.					
3.					
4.					
5.					
6.					
7.					

15. **Non-Governmental Organisation (NGO)**

15.1 Is any NGO active in the village? [Y/N] [ ]

15.2 If yes, what are its functions?

15.3 No. of beneficiaries (functions-wise):

16. Village Co-operative[1]

16.1 Is there any co-operative society in the village? [Y/N]

If yes, what is it called?

16.2 Membership of the Cooperative Society:

Name of Cooperative	SC	ST	OBC	Women	Others

16.3 Financial Statement of the Cooperative (Amount in Rs.)

Name of Coop.	Share Capital	Working Capital	Volume of Transaction	Loan	Overdues	Sale	Profit	Dividend declared

1. To be collected from Co-operative Secretary at Block Level. Write the name of the society at the back of the page and also give atleast 5 points of significance regarding co-operatives in the village. Where the Society is running at a loss examine the reasons for the same at the back of the page.

Part II—Poverty Alleviation Programmes

A. Swarnajayanti Gram Swarojogar Yojana

1. Note down the total number of families (both in absolute and percentage term) in the village included in the BPL list. Do a test check on 10 such families as to whether they are actually below the poverty line.

2. When was SGSY implemented in the block in which the village is located.

Month	Year

B. Key Activities

3. List out the key Activities, which have been identified under SGSY in the District

Activities under SGSY					
	Farm based	Non-farm based		Other artisan class based	
1.		1.		1.	
2.		2.		2.	
3.		3.		3.	
4.		4.		4.	
5.		5.		5.	
6.		6.		6.	

4. (a) Give details of key activities undertaken in the village under SGSY scheme.

Activities under SGSY					
	Farm based	Non-farm based		Other artisan class based	
1.		1.		1.	
2.		2.		2.	
3.		3.		3.	
4.		4.		4.	

5. Do you think the key activities identified are appropriate in terms of :

(a) Existing infrastructure facilities Yes ☐ No ☐

(b) Marketing facilities Yes ☐ No ☐

(c) Availability of raw material Yes ☐ No ☐

(d) Availability of skilled labour Yes ☐ No ☐

C. SHGs under SGSY

6. Total number of SHGs groups in the village: ☐

7. Details about the Self Help Groups (SHGs) in the village

Sl.No./ Name of the Group	No. of Members	No. of women members	No. of SC/ST members	*Nature of group	Date of formation	** Regi-tered Under Act	Date of opening of Bank Account	Mont-hly cont-ribution	Frequ-ency of meeting held	Whether group has been graded (Yes/No)	The grade passed *** (0/I/II)	Revolving fund availed (Yes/No)	Bank credit availed (Yes/ No)
1.													
2.													
3.													
4.													
5.													
6.													
7.													

* Whether the SHG is caste based, exclusive women or mixed type.

** Provide under which of the Act the SHGs are registered, 1-Society Act, 2-Cooperative Act and 3-Informal

*** The grade point 0=Not graded

8. Financial Performance of SHGs in the village under SGSY (Rs. '000')

Sl. No/Name of the Group	Amount of saving by the SHG	Revolving fund availed	Total fund of the SHG	Amount lent to the members	Recovery%age of member to society	Repayment % age of the SHG to bank	Income of group per month per member
1.							
2.							
3.							
4.							
5.							
6.							
7.							
8.							
9.							

9. Is there any facilitating agency for formation and monitor of SHGs in the village? If yes, mention its name.

---

10. Whether the SHG members and group leaders have under gone any training? If so how many?

D. Individual Families covered under SGSY

11. How many individual families have been identified for different key activities in the village for the assistance under SGSY? [ ]

12. Individual details covered under SGSY

Total No. of Swarojgari	No. of beneficiaries coming from						
	SC	ST	Women	Assignees of surplus land	Freed bonded Labour	Handi-capped persons	Others

13. Credit details of the individual benefited from SGSY:

Total Disburse-ment	Out of total credit disbursed, disbursement of Swarojgari coming from						
	SC	ST	Women	Assigns of surplus land	Freed bonded labourers	Handi-capped persons	Others

14. Whther the coverage of SC/ST/Women)* as per norms.

    Yes [ ] No. [ ]

15. Amount released for infrastructure activities under SGSY (Amount in Rs. Lakh)

16. Details of work taken up under SGSY (2000-2001) (Infrastructures)

Sl. No.	Name of Work	Estimated Expenditure (in Rs. Lakh)
1.		
2.		
3.		
4.		

17. Besides the SHGs when was the last household survey for identification of beneficiaries to be assisted under SGSY was conducted. [ ]

18. What type of procedures was adopted for the identification of individual families suitable for each key activity of SGSY? Write in few lines.

    ____

    ____

    ____

19. Is there any special project under SGSY financed by MORD running in the village?

    Yes [ ] No [ ]

20. If yes, then give the estimated amount sanctioned and utilized (write a detailed note on the project in your report)?

    ____

Jawahar Gram Samridhi Yojana

1. When was the programme initiated in the village? [ ]
2. a. Allocation of fund to the panchayat during 2000-2001: [ ]

b. Amount actually received by the panchayat during the same period.

3. a. Earmarked funds for SCs/STs during 2000-2001:

   b. Amount utilised during 2000-2001:

4. Whether the JGSY fund was diverted to other departments during 2000-2001? (Y/N)

   If yes, to which departments?

5. Was any work entrusted to contractor(s) during 2000-2001? [Y/N]

6. If yes, describe the work, workforce used, wage component and whether contractors were engaged? Was any of the contractors engaged relative of the Sarpanch?

7. Physical Progress of JGSY During 2000-2001

Item of work		Unit	Physical Assets	Total Expenditure (Rs. in lakhs)	Employment generated (Mandays)				No. of beneficiaries			
					SC/ST	Women	Others	Total	SC/ST	Women	Others	Total
7.1	**Directly Productive Economic Assets**											
1.	Irrigation Wells	Nos.										
2.	Irrigation tanks	Nos.										
3.	Field channels	Kms.										
4.	Flood protection works	Hects										
5.	Anti-waterlogging	Hects										
6.	Soil conservation land reclamation	Hects										
7.	Construction of village tanks/ponds	Nos.										
8.	Land development	Hects										
9.	Other works	Nos.										
7.2	**Socio-Economic Community Welfare Assets**											
1.	Provision of drinking water wells and other water sources	Nos.										
2.	Rural Roads	Kms.										
3.	School Building	Nos.										
4.	Development of House sites	Nos.										
5.	Construction of houses	Nos.										

	Item of work	Unit	Physical Assets	Total Expenditure (Rs. in lakhs)	Employment generated (Mandays)				No. of beneficiaries			
					SC/ST	Women	Others	Total	SC/ST	Women	Others	Total
6.	Panchayat Ghars		Nos.									
7.	Construction of buildings		Nos.									
8.	Mahila Mandals		Nos.									
9.	Construction of Sanitary Latrines		Nos.									
10.	Other Works		Nos.									
7.3	**Indira Awass Yojana**											
	No. of Houses completed for											
1.	Scheduled Castes		Nos.									
2.	Scheduled Tribes		Nos.									
3.	Freed Bonded Labourers		Nos.									
	No. of Houses in Progress		Nos.									
7.4	**Social Forestry**											
1.	Farm Forestry (Trees Planted				No.							
2.	Plantation on Forest Lands (Area)				Hect.							
3.	Plantation on village community land (Area)				Hect.							

8. **Maintenance of Assets created under JGSY during 2000-2001**

Sl. No.	Assets created	Maintenance to be done by*	Expenditure (Rs.)

9. Wage Component

9.1 Notified minimum wages for unskilled agricultural workers:

9.2. Is there any evidence of violation of Minimum Wages Act? [Y/N]

If yes, provide the wage differential.

9.3. Is there any disparity between the actual wage paid** and that entered in the muster roll? [Y/N]

9.4 is there any disparity between the wages paid to female and male workers?

9.5 Wage and non wage component during the period (2000-2001)

Sl. No.	Work Undertaken	Total expenditure	Expenditure on wages of unskilled labour	Expenditure on non-wage component

* Write which Govt. Department is held responsible for maintenance. If the Panchayat itself is responsible for maintenance of any asset created under JRY, mention 'Pancyat'.

** Cross check from the household interview and the muster roll record.

9.6 Whether the functionaries of the Panchayat were trained for undertaking JGSY activities? [Y/N] ☐

9.7 Who took the decision regarding

a. Work to be undertaken:

b. Selection of beneficiary:

9.8 Is record keeping* at the panchayat level as per norms?

[Y/N] ☐

If not, what are the anomalies?

9.9 Is any NGO involved in implementation of JGSY? [Y/N]

If yes, describe its role ☐

9.10 Whether any project under JGSY amounting Rs. 50000/- was executed by the Panchayat on its own? If yes, state whether any external agency or other was involved for the evaluation of the project or for preparing project plan?

____

____

____

---

* Village Panchayats should maintain a Muster roll indicating the details of the labourers employed, their record of attendance and the wages paid to them. The muster roll will clearly indicate the SCs/STs, landless and women separately. Village Panchayat should have complete inventory of assets created under JRY giving details of the date of the start and date of the completion of the project, cost involved, benefits obtained, employment generated and other relevant particulars.

Land Reforms

1. Ceiling and redistribution of land[1]

1.1 Land covered under ceiling laws in the village (area in ha.):

Initially declared surplus	Finally declared surplus	Land released	Land pending under litigation

1.2 Group status of landowners covered under the ceiling laws (area in ha.):

SC		ST		OBC		Other Castes	
No./Area		No./Area		No./Area		No./Area	

1.3 Land Ceiling and Distribution from the cut-off-date[2]:

Land declared surplus (ha)	Land taken possession by the Government (ha)	Land distributed (ha)	Land in actual possession of beneficiaries (ha)	No. of beneficiaries who got possession of land (no.)

1. Record information from Patwari.
2. Every state had set a cut-off-date by which landowners were required to declare surplus land owned by them.

1.4 **Classification of beneficiaries who got possession of land (area in ha.)**[3]**:**

SC		ST		OBC		Others	
No. of beneficiaries	Land area under possession	No. of beneficiaries	Land area under possession	No. of beneficiaries	Land area under possession	No. of beneficiaries	Land area under possession

1.5 Land area under litigation (area in ha.):

As on the day of survey		Original Court		First Appeal	
Total area Under litigation	No. of Cases involved	No. of cases involved	Area declared surplus	No. of Cases Involved	Area declared surplus

Revision		High Court		Supreme Court	
No. of Cases involved	Area declared surplus	No. of Cases involved	Area declared surplus	No. of Cases involved	Area declared surplus

3. From the cut-off-date.

1.6 Landholders holding land in excess of the ceiling surplus land not covered under ceiling land act4:

No. of landholders holding land in excess of ceiling surplus land (No.)	Total Surplus area	Why not brought under the ceiling law							
		Case not started at all		Case wrongly decided in favour		Acquired land subsequently		Others	
		No.	Area	No.	Area	No.	Area	No.	Area

2. Tenancy[5]

2.1 Total tenants in the village (in terms of Households)6

Total Tenants No/Area		Owner-cum-tenants No/Area		Pure-tenants No/Area		Unrecorded tenants No/Area		Recorded tenants No/Area	

2.2 Area under Self-cultivation and Tenancy:

Area under self-cultivation of the landholders (ha.)	Area owned by absentee landholders (ha.)	Area leased in by tenants (ha.)	Area leased out by the landholders (ha.)	Area leased out by the absentee landholders (ha.)

4. As on the day of survey. In case the Patwari fails to provide information, collect information from village elders. Write detailed notes on the five biggest landholders who have been left out of the ceiling process or own land otherwise beyond the ceiling surplus land.
5. Status as on the day of survey. Collect information from Patwari and village elders.
6. Collect information from Patwari, village elders or any other reliable sources.

2.3 Forms of Tenancy in the village (tick)

Fixed Cash rent	Share cropping	Fixed Produce	Usufructuary mortgage	Others

2.4. **Write a detailed note on status of tenancy in the village [attach extra sheet(s)]**

3. **Government Land**[7]

3.1 Extent of Government Land:

Extent as on 1-1-1991	Extent as on 1-1-2001	Extent as on day of survey

3.2 Area of Government land put in various uses (ha.):

Wasteland	Barren land	Homestead	Cultivation	Grazing/pasture	Others

3.3 No. and extent of Government land allotted.

Number of allottees (Nos.)

ST	SC	OBC	Women	Others	Total

Area alloted (ha.)

ST	SC	OBC	Women	Others	Total

7. Collect information from Village Records, Patwari and village elders.

3.4 Encroachment of Government Land

Total area encroached (ha.)	Castewise encroachment				No. of cases recorded	No. of cases unrecorded	No. of cases regularised	No. of cases where order issued	No. of cases where no decision taken
	ST	SC	OBC	Others					
.									

3.5 Encorached land put to various uses and duration of encroachment:

Uses of encroached land (ha.)			Duration of encroachment (no. of cases)			
Area under Houseshed	Area under cultivation	Others	0-1 year	1-2 years	3-5 years	>5 years

4. Tribal land (area in ha.)8

No. of Tribal h.h.	Total land held by the Tribals at Time of last survey	Total land held as on the day of survey	Area alienated by			
			Fraudulent sale	Lease	Forcible occupation	Total

Area in respect of which restoration proceedings started	Area in respect of which restoration order passed	Area in respect of which physical possession given	Area in respect of which claims rejected	Area in respect of which order passed but possession not given

---

8. Collect information from Patwari/Village Chief.

5. **Land consolidation**[9]

When Consolidation notified	Total Number of Khatas before consolidation	No. of Plots before Consolidation	No. of consolidated Plots	Total Number of Khatas after Consolidation	Date of final Publication	Whether People have moved to the new plots (1/2)[10]	Total Number of Khatas move to the New Plots

6. Status of Land Records[11]

Day of last Survey operation	Whether final publication done (1/2)[12]	Whether the new record of rights is operational (1/2)[12]	Whether patta passbook distributed (1/2)[12]	Whether land records computerised (1/2)[12]	If yes, Whether computerised copy of Khatauni is available (1/2)[12]	If no, stage of the process of computerisation (1/2/3/4/5/6)[13]

9. Record information from Patwari.
10. 1. Yes 2. No.
11. Record information from Patwari.
12. 1. Yes 2. No.
13. 1. Computerisation process not begun 2. Data entry stage 3. Data entry completed but not operationalised 4. Operationalised 5. Operationalised but out of order 6. Others

Appendix II

Household Schedule

1. Name of the Village:
2. Name of the Block:
3. Name of the District:
4. Name of the State:
5. Respondent's Name:
6. Relation with the Head of the Family:
7. Religion:
8. Caste (in case of a Scheduled Tribe, name of the tribe):
9. Date of investigation:
10. Name of the Officer Trainee:

House Hold Schedule-General

1. Name of the Head of the Family:
2. Family structure:

   [joint family-1; nuclear family-2]
3. Particulars of the inmates of the household (including the head of the household):

Sl. No.	Name	Relation with hh head[1]	Age	Sex M/F	Marital status[2]	Educational status of above 14 yrs[3]	Educational status of children 6-14[4]	Occupation[5]			Migrant status[6]
								Main	Subsidiary 1st	Subsidiary 2nd	
1.											
2.											
3.											
4.											
5.											
6.											
7.											
8.											
9.											
10.											

1. Self-1; husband/wife-2; son/ daughter -3; wife/husband of son/daughter-4; grandson/daughter-5; father/mother-6; brother/sister-7; mother/father-in-law-8; sister-in law-9; nephew/niece-10; uncle/aunty-11; other relatives-12; servant/employee/others-13

2. Unmarried-1; married-2; widow/widower-3; divorced/separated/deserted-4

3. Illiterate-1; below primary or informal education-2; primary-3; middle-4; matric/high school/secondary-5; higher secondary/pre-university/intermediate-6; pre-graduation diploma or certificate below degree-7; degree/equivalent to degree (graduation level)-8; post-graduate degree/diploma/certificate-9; technical degree (medical, engineering etc.)-10

4. Never enrolled-1; dropped out after enrollment-2; enrolled but doesn't go (or irregularly goes) to school-3; goes to informal institutions-4; enrolled in government school and is regular-5; goes to private school-6

5. Self-cultivator-1; tenant-2; casual labour in agriculture-3; attached agricultural labour-4; casual labour in rural non-farm-5; industrial casual labour (engaged in manufacturing, construction, mining etc.)-6; industrial regular labour-7; self-employed mechanic-8; engaged in traditional occupations/artisan-9; engaged in self-business based on agriculture & allied activities (animal husbandry; poultry, aqua-culture etc.)-10; politicss 11; small business/trade/shop/contract work-12; big business/trade/shop/contract work-13; collection of fodder/cutting wood from jungle and selling-14; begging/dependent on doles-15; unemployed-16; student-17; only domestic work-18; retired/very old-19; disable/handicapped/sick-20; domestic servant-21; [white collar jobs] class I-22; class II-23; class III-24; class IV-25; none-26; others (specify)-27

6. General residential status) resident of the village who resides in the village for most parts of the year-1; out migrates for less than 3 months-2; outmigrates for 3 to 6 months-3; outmigrates for 6 to 9 months-4; resides out of the village for most parts of the year-5; inmigrates for less than 3 monghs-6; inmigrates for 3 to 6 months-7; inmigrates for 6 to 9 months-8; resides out of the village for most parts of the year-9; non-resident of the village but resides in the village for most parts of the year-10)

4. Housing Status

Type of house?	No. of Rooms	Details of homestead land[8]	Whether the house electrified [yes-1; no-2]	Main source of light in the house[9]	Source of drinking water[10]	Place of defecation[11]	Main source of fuel used for cooking in the household[12]

5. Land and Agriculture

5.1 Land Details (in acres and decimal)

Total owned land (all types)	Total cultivable land		Net sown Area (last year)				Land Mortgaged	
	Net sown Area (last year)	Fallow land (last year)	Irrigated area	Single Cropped area	Double Cropped area	Multi Cropped area	Mortgaged -in	Mort-gaged out

5.1.1 If any of your land lying fallow (if given under 5.3.3), reasons thereof [for crop rotation-1]; lack of resources for cultivation-2; area under litigation-3; conflict-4; family division-5; absenteism-6; economic blockade-7; others (specify)-8]

5.1.2 Source of Irrigation ☐

[Private tubewell-1; public tubewell-2; canal-3; well-4; tank-5; ahars/pynes-6; river-7; exclusively rain water-8; others (specify)-9. If there are more than one sources, mention the main source first and the other two sources subsequently.]

7. Straw thatched hut-1; katcha-2; pucca-3; kutcha-pucca-4; tent-5; no house-6; others-7
8. Inherited own land-1; purchased land-2; govt. land with purcha-3; govt. land with purcha-4; landlord's land-5; other (specify)-6
9. Dhibri-1; k.oil lantern/lamp-2; k.oil petromax-3; gas petromax-4; electric bulb/tube-5; solar lantern-6; bulb/tube run by solar energy-7; others-8
10. Own handpump/tubewell-1; public hundpump/tubewell-2; tap in dwelling-3; public tap-4; own dugwell-5; public dugwell-6; pond/river/stream-7; tanker/truck supplied-8; others (specify)-9
11. Modern latrine (with or without flush)-1; pit latrine-2; service latrine-3; open field-4; others (specify)-5
12. Wood-1; coal-2; k.oil-3; hay/leaves-4; cowdung cake-5; agricultural waste-6; gobar gas-7; liquid petroleum gas-8; others-9

5.2 Land Transaction

Give details if you have sold any of your land during last 5 years:

Serial No. of selling	Year of selling	Area of land sold	Caste of purch-aser[13]	Reason for selling[14]	Serial No. of purchase	Year of purchase	Area of land purchased	Caste of seller[13]

5.3 Employment of labour in agriculture (put a ✓ mark on whichever is applicable)

Only family labour	Mainly family labour	Only hired labour	Mainly hired labour	Exchange labour

5.4 Agriculture and Allied activities

[If not indicated otherwise, take information only of previous year]

5.4. 1 Level of technology in agriculture and constraints

a. Means of ploughing* ☐

[*tractor = 1, bullock plough = 2, other = 3]

b. Whether using HYV seeds/ [Y/N] ☐

c. If not, reasons?

i. lack of money / high cost

ii. non-availability

iii. lack of information

iv. preference for traditional seeds

v. poor output (as experienced)

vi. other reasons (note details):

13. Upper caste-1; OBC-2; SC-3; ST-4; others (specify)-5
14. Repayment of debt-1; marriage/social ceremonies-2; meeting basic necssities-3; illness-4; education-5; far away land-6; difficult to manage-7; no interest in cultivation-8; to purchase other land-9; others (specify)-10

5.4.2 Input cost for two major crops (Rs./acre)

Crop Name	Ploughing Seed	Fertilizer	Irrigation	Harve-sting	Storage	Hired Labour	Other	Total
1.								
2.								

5.3 Productivity and marketing of agricultural produce

Name of major crops*[1]Prod-ced by the h.h.	Area under the crop	Total production	Produce marketed (quintal)	Market price of selling (Rs/qnt.)

[*[1] list out at least 4 crops, if grown by the h.h]

5.4 Sale of agricultural produce (indicating distress sale, storage period, market outreach of the farmer) for 4 major crops:

Crop name	Time of selling*	Place of selling**	Purchaser***

[* Immediately after harvest = 1, three months after harvest = 2, six months and above after harvest = 3]

** At doorstep = 11, nearest hatt = 12, local big market = 13, bazaar samiti = 14, other secondary market = 15.

*** To middleman = 21, trader = 22, consumer = 23, other = 24]

6. Livestock (List out different kinds of Animals under the categories provided)

Milch animals	Drought animals	Other animals	Small animals Annual Income	App. Average

7. Household Income

[Given the details of occupations, land, agriculture & allied activities, carefully enquire about the household annual income from different sources in past one year (in Rs.)]

7.1 Ownership of Productive Assets

Sl. No.	Assets	Number	Other Assets	Number
1.	Plough		Assets	
2.	Tractor		Palang/Cot	
3.	Power tiller		Table	
4.	Threshing machine (Wheat)		Chair	
5.	Threshing machine (paddy)		Almirah	
6.	Pump set (diesel)		TV	
7.	Pump set (electric)		Radio	
8.	Bullock cart		Cycle	
9.	Tractor Trolly		Motorcycle	
10.	Fodder Cutter (electric motor operated)		Car/jeep	

11. Fodder cutter (Manual)	Pressure cooker
12. Rahat	Watch
13. Latha Kuri	Electric Fan
14. Karing	Stoves
15. Thela	Lanterns
16. Sewing machine	Others (specify)
17. Others (specify below)	(i)
i.	(ii)
ii.	(iii)
iii.	(iv)
iv.	(v)

8. Public Distribution System

8.1 What items you use to purchase from the PDS shop?

Sl.No.	Items year [Y/N]	Purchased in a last month (kg.)	Quantity purchased

8.2 Are you satisfied with PDS functioning [Y/N]

If no, why?

8.3 In your (respondent's) opinion what items should be made available through PDS shop?

9. **Credit details** (Consider all types of borrowings as loan]

9.1 Do you owe any loan at present [Y/N]

[If no, then move to section 11]

Amount of loan-purpose and sourcewise

Sl. No.	Amount	Year of borrowing	Rate of interest	Source*	Purpose**	Amount repaid	When was last Installment paid

[*Money lender=1, Govt. PAPs = 2, PRY = 3, PACS = 4, Bank = 5, Post Office = 6, Family relatives & friends = 7, Other = 8. If more than one source, mention all.

** Enterprise (including poultry, fishery, sericulture) = 1, cropping = 2, children's education = 3, Outmigration = 4, Treatment of illness = 5, Repayment of another loan = 6, Social functions (marriage, birth, death) = 7, Festivals = 8, House construction =9, Purchase of agricultural implements = 10, Purchase of cattle = 11, Food = 12, Other = 13]

10. **Health**

10.1 Fertility and acceptance of family planning

Eligible couples* in the family (name of husband & wife)	FP Methods currently adopted			No. of Children	
	Temporary (M/F)	Permanent (M/F)	None	Living	Dead

[* eligible couples indicate those in fertility age group]

10.2.Births in the family in past one year

Name	Date of Birth/ age	Sex	Place of delivery*	Personnel conducted Delivery**	Survival at present [Y/N]

[*Home = 1, Govt. Hospital = 2, Pvt. Hospital = 3, PHC/Sub-centre = 4, Other = 5,

** Trained = 1, Untrained = 2]

10.3 Mortality in the family in past one year

Name	Age	Sex	Was it a maternal mortality* [Y/N]

[*Maternal mortality means death during pregnancy to 6 weeks within delivery]

10.4 Maternity coverage (for mothers who have delivered in the last 12 months)

a. Did you undergo minimum 3 check-ups during last pregnancy? [Y/N] ☐

b. Were you given TT immunisation? [Y/N] ☐

If yes, how many times*? ☐

[*Twice = 1; None = 2; Once, but received full schedule in previous pregnancy = 3; Once, but no immunisation before = 4]

10.5 Immunisation (for child of age 12 to 23+ months)

Immunisation status of the child* ☐

[*Fully immunised = 1, Partially immunished = 2] No. immunisation = 3. Here, fully immunised means 1 dose of BCG, 3 doses of OPV & DPT and 1 dose of measles]

10.6 Generally which is your first point of contact* in case of illness? ☐

[* PHC/Sub-centre=1, Other Govt. facilities = 2, Local quacks = 3, Private facilities = 4, Other = 5]

11. **Non-agricultural Activities**

11.1 In case of household enterprise (rural industry, traditional trade or craft), scale of operation.

a. Name of the enterprise:

b. Initial fixed cost:

c. Current working capital:

d. Manpower employed:

e. Profit margin (in net amount):

f. Market avenues utilised:

11.2 In case of family members being engaged in wage labour, wages received per day:

[Take notes in detail of wages for each type of work, either in the form of cash/kind/food. Also take care to note down seasonality factor]

INDEX